SPLENDID FUN

The Story of One Hundred Years of Devon Girl Guides

Rosemary Howell

HOWELL
LUKESLAND   IVYBRIDGE   DEVON

By the same author:
The Ponies Loved It Too, Rosemary Griffin and Paddy Miles (Blackie &
    Son Ltd, 1948)
Cheers for the Ponies, Rosemary Griffin (Blackie & Son Ltd, 1950)
The Ponies Camped Too, Rosemary Griffin (Blackie & Son Ltd, 1956)
Fountain Forestry: The First Fifty Years (Arthur H. Stockwell Ltd, 2008)

Quotations taken from the Scout and Guide publications are reproduced with the kind permission of the Scout Association and Girlguiding UK.

ISBN 978-09559393-1-0
Printed in Great Britain by
Arthur H. Stockwell Ltd
Torrs Park   Ilfracombe
Devon EX34 8BA

Contents

Foreword

'I was there. . . . I remember that. . . . Goodness – no idea she did all that. . . . I never knew that. . . .' And so it's been as I've read Rosemary's amusing, charming and easy-to-read book. And if you've ever been involved in Guiding, I expect you'll find the same.

But *Splendid Fun* can be enjoyed by anyone; it gives a unique opportunity to glimpse the history and evolution of Guiding against the changing backdrop of society. As a past Chief Guide I am very conscious of that evolution, and of the necessity of ensuring Guiding continues to change and remain relevant to the society around it. And in this book Rosemary has vividly traced the path of the organisation in Devon, from its beginnings up to the present; through the linking of events and individual accounts she illustrates its development, as well as the tremendous support and commitment of all those involved.

Personally, I have found the book helpful in understanding some aspects of my childhood; my mum was a Guide and Sea Ranger in Exmouth during the war years and she's only ever told me tiny snippets about that part of her life. But now, thanks to this lovely book, I've a much better idea why she loved it so – and why she strongly encouraged my sister and myself to become members as soon as we were old enough. Little did I imagine that from that early start at the 2nd Countess Wear Brownies I would one day become Chief Guide!

And, like me, you'll probably remember odd things from events which Rosemary's account will set in context. For myself, I've long remembered spending a whole day as a Guide in pouring rain at Powderham Castle – maybe you were there too? But now, thanks to Rosemary, I know why I was there: it was County Day in 1970, a huge county-wide celebration to mark the Diamond Jubilee. I'd completely forgotten the day's purpose – and that the Royal Marines were there – but not that it poured all day! And now in this book there's the event faithfully reported, with the words 'but the very large numbers with no wet-weather shelter meant that the day was not an unqualified success'. Perhaps I'd have put it less diplomatically, but it certainly chimes with my memory! And today we'd almost certainly have a marquee just in case – underlining again the progression of Guiding over the intervening years.

Being about Guiding in Devon, with its extensive coasts to both north and south, there is a strong theme of activities on or near the sea. Many of these involved Sea Rangers, such as myself, and when I was Chief Guide it was always nice to meet former Sea Rangers. Like others mentioned in the book, I also regret the sad decision in 1973 to disband the separate Ranger sections, and it's lovely to revisit so much sea-based activity in Rosemary's book.

It's evident that the need to recruit new leaders to enable more girls to join is nothing new. In many ways it's a great problem to have and it's still one we have today. At the same time, there's been a continuing focus on growing Guiding, recruiting more girls and young women, and Rosemary has highlighted several different approaches, some of which could still work today. For example, Rosemary records details of a day camp run for thirty-six eleven-year olds – who were not in Guiding – to promote Guiding to them. This initiative could easily have been proposed yesterday . . . but it wasn't, of course – no, it was 1975! But the idea could still be useful.

We can see that Guiding has most definitely changed over the years, not only in the provision of marquees for all-day events, but in the way leaders are supported and trained; increasing use is made of professional support, and far greater attention is paid to communications with the media, with parents and with our members. Many facets will have contributed to this, from the changing availability of volunteer leader time, to the growth of competing activities and the immediacy of communication in the modern world. Guiding now needs to present a consistent brand and image to a far greater extent than was ever necessary in the past described in this book.

We can see that Rosemary has tirelessly researched hundreds of service projects, unique visits and occasions, international trips and stories of home stays in the production of this book. Devon is exceedingly fortunate to have this outstanding record of its significant and notable history in such a concise and readable format. And Rosemary really is to be congratulated on this huge achievement!

Rosemary's infectious sense of humour and affection beautifully sets out a compilation of tales of great adventures, amusing times and inspirational activity. It's a book either to read as a narrative or to dip into from time to time – or even as a reference. It's full of ideas, some of which are still relevant and totally doable today. It will be enjoyed by Guiding members as well as by people with an interest in the changing role of women in society. I hope that you will enjoy this superb account of the splendid fun enjoyed by members of Girlguiding Devon over many decades.

Gill Slocombe, CBE,
Chief Guide and Chair of Trustees of Girlguiding, 2011–16

Preface

Many wonderful women have contributed to this book – those I have written about or quoted, those who have answered endless questions on the phone or by email, those who have written about their Guiding lives, and those who have given me encouragement to complete the job. To all those I give my warm thanks.

It has been a fascinating journey, from the keenly adventurous but restricted lives of the early Girl Guides to the freer lives of the millennials, but underlying it still the aims and values of the founder. From her letters to the Guiders of Devon, I became very fond of Lady Clinton, who started and inspired Guiding here, and my thanks go to the present Lord and Lady Clinton (the latter our patron) for their help and encouragement.

I also thank Gill Slocombe for writing the foreword. Gill started her Guiding life in Devon, was Region Chief Commissioner for South West England from 2006 to 2011 and was Chief Guide from 2011 to 2016, My thanks also go to the Stockwell family for their help in publishing this book.

I have hardly mentioned the Trefoil Guild, which is Guiding for adults, because its history is a subject in itself, for someone else to write. But I do thank a Trefoil Guide member from Newton Abbot – Chris Holman – who kindly shared with me the research she did on the Sea Rangers.

The title – *Splendid Fun* – is a quotation from the editor of *The Scout* magazine of 1909 – see page 9.

There will inevitably be mistakes and inaccuracies, and omissions of events and people that perhaps should have been included, and for these I apologise.

I dedicate this book to the many Guiders who have inspired, helped and befriended me over very many years.

Rosemary Howell, Lukesland, 2019

Chapter 1: THE BEGINNING

General Baden-Powell looked in amazement and some dismay at the small group of girls in white blouses and blue skirts and Scout hats and scarves and carrying broom-handle staves, as he moved among the thousands of Boy Scouts at the Crystal Palace Rally in September 1909.

"We are the Girl Scouts," an eleven-year-old told him.

Baden-Powell had already had letters from girls who had formed patrols and were trying to do much the same as the Boy Scouts – tracking and fire-lighting and signalling and first aid. The editor of *The Scout* magazine in July 1909 in an article headed 'Is Scouting good for girls?' wrote that Scouting is 'splendid fun', exercising the mind and the body; 'One only has to see a Patrol of Girl Scouts at work and play to be convinced of the excellent thing it really is.' He added that General Baden-Powell was writing a book, *Scouting for Girls* (which was never published). When Baden-Powell realised the determination of the girls to belong to his new and fast-growing movement, he decided to set up an organisation similar to the Scouts but more suited to girls of that time. He gave them the name Girl Guides, after a famous corps of guides in India, 'distinguished for their general handiness and resourcefulness under difficulties, and their keenness and courage . . . a force trained to take up any duties that are required of them, and to turn their hand to anything'. Guides, for instance in mountain areas, are also known for their ability to know the way and lead others in the right direction. He persuaded his sister Agnes to take over the Girl Guides.

Meanwhile in Devon, as in other parts of England, at least one group of girls was among the first to pioneer Girl Guiding – in Teignmouth. The following letter was written in response to a request for early memories which were published in *The Story of the Girl Guides* by Rose Kerr in 1932:

As one time Lieutenant of 1st Teignmouth Patrol of Girl Guides, registered in December 1911, I have been trying to remember what we did in those early days of Guiding.

We had no rules or regulations, no handbook even, and nobody to help us, but we felt immensely patriotic and – whisper it low – distinctly martial in spirit. We had "Officers" (not Guiders) and "Corporals (not Seconds).

This martial spirit may have been due partly to the thrill of evolving a uniform, and the courage it took to walk along the street in it when we had evolved it!

I remember to this day the open-mouthed astonishment of an old lady as I walked past her in the full glory of my – in those days – SHORT blue skirt, white blouse, belt of gold braid (filched from part of my brother's uniform), navy-blue hat, with a chin-strap, turned up at one side with a bit of my mother's feather boa, long gloves, a haversack on my back, and grasping a stout pole about 5ft long. I wonder now how I dared to do it!

Short skirts for older girls were a stumbling-block to mothers in those days, and led to misunderstanding; one mother declaring that "SHE wasn't going to have HER maid trapezing about the moors with bare knees like the Scouts". "Maid Scouts" was one of our names.

The poles that we carried were rather embarrassing and great encumbrances, but we clung to them tenaciously except at rallies, when nervous people let them fall with a great clatter. We made bands of webbing which we carried in a haversack, and these with two of the poles made an effective stretcher – or so WE thought, but not so the patient, I fear. Then, when out on a picnic, we lashed three poles together for a tripod, not very resourceful, or we shouldn't have needed to carry our tripod with us. We also had a great idea that these poles would be useful to help us to jump across rivers and even to make bridges, but I don't remember ever actually attaining such heights of accomplishment.

We were fortunate in having a very friendly coastguard, who taught us cutlass drill, and also to signal with great rapidity. Poor man; we ill-repaid his kindness. One day when the captain and I were on board one of H.M. ships in the bay, she "borrowed" the ship's semaphore, and having induced the signalman to hoist the coastguard signal, she spelt out "England expects that every man will do his duty," to the bewilderment of our friend, who thought the Navy had gone mad!

We afterwards had the privilege of sending him cigarettes, etc, during the war, and were proud to know that he came through Zeebrugge.

Our first camp would have rendered any present-day Camp Adviser speechless. We decided it would be great fun to camp, so to camp we went, with no camping knowledge and practically no equipment, but laden with food and enthusiasm. We had the use of a long barn with a cement floor and large doors in the centre on both sides. One half was the bedroom where we slept on loose straw with a pathway up the middle – Officers on one side, and Guides the other. The lower half of the barn we used for washing and running about, and a turnip cutter, standing near the door, served as our larder. Not very ideal, but we all came home alive, though very dirty, having had an adventure to remember for many a day.

I think we did more drill in the early days, and we were fond of displays of physical jerks; ambulance, stretcher work, and signalling were our chief subjects, as badge work was in its infancy. Officers' resourcefulness and imagination were taxed to the uttermost; we stood or fell on our own merits, rather lonely souls, and lacking the ESPRIT DE CORPS which is such a feature of Guiding today.

(Reproduced by kind permission of the Girl Guides Association.)

Devon was off to a good start!

Olave Baden-Powell came on the scene in 1912. Born Olave Soames, she had spent some of her teenage years in Devon. Her father rented Luscombe Castle, near Dawlish, from the Hore family for a year (the Hore family still lives there), and here she and her sister Auriol enjoyed an outdoor life with dogs and horses and swimming in the sea. Another year they rented Bradfield, an Elizabethan manor near Cullompton owned by Lord Waldron, where again she enjoyed an adventurous country life, hunting and shooting and playing 'bath polo' in tin baths on the lake with Auriol and friends. In 1907, just before her eighteenth birthday, she had a grand coming-out ball in the Great Hall. She loved Bradfield, and in her autobiography of 1973 she said how sad it was that the house was now a school for 'maladjusted boys'. In the family flat in London and their next country home in Suffolk she played the piano and violin and had singing lessons – she loved music, and eventually her violin was bequeathed to the Guides.

It was on a cruise to the West Indies with her father in 1912 that she met Lieutenant General Sir Robert Baden-Powell, who was embarking on a world tour for the Scouts. Although she was only twenty-three and he was fifty-five, they found they had a lot in common; they fell in love, he proposed at the end of the cruise, and they were married later that year. She was not officially involved with the Guides at the start of her married life.

Agnes Baden-Powell had produced her version of *Scouting for Boys* in 1912; it was called *The Handbook of the Girl Guides, or How Girls Can Help Build Up the Empire*. But by 1914 Agnes and her committee, still set in rather Victorian ways, had not given the Guide movement the strong and imaginative leadership that Baden-Powell had expected, so he reorganised it and in 1915 the Girl Guide Association was granted a Charter of Incorporation, which gave it official recognition. The original committee was changed into a council, which elected a strong executive committee, who insisted that Baden-Powell chaired it, with Agnes staying as president. Olave offered to help, and in 1916 was appointed County Commissioner for Sussex, where she lived. With great energy she set about organising the county, visiting all the existing Guide companies and appointing the necessary local Commissioners, and went on to do the same for the whole country.

> All the many friends I had made – and kept – from Devon to Sussex – from Cumberland to Berkshire, during family peregrinations, were to help me now as I travelled from one end of the country to another finding Commissioners, organizing, coaxing, enthusing, 'spreading the word'. Even if the friends were not themselves prepared to put on uniform, they could often introduce me to someone who would.

Her enthusiasm, efficiency and popularity were such that following the first GG Commissioners' Conference in Matlock in 1916 Olave was made Chief Commissioner, and in 1918 Chief Guide.

Meanwhile the first Commissioners' warrants had been issued in May 1914, and that year Lady Clinton was one of the first County Commissioners to be appointed, for Devon. Possibly she was a friend of Agnes or of one of the members of her committee, as it seems likely that women of standing (usually among the gentry) in the counties were asked to start up and organise the Guides. This they did by persuading THEIR friends to become involved and start up units in their areas.

Lady Clinton not only organised Guides in Devon, but also during the 1914–18 war in Kincardineshire and in Norfolk, where the family had residences. In her book *The Story of the Girl Guides*, published in 1932, Rose Kerr stated that, together with Miss Mary Royden of Cheshire, who was slightly senior to Lady Clinton,

These two County Commissioners played a great part in the Guide Movement, and were loved and honoured not only by the Guides of their own counties, but far beyond the bounds of these.

In 1918 Baden-Powell's manual *Girl Guiding* was published, to replace the now outdated book by Agnes Baden-Powell *How Girls Can Help Build Up the Empire*. *Girl Guiding* included a programme for younger girls, who had originally been called Rosebuds but were now Brownies, and one for Senior Guides, who were later called Rangers. This year Lady Baden-Powell was made Chief Guide.

There is another mention of Lady Clinton in Rose Kerr's book. In 1919 she organised a conference in Sidmouth at which her sister-in-law Lady Mary Trefusis, who was president of the English Folk Dance Society, gave a speech on country dancing. This enthused the Guide leaders so much that country dancing became an important and popular part of the Guide programme, and they were helped and encouraged by Cecil Sharp, who had been rediscovering English folk dances. Apparently, though, the girls' dancing never came up to his high standards!

In 1922 it was decided by the County Commissioners to give the Chief Guide her own personal standard. A beautiful design was made and embroidered over a period of three years by Guiders and their friends, and it was presented to her at the annual meeting of the Girl Guide Council in 1925 by Lady Clinton on behalf of all the County and Overseas Commissioners. Lady Baden-Powell was delighted with it and always very proud of it.

Meanwhile Guiding was growing in Exeter and other parts of Devon, but not in Plymouth until in 1917 Nancy Astor, wife of the MP for Plymouth and well known as a leader in the suffragette movement, decided to do something about it. "No town in Europe wants companies of Girl Guides more than Plymouth," she said. She organised a big meeting of local VIPs and representatives of other girls' organisations – for instance, the YWCA – and churches and schools; it was attended by Lady Clinton and Miss Townsend from the County Executive and various local dignitaries, including Lady Mary St Aubyn. Following this highly successful meeting, many companies were started, Nancy Astor being Division Commissioner. The Astor family, together with the local landed gentry, contributed funding. In less than two months 4,000 girls in Plymouth had joined the Guides, and Nancy Astor spoke to the press, saying that the war, which was still going on, had shown how women could not only do men's work, but often showed them how to do it.

> The head of a large shipbuilding firm told me that women had done certain work not only as well as men, but had produced five times the amount. This, I think, is because women went into their work with a different spirit.

She went on to say that Guiding provided

> a wonderful chance to do a great deal towards improving the moral tone of the town. Obedience does not mean servility; it is amazing how some people seem to be getting positively terrified of their children. The movement is one of the most important things that has happened to Plymouth in recent years.

In Tiverton, as early as 1911, a meeting had been held in the town hall to discuss the possibility of forming a Guide company in the town. However, it was not until 1917 that the 1st Tiverton Guide Company was registered in conjunction with the YWCA. The same year the 2nd Tiverton Guide Company started up at the Greenway House School, a day and boarding school mainly for Anglo-Indian children and colonial families, and only girls at the school could join. Over the years, Tiverton Division has enjoyed the use of the extensive and beautiful grounds of Knightshayes Court for outdoor activities, including camping, thanks to the kindness and interest in the Guides and Scouts shown by Sir John and Lady Amory while they lived there. In the 1960s and '70s County Training Camps were held there. Tiverton's first Division Commissioner, from 1917 to 1930, was Mrs Charles Carew, who had been a Miss Heathcoat-Amory. Lady Amory was Division Commissioner from 1947 to 1958, and was County President from 1967 to 1978.

A few copies of the monthly newsletter for 1928 and 1929 have survived. Headed 'Devon Girl Guides Association', it is the size of *Devon Star*, with a blue cover on which is a nostalgic picture of a Guide camp (with bell tents) by the sea. On the rest of the cover, inside and out, are advertisements for shops, mostly in Exeter. It is headed by a list of VIPs, many of whom are titled: President – the Duchess of Bedford (whose family owned property in West Devon); County Commissioner – Lady Clinton. The Division Commissioners were

1. Plymouth – Lady Clinton.
2. Totnes – Lady Mildmay.
3. Torquay – Mrs Thompson.
4. Exeter – Miss Leeke.
5. Honiton – Miss Williams.
6. Tiverton – Lady Acland.
7. South Molton – Mrs Vinson-Thomas.
8. Tavistock – Lady Albertha Lopes.
9. Barnstaple – Miss Davie.
10. Ashburton – Lady Cable.

The County Secretary, who also edited the newsletter, was Mrs J. H. Foster of Budleigh Salterton; she had an assistant, and there was a County Badge Secretary and a County Lone and Post Secretary.

There was always a letter from the County Commissioner.

Writing for the September 1929 newsletter on 19 August from Fettercairn House, her home in Scotland (she divided her time between her Devon homes – Bicton and Heanton Satchville – and Fettercairn and her home in London), Lady Clinton said:

Dear Guides,

I returned early in August from France where I had been having vein treatment and came back feeling so much better. I hope by the late autumn or winter to be back in Devon doing my ordinary work as before my illness last year. I am hoping to see a great many Companies this autumn and winter – some Companies I have not seen for a long time and I want to be asked to come and see them even if only on an ordinary Guide evening.

We are very proud of our County President, the Duchess of Bedford, who flew to India in 58 hours, taking control of the machine herself for part of the time. It seems almost incredible to think of covering that huge space in such a short time. I take two days to go to Paris, as being a very bad sailor I prefer to go from Southampton to Cherbourg in the great Atlantic liners, which takes almost as long a time as the Duchess took to fly to India, as one has to wait at Cherbourg till the next morning to get a train to Paris. I saw a great many Scouts of all nations passing through Paris for the great British Jamboree. We are very proud that the King has conferred a peerage on our great founder, Sir Robert Baden-Powell. He has, through the Boy Scouts and Girl Guides, brought an enormous amount of joy and fun into the lives of hundreds of thousands of boys and girls and what is better still helps them to be more efficient thus enabling them to help others in the best way and bring happiness into their lives and so carry out the Scout and Guide Promise.

Yours in Guide affection,

JANE GREY CLINTON

(This is one of the very few times she used her Christian names – she usually signed her letters J. G. Clinton. In those days women were addressed as Mrs or Miss and the use of Christian names was rare.)

Her letter in the January 1929 magazine is interesting:

Sister Guides,

Once more I take up my pen to wish you all a very happy New Year. Let us remember that the more we try to help others and make them happy the more sure are we to find happiness ourselves.

In looking back over the past year, the Devon Guide world has been full of interesting events. The Crowning Glory was the visit of our Royal President, Princess Mary, to the wonderful rally at Plymouth, for which I should like once again to praise every section of Guides, Guiders, Commissioners and all who helped so splendidly to make the day the great success it was, and not least, those who so gallantly bore the trying heat in a truly Guide manner.

To me the year includes one of the most thrilling and touching moments of my life – the gift of the glorious Standard from all my beloved Guides in Devon, from Commissioners to Brownies. Thank you and bless you once more. . . .

We are increasing in numbers and in efficiency (30 new Companies and 18 new Packs having been formed last year), and I think also in the spirit of Guiding, which is of still greater importance.

We must have good work, bad work and a slack Company cannot help anyone; but above all, we want to strive for the spirit of love and loyalty. It is the want of these that makes a rift, and our aim is to stand united like one big happy family.

Yours in true Guide affection,

JANE G. CLINTON

From the last paragraph, it would seem that there had been a problem with units somewhere, but no doubt it was sorted out!

The last newsletter we have from Lady Clinton was in June 1943. She had just resigned as County Commissioner, but a new one had not yet been appointed. She expressed her sadness at missing the Commissioners Conference, held over a weekend at the home of Captain and Mrs Tyler at Elm Park, Broadhempston, which was attended by Lady Cochrane, the Chief Commissioner for England, because she was addressing a meeting of the St John Ambulance Brigade, of which she was County President.

I had the pleasure of meeting the Chief Commissioner at the station in Exeter, and had eight delightful minutes of talk with her. She was travelling six a side in a carriage in great heat, but appeared quite happy and unruffled, a real example of Guide selflessness and of carrying out the eighth law!

County affairs were to be conducted through County Court of Honour, composed of the Division Commissioners and chaired by Mrs Kennaway, until a new County Commissioner was appointed. This was to be Mrs D. M. Ledger who had been Division Commissioner for Plymouth. In the November 1944 newsletter, her piece, headed 'From the County Commissioner's Notebook', was purely factual and lacked the warmth of those written by Lady Clinton – who was now County President, with Countess Fortescue, of Castle Hill, near Barnstaple, as vice-president. Mrs Ledger wrote about a Guide Guiders' Conference in London which had impressed her. Lady Cochrane chaired it, supported by the Chief Guide and Lady Somers, and it was addressed by Sir Stafford Cripps, who emphasised that women in the future could and should do much to build up a Christian way of living and a true democracy. There were discussions on the difficulties and psychology of the adolescent girl, and on the work and difficulties of the Guider. Mrs Ledger said that she hoped that the two forthcoming County Conferences would be well attended.

Excerpts from Ivybridge Guides' logbooks

In 1930 four Ivybridge Guides joined others for a camp at St Minver in Cornwall.

> They left by the 8.30 train and rode up on Mr. Jeffery's lorry. He kindly took their luggage to the station at the same time. Guides from Plympton joined them on the train at Plympton and they all had a very long journey before them. At Bodmin Road they had to wait for an hour and a half. . . . They went for a long walk in the woods. When they reached Wadebridge another ride in a lorry took them to the camp site.

The job I liked best was Mess. We had to pass around all the meals and cut the bread and butter for tea. It was fun having to sit on groundsheets to have our meals.

They had sports one day.

The Guiders' race was exciting – they had to balance a mug of water on their head and walk about 20 yards. Of course they had to wear mackintoshes in case they were bad at balancing. After walking the 20 yards they had to drink their water and eat a very dry biscuit. Our Captain was first.

In 1934 a secret message was sent from the Isles of Scilly to the Chief Guide in London –

Signalled in morse or carried by runners through Cornwall and at Plymouth a Ranger signalled it across the water to a Plympton Guide.

It was passed through Ivybridge to South Brent and on to Totnes, and reached the Chief Guide on 17 May. It read, 'All loyal greetings from Scilly, West and South.'

In 1934 a Guide wrote:

I feel terribly sad to have to relate the death of Phyllis Leach, beloved Second of the Pansy Patrol. [She died of pneumonia.] The Guides marched to the funeral of the dearly beloved Pansy Second whose belt and tie were thrown in on the coffin.

Chapter 2: THE WAR YEARS AND BETWEEN, 1914–45

At the outbreak of the First World War in 1914, Guides all over the country, thinking of their promise to serve their king and country, were keen to help in whatever way they could. Headquarters issued suggestions: they could offer their services to the local Red Cross or St John Ambulance or hospitals, they could help in soup kitchens or crèches, etc., or they could knit socks or balaclavas for the troops. In 1915 a War Service badge was instituted: Guides (or Guiders) had to give at least twenty-one days' special service to hospitals, etc., OR make personally at least fifteen articles of clothing ('Knitting and needlework already done for sailors, soldiers, Sea Scouts, Belgian refugees, etc., may count.'), OR do twenty-one days' work on a farm or dairy or market garden or clothing factory, etc. Much enterprising work was done by the girls over the four years of the war, including raising money for a recreation hut for troops in France similar to one provided by the Scouts, which proved to be a great asset.

Early in 1918 Lady Baden-Powell was acclaimed as Chief Guide, a title she preferred to Chief Commissioner, and she was presented with the Gold Fish by the ninety-five County Commissioners of the British Isles. She became vice-chairman of the executive committee, which Baden-Powell still chaired. The same year his handbook *Girl Guiding* was published, and there was a big London rally in Hyde Park attended by Queen Alexandra and Princess Victoria. Among the displays given by the divisions was a trek-cart race and a fire-drill display, which involved Guides running up a ladder and jumping from the top rung into a tarpaulin held by other Guides. In November 1918 came the Armistice, and Rose Kerr in *The Story of the Girl Guides* writes:

> The Guides had carried on valiantly during the war in the face of great difficulties, and they had proved in many ways, large and small, that their training could fit them for service to their country.

Meanwhile by 1914 the Guides' younger sisters were clamouring to join, and the first groups were called Rosebuds. But this name was not popular and in 1915 Baden-Powell came up with the name Brownies, who in folklore are little people who help adults with surprise 'good turns'. Then by 1917 Senior Guides had come into existence to cater for the older Guides and older girls who wanted to join. Once again Baden-Powell came up with the name Rangers for this section, to complement Rover Scouts. The Chief Guide wrote:

> To range is to set in proper order, to roam, and this might well mean that you are going to tread ground as a Senior Guide that as a Guide you have not yet passed. Distance of vision . . . again shows that as a senior member of the community you are expected to look farther afield for good, and work that you can do for the community.

The name was approved in 1920, by which time there were also Cadets, Lone Guides and Sea Guides.

Cadets were Guides over sixteen who wanted to train to be Guiders, and many girls' schools had Cadet companies. The Cadet Promise was 'to train for service in the Guide Movement'. The name Cadet was eventually changed to Young Leader. Lone Guides were (and still are) girls who live too far away to be able to join an active company or girls at boarding schools where there are no companies. They worked at Guiding by themselves, being monitored by a captain who wrote them a monthly letter, and they met up occasionally, sometimes at a special camp. They would sometimes be invited to join an active company for camp. (Devon has always had Lone Guides – see further on.) Sea Guides were set up in 1920 at the request of many girls who wanted to concentrate on maritime activities, and their companies were often run by ex-WRNS. Companies took the names of famous ships, and with their distinctive smart uniform and often upper-class connections they were very popular. The name changed to Sea Rangers in 1927.

Guiding had started up in various other countries before the 1914–18 war, and after the war Lady Baden-Powell formed the International Council to regain and maintain contact with Guides and Girl Scouts in foreign countries. In 1928 this was replaced by WAGGGS – the World Association of Girl Guides and Girl Scouts.

HRH Princess Mary, the daughter of King George V and Queen Mary, took a great interest in the Guides and was County President for Norfolk, often attending meetings of the village company at Sandringham and attending rallies all over the country. In 1920 she became President in place of Miss Baden-Powell (who became vice-President) and was a popular and hard-working holder of this role. The following year she became engaged to the Earl of Harwood, and 215,000 Guides and Brownies subscribed one penny a head to give her a wedding present. One present was a diamond-and-ruby Tenderfoot badge, the trefoil of which was platinum. In addition, all the Marys of the empire contributed towards a present, and this money was used to furnish and equip Foxlease as a training centre for Guides. Foxlease, in the New Forest, had recently been offered to the Girl Guides for training and camping by an American admirer of the Guide Movement, Mrs Archbold. Princess Mary gave more of her wedding-present money to the house, which became known as The Princess Mary House.

Devon was delighted to welcome Princess Mary on 21 July 1928, when she attended a Devon and Cornwall Rally at the Royal Naval Barracks in Devonport. Every company in the county was expected to attend, and a scheme was worked out with the railway companies, Great Western and Southern, whereby the Guides travelled to Devonport by train from stations all over Devon and Cornwall at a reduced rate. In those pre-Beeching days there were stations long since gone in very small places like East Anstey, Up

Exe Halt, Trusham, Gara Bridge, Shaugh Bridge Platform, etc., where the local Guides, with their Guiders, would entrain. In the June 1928 news-sheet there is a plea from the County Secretary that they rehearse the songs for the rally:

Will Guiders impress on their Guides that they must keep time with the beat of the conductor. We shall be over 6,000 at the Rally, and if Companies are going to sing 'just their own way' I dread to think of the result.

There was also an 'Alteration in Programme' notice:

Please note that 'Daughters of England' will not be sung at the Rally. The hymn, 'O God our help in ages past', will take its place.

Another piece in the news-sheet is interesting. Headed 'Devon memento for the Rally', it reads:

1st Tavistock Rangers have the honour to provide the memento to be presented to H.R.H. Princess Mary for her eldest son. It is to be a kite *that will fly* – made by themselves. We had many splendid suggestions from Ranger Companies, and the County Commissioner found it hard work to choose the most suitable gift.

Some memories of Guiding in Plymouth in the 1920s were provided by Mrs Dorothy Nicholls, who joined the 3rd Plymouth Mount Gould Methodist Church Company as a ten-year-old in 1926. She remembered summer evenings when they went out on to Dartmoor by train from Millbay Station, and going to camp in Cornwall by train. She described how on arrival they had to fill bags with straw (to act as mattresses – they were known as palliasses) and they slept in a hut with an outside toilet, and she remembered campfires and visitors' day. The uniform was navy-blue skirt and blouse with belt and lanyard, and when she joined the Rangers at sixteen she exchanged her blue tie for a red one. All her life Dorothy supported local Guiding, especially when her daughter Valerie (Faulkner) became a Guider and Commissioner. Val reported that her mother (whose birthday was on 22 February) lived to see the Guide Centenary and from a wheelchair witnessed the celebrations on Plymouth Hoe.

Rita Hore, writing in 2012 from Budleigh Salterton, remembers her early Guiding days; she was thirteen when war was declared in 1939 and her family left London to live with her grandmother in Exmouth.

I joined the 1st Exmouth (Clinton) Company named after Lady Clinton who I believe was a close friend of Lady B-P. The Captain was a Colonel's wife and the Lieutenant came from a prominent local business family. When they both moved on to do war work, another lady took over, but soon left to look after aging parents. By then I was 16 and was made acting Captain – no warrant because I was under age. Because many Guiders had joined up, I understand this was done in several other Companies. We met in the Scout Hut. I don't remember being there after dark – we probably finished meetings before "black-out" time when all lights had to be hidden; dark curtains, no street lights, subdued car and cycle lights, etc. Our main war effort was collecting waste paper: 100 hours shown on a signed card earned a special badge. I was driven by an old lady who used her petrol ration to take me every Saturday morning to some of the big houses in "the Avenues". I had to wear my uniform and go to the back door where I would pass over a clean sack in return for the full one – this was done by a uniformed maid or even a butler in most of the homes. Sacks were then taken to a depot where Guiders and other adults would empty out the contents. We also did knitting – mitts, balaklavas, scarves, according to our ability. Camping under canvas was forbidden – we could have been mistaken for a military unit. We had some day camps on a local farm and thoroughly enjoyed constructing shelters from branches, bracken etc. We cooked on open fires and had to be very careful that they were fully extinguished before going home.

In 1942 or 3 Lady B-P came to Exmouth and inspected Guides and Brownies in a local church hall. Later she met Guiders in the District Commissioner's home. I was privileged to be included, a fact that she commented on as I was still only a teenager. Lady Clinton also came. Being a tall girl, I was surprised how short they both were! (Not like the present Lady Clinton who is very tall!)

Uniforms cost clothing coupons, so we made do as best we could by wearing a navy skirt and the top of our uniform if the skirt section was too short as we grew.

A VIP from HQ came and enrolled a few of us as the first Sea Rangers in Exmouth, and I joined as well as still running the Company. We learnt to row, round and round the little harbour, and once a little way out to sea. Our tutor was a local fisherman who was reprimanded for letting us go so far – the Naval Officer in charge of the area had seen us! We also rowed on Exeter canal.

In November 1941 there was an all-day training event for Guiders in Exeter (this was before Exeter was bombed); it was opened by Lady Clinton with an inspiring talk in which she emphasised the importance of Guiding in the present time. Demonstrations were given to show the importance of the patrol system and the way children were trained to responsibility by its means. There were also demonstrations in the running of company meetings – the 'bad company' causing much amusement with its riotous Guides, dithery captain, ineffective lieutenant and ignorant recruit who was allowed to wander at will (the latter was played by Miss Candler, Exeter's Division Commissioner). The 'well-run company' had proper training of leaders, who passed on instructions to their patrols, there were properly run games and there was a model reception of a visiting Commissioner. This event was completely different to training sessions of former years and was apparently particularly enlightening and helpful. The trainers were Miss Cobham, Miss Bindloss and Miss Glenister, all of whom went on to give many years of inspiring leadership for Guiding in Devon and beyond. (Miss Bindloss became the first Chief Commissioner for South West England when regionalisation took place in 1971.)

Also towards the end of 1941 Lustleigh District Guiders had an evening 'gathering', arranged by Miss Earle who was acting as District Captain in place of Miss Bradford, who had joined the WRNS. They had training in camping, which included listing the right sorts of wood to start a campfire and to keep it going. They also considered several questions

concerning the moral training of the Guides and the best way for a Captain to help them when various difficulties presented themselves. These questions caused interesting discussions and many helpful and constructive suggestions were forthcoming.

These reports were in the January 1942 newsletter, along with the following:

KINGSBRIDGE GUIDES recently did a novel good turn in undertaking the distribution of the Pink Ration Books to people in their parish. In the case of old or invalid people the guides called for the old books, took them to the Food Office, and duly returned them along with the new ones.

TORQUAY RANGER CHALLENGE. Competition in the Torquay Divisional Annual Challenge was as keen as ever. Companies from Dartmouth, Brixham, Paignton and Torquay, both Land and Sea Rangers, took part, and the result was a win for the Torquay Sea Ranger Crew S.R.S. "Delight" (Skipper Miss S. Clarke), who snatched a one point victory from 2nd Torquay Rangers (Captain Mrs. Colwill), third place being taken – only one point again separating them – by 2nd St. Marychurch Rangers (Captain Mrs. McManus). The programme of events was very varied, and included the best crop of potatoes grown from six stalks; Company Drill, taken by one of the Rangers themselves; a Handicraft entry, all exhibits to be made from natural objects; the invention and running of a team game; and what caused the most interest, a Comb and Paper Band.

(The latter caused the judge some difficulty because she had "no standard to go on"!)

Also mentioned is a training for Commissioners and Ranger Guiders, to be taken by Miss Hacon (Chief's Diploma), who had recently attended a Ranger Conference at Foxlease and who would explain the new Ranger Training scheme. Miss Rosalie Hacon was another great personality in Devon Guiding.

Mrs Hilda Mitchelmore's memories of Guiding in Exeter in the war were still vivid when she was ninety. Hilda and her school friend Peggy Sawicka (who later was very involved in Guiding in Paignton and who edited *Devon Star* for many years) were sixteen when war broke out, and automatically moved from Guides into Rangers. Every Saturday evening they helped bath evacuee babies in a large house called Southlands, and between 6 and 8 p.m. on Wednesdays they prepared dressings for the operating theatre at the Royal Devon and Exeter Hospital (which was then in Southernhay East); other Rangers did this on other evenings, and they always wore their Ranger uniform. They took trek carts round the big houses, collecting unwanted saucepans, which were sold to raise money for the Guide International Service, the metal going, they were told, to help build Spitfires. Metal railings throughout the country also went to help the war effort. The evacuee girls joined the Guides in the Heavitree Church Company, which is the company that Hilda was involved in through all her Guiding days.

Hilda worked in the Devon and Somerset Stores and was involved in fire-watching during the 'Baedeker raid' of 29 April 1942, when Paris Street and Sidwell Street were hit. She remembers that the telephone exchange had to be saved at the expense of shops, which burnt as a result of the incendiary bombs. Her mother was a first-aider for her street. Each street also had a Morrison shelter, and Hilda's Guide-age sister always put the company colours in the shelter every night for safety.

Hilda remembers camping with a huge camp at Hartland in 1935 or 6, when they sat on the beach in full uniform in great heat! There was no overnight camping during the war, but Mrs Thomas at Coaver House (where County Hall is now) let the Guides have day camps in the large garden; the Cook Patrol had to be there by 6.30 a.m. to cook breakfast! After the war Hilda gained her camping licence at Knightshayes, being tested by a formidably strict Camp Adviser called Miss Dyson, who was also the District Commissioner and who had brought her school from London at the outbreak of war and stayed on in Devon. At this test camp the County Commissioner also camped with them.

Hilda's memories include going as a Guide to a big County Rally attended by Princess Mary in about 1935–6 in Torquay, at which the divisions had to dress up and perform a song or dance. Exeter Division chose 'Widecombe Fair', and the Guides travelled by train from Polsloe Bridge Halt dressed as farmers in calico smocks.

Hilda was captain of the 14th Exeter Heavitree Church Company for thirty-five years. She started Division Ranger units, and organised activities with the Rovers, including camping. (There were age discrepancies as Rovers could carry on till twenty-five, whereas Rangers had to leave at twenty-one.) During the 1960s, with the help of Division Commissioner Margaret Branch, Hilda started a new company, 26th Exeter St Paul's, in a run-down part of Heavitree, which was challenging to say the least. Most parents were illiterate and could not fill in forms. The girls, with nothing else to do, came along, but had no sense of discipline and played up the Guiders by doing things like putting the plugs in the washbasins and turning the taps on until the hall was flooded. Hilda was not deterred and did not give up, believing that Guiding could help these girls; gradually she won their respect, and, when Moreen Folland took over the company, assisted by Hilda, they even managed to take them camping at Dawlish. An interesting fact is that Gill Slocombe, who became Chief Guide in 2011 and who started her Guiding in Exeter, helped Mrs Joyce Dobson run the Brownies at St Paul's.

Hilda was County Secretary from 1977 to 1992, the indispensable right-hand woman for County Commissioners Angela Graham, Rosemary Howell and Mavis Budden.

Another stalwart Devon Guider who lived through the Blitz in Plymouth was Muriel Boatright, known affectionately by her many friends as Boaty; when she was a young Guider the Patrol Leaders were allowed to call her Boaty, but to the Guides she was Captain. She was a Guide from the age of eleven and remembered being enrolled on Polhawn beach, having walked from Cawsand in full uniform and carrying the colours. She also carried the colours on the occasion when Lady Clinton came to enrol the mentally handicapped daughter of Mrs Welby, who was the WRNS Superintendent of the Western Approaches and a Guide Commissioner in Plymouth.

Boaty left school at seventeen in 1939 and joined the WRNS as a shorthand typist. She lived in Eggbuckland and remembered incendiary bombs falling on three nights of full moon, windows being blown out and lights being put in fields and gardens to lure the bombers away from houses. The cat always knew beforehand when the sirens were about to sound. Boaty ran the Emmanuel Church Guide Company at the age of seventeen, as would-be Guiders had been called up or evacuated. Once they had permission from the army to camp on the vicarage lawn in camouflaged tents, and there was a bad raid on the Saturday night, so they all went into the Anderson shelter and sang songs. She said that people just got on with things as best they could – she remembered cooking meals in the grate at times. The parish hall was a reception area for those who were bombed out; it was manned by the WRVS and the Guides helped, giving out blankets and holding people's hands to comfort them after the trauma of losing their homes. Guides knitted golliwogs with safety pins on the back, which were sold for the Spitfire fund. They knitted socks and gloves for the troops for their Knitters badge and they made nightdresses for babies for their Needlewoman badge. They picked rose hips to make syrup (in the absence of oranges during the war, rose-hip syrup was a good source of vitamin C). Patrol Leaders and Cadets did canteen duty for service people at North Road Station.

Boaty was a Cadet with Valerie Dampney under Rosamond Stevens, both of whom left their mark on Plymouth Guiding. After the war she became District Commissioner for the new Compton District at only twenty-four, and was invalided out of the WRNS at twenty-five due to increasing deafness. She said that her Guides were always very good at looking after her when her deafness caused difficulties, and the fact that she was a young Commissioner attracted young Guiders. In later life Boaty was County Registrations Secretary for at least fifteen years.

From Exeter Division's annual report for 1942 comes the following report of the war work undertaken by the Guides.

North Districts: 20 Guides took a course in Home Defence with practical experience in Fire Fighting. A number worked on the College allotments. They acted as messengers after the heavy raid. . . . The Guides have collected salvage; mended for the Babies' Home; renovated toys for the Nursery Centre; helped at the Emergency Centre after the Blitz. . . .

St Thomas: Guides collected razor blades, cotton reels, custard tins, electric light bulbs, books and papers. Picked fruit, collected and dried nettles. Helped at the Dunraven Babies' Home, two Guides going each evening to help with the children. . . . One company is responsible for the salvage of bones in the village. Four Rangers helped at the Exeter Emergency Centre after the Blitz. . . . Two or three go regularly one evening each week to help with the washing up at the D. and E [Hospital].

South District: Guides are helping at the Eye Infirmary and Civic Hall. Sewing and knitting for a Babies' Home. . . . Hip picking, collected chestnuts, cotton reels. Provided Christmas parcels for six needy families. . . . The Brownies brought gifts for the Cathedral Christmas Tree, gave an entertainment and sent the proceeds to the Red Cross; they also collected salvage.

Heavitree: The Rangers and Guides have done daily hospital work at the D. and E. and the Orthopaedic Hospital and are helping at the Eye Infirmary. . . . Helped with National Savings, knitted for the W.A.A.F. Collected chestnuts and cotton reels. . . . Collected vegetables for Mine Sweepers. One Company made £30 by a Bazaar and the proceeds were given to Prisoners of War Fund and the B. P. Memorial Fund.

From all the Districts toys and books were sent to the Mayoress' Depot and given to the children who had lost their toys in the blitz.

Among all the badges gained during the year in the Division were forty-eight War Service badges. The Mayor of Exeter inaugurated a collection of books to replace those lost in the Plymouth Blitz, and at his request the Guides collected, sorted and helped pack up for Plymouth about 6,000 volumes.

Guiding carried on as normally as possible during the war, and in May 1943 Commissioners and secretaries from all over Devon gathered for a weekend training and conference at the home of Captain and Mrs Tyler in Broadhempston, near Totnes. The Chief Commissioner for England, Lady Cochrane, joined them and talked about the many interesting ideas that were being tried out in Guiding, including suggestions for a 'Fourth Branch' for the girls and women too old for Ranger companies. She described the arrival at Guide Headquarters on Thinking Day of messages of greeting, brought (with the help of the army) by carrier pigeons, and how sums of money, sometimes quite small, from small and isolated Guide companies were arriving at Headquarters from all over the empire towards the Baden-Powell Memorial Fund. (This had been launched by the Scout Association to erect in London a meeting place and hostel for British and overseas Scouts, as a permanent memorial to the Chief Scout.)

Also at the conference, Miss Oliver from Dartmouth took a session on sex education, leading a discussion on problems arising out of war conditions, particularly the importance of interesting girls in home and housecraft subjects through badge work, "to give them stay-at-home interests to counteract the growing tendency to seek entertainment outside their homes". She deplored the modern tendency to treat homes as "filling stations by day and parking places by night". Among many other training sessions, Miss Cobham recounted her experiences while training for the Guide International Service.

In the June 1943 news-sheet there is a camping section written by the County Camp Adviser, Miss E. K. Parker (who later became County Commissioner): 'I am sorry to tell you that I am shortly resigning as C.C.A. Now that I have no ties, I feel that I should like to do a whole time war job, and I have volunteered for the W.R.N.S.' She had organised a Camping Committee and a Camp Recorder to take over her work when she was called up, but it shows difficulties faced by Commissioners trying to fill posts with competent women to keep Guiding going.

Also in the June 1943 news-sheet is a report of the annual meeting of Ilfracombe District Local Association, which the vicar chaired. This seemed to be the usual pattern – Guide districts were supported by strong Local Associations of interested and influential local people, including clergy, gentry, shops and businesses, who subscribed to district funds as well as helping in other ways, especially fundraising. As time went on and well-wishers had less leisure time to support Guiding, Local Associations dwindled in number, especially after the apparently unpopular change of name to Friends of Guiding in the 1980s, although some districts still have a loyal band of supporters in the Local Association. At the Ilfracombe annual meeting the speaker was Miss Sylvia Clarke,

Assistant Commissioner for Rangers (Sea Rangers), who gave 'a most inspiring talk on Rangering', referring particularly to Sea Rangers, as a crew had been formed in Ilfracombe recently.

An article headed 'American Girl Scouts help Britain' from the *English Speaking Union News* told how the Girl Scouts of America had sent 3,000 gifts to the Girl Guides of England, with Christmas cards attached. Showing enterprise, one group had made lapel ornaments, which they sold and contracted with a manufacturer to make twenty woollen sweaters. One story is very touching:

> A little Scout in a West Virginia mining town – one of a large family with an out-of-work father – carefully washed two of her skirts, pressed them, and sent them with a little note saying she greatly wanted to send a gift and her own little skirts were all she had to send.

In the November 1944 *Devon Supplement* is a report of a farewell party for Paignton District Commissioner Miss Hughes, who had been appointed as a Team Leader in the Guide International Service.

> After . . . giving the best of her thorough Guide knowledge for over nine years, first as Guide Captain, then as District Captain, and finally as Commissioner, her inspiring leadership and cheerful personality will be sadly missed, but the Division was proud to know that Miss Hughes was the only Guider in the West, as yet, to embark on such an adventure.

(District Captain was a rank that was later abolished; she ran the district as District Commissioners do now. In the early days of Guiding, District Commissioners were quite grand ladies who dealt with the District Captain rather than the Guiders. An elderly Guider told the author that no working-class woman would ever become a District Commissioner.)

Devon sent two delegates to an International Conference for Guide Guiders in London in October 1944, which was opened by Sir Stafford Cripps, who congratulated the Guide Movement on foreseeing the necessity of training in citizenship, "so that women will be able to take their rightful place in the control of the nation". There were discussion groups, and ideas from the counties were pooled. At a rally on the Saturday evening Lady Baden-Powell and Lady Reading spoke, and Miss Elizabeth Hartley, Headquarters Trainer, who later came to live in Devon, showed how a Guide company can present campfire songs and folk dances to an audience "in a very attractive manner". The performers were in Elizabethan costume.

Chapter 3: AFTER THE WAR – THE 1940s AND 1950s

In 1947 there were several notable visits to Devon, as described by the County Commissioner, Miss E. K. Parker in her annual report. The Chief Commissioner for England, the Honourable Lady Cochrane, came and met many Commissioners, secretaries and Guiders in Exeter and Plymouth. Then Lady Fryer, Imperial Commissioner for Auxiliaries, came to visit the Guide and Ranger companies at Ryalls Court School, Seaton.

> This section of the Guide Movement [wrote Miss Parker] brings the interest and happiness to be found in Guiding to the girls in approved schools or voluntary homes. It is not always realised that many of these girls are not delinquents, but are sent to the schools for care and protection.

Lady Alethea Eliot, Commissioner for Extensions in England, came to see Devon Extension Companies. 'Guiding is the Youth organisation which caters for invalids and handicapped girls (in their own homes and in hospitals and institutions) as well as the physically fit, and doctors and nurses pay tribute to the very real benefit that they derive from Guiding,' wrote Miss Parker.

Five Devon Guides gained the Queen's Guide Award this year. The Queen had given permission for this award, which aimed at producing the best type of all-round person, with qualities of skill, ingenuity, pluck and endurance. The Queen's Guide was expected to live up to the ideals given by Lord Baden-Powell and to the honour of wearing a royal badge. Over the years the syllabus was altered and made harder and the age range altered slightly. It has always been a very prestigious award.

The Ministry of Food had appealed for the collection of jam jars, and Guides collected many thousands. Some companies used the money they made from selling them to buy camp equipment; others used it for their quota for the Headquarters Development Fund, or to provide Christmas good turns for old people and needy children.

It was a good year for camping as the weather had been 'wonderful' with some reports showing that campers had felt the heat and drought a lot. There were thirty-five Devon camps and two holidays abroad. 'The standard of camping was very good, and there were no bad reports from Devon camps,' wrote Camp Adviser Miss D. Page.

The County Commissioner reported with pride that Miss Sylvia Clarke, Division Commissioner for Torquay, had been appointed Assistant Commissioner for Rangers (Sea Rangers), IHQ, and had been awarded the Beaver in recognition of her work for the Sea Section, and in connection with the Sea Ranger Training Ship MTB *630*, moored at Dartmouth.

Six new Ranger companies had been formed in 1947, including one Sea Ranger crew and two Air Ranger flights. The new Ranger Service Star was being worked on by most units and was proving interesting and adaptable. There were 147 Rangers in the county, 283 Sea Rangers and twenty-nine Air Rangers.

In 1948 Mrs Woolner of Bradley Manor, Newton Abbot, gave the county the opportunity of renting North End, Bradley Manor, as a centre for Devon Guiding. It consisted of a large living room, two bedrooms, bathroom and kitchen, providing accommodation for nine people. This lovely old house, some of it dating back to 1450, and set in Bradley Woods, gave great scope for trainings and outdoor activities.

During the war the Girl Guides Association had raised over £100,000 for relief work abroad, and now money had to be raised for the Imperial Headquarters Development Fund. A voluntary rate of one shilling per head for every member, to be raised over three years ending in 1948, meant a total of about £1,000 for Devon, which was of course in addition to local and county needs. By the end of 1948 almost all this had been raised.

By the mid 1940s Cadet companies were in existence. For girls of Ranger age (sixteen plus) who were training to become Guiders, the promise had an addition, "to be of service to the community". In 1948 there were three Cadet companies in Devon: one in Tiverton, run by Miss Murdoch, with eleven girls, who had spent a year on Guide second- and first-class test work and were now studying for the Ranger Citizen Certificate and took an active part on the local Youth Committee. The 13th Plymouth YWCA Cadet Company, with six girls, was run by Captain Miss Rosamond Stevens and Lieutenant Miss Valerie Dampney. The Cadets had run Patrol Leaders' trainings for the district and went on weekend hikes to youth hostels and were making lightweight camping equipment. Pat Fourte attended the Cadet Conference in London and gave an interesting account of it on her return. The 1st Newton Abbot Cadet Company, with ten girls, camped with their captain, Miss Betty Bindloss (who was also the Cadet Representative for the county) and were now on Brownie training. It was hoped that six applicants from North Devon would form the nucleus of a County Cadet Company.

Betty Bindloss wrote:

> We feel that our Cadet Companies, though few in number, are contributing to the quality of Guiding, by producing keen, trained, young Guiders with wide interests and a balanced outlook.

In 1950 the 13th World Conference was held at St Hugh's College, Oxford. It was the fortieth anniversary of Guiding, so very important, especially as the USA had done WAGGGS proud in 1948. How to involve everyone countrywide was the challenge. This was solved by the 'Message Scheme'. Scrolls of Friendship, beautifully written and designed, all by hand, were passed from hand to hand from the furthest corners of the UK until they reached Oxford on the appointed day. They were then presented by Princess Margaret at a monster campfire, at which 10,000 Guides were present, to the leaders of all the national delegations to take back to their own countries. The organisation had been hard work, but the Guides thought it wonderful and the scrolls travelled by punt, flying, sailing, in hay wagons, on penny-farthing bikes, on an elephant and so on. It was an amazing PR stunt as well and people came out to see the passing of the scroll wherever it went. The scrolls were received in stately homes, churches, town halls and castles, where they were looked after overnight before going on their way. Logbooks illustrating the history and beauty spots along the way were also presented to the delegates. The scrolls were received with enthusiasm by the delegates and taken home, and this resulted in many invitations and exchange events. Canada's scroll toured Canada and they sent a beautiful logbook back, which finally came to rest in Hampshire. (See page 194 for Devon's participation.)

No annual reports or other records of the early 1950s seem to have survived, or at least not in the county archives.

In 1956 Mrs Shelagh Eastley, MBE, JP, was County Commissioner. As 'Mrs Exeter' she modelled smart clothes for middle-aged ladies in Vogue magazine. She suffered from poor health and had to spend winters abroad, which meant that one of her Assistant County Commissioners, Betty Bindloss (who followed her as County Commissioner) had to stand in for her. (The other assistant was Miss M. Wheen of Lee Abbey, near Lynton.)

The Countess Fortescue, JP, of Castle Hill, was County Vice-President and the County President was the Honourable Mrs John White, JP, who as the Honourable Helen Mildmay had grown up with Guiding, as her mother, Lady Mildmay, had been Division Commissioner for Totnes.

There were still twelve divisions; Barnstaple had become North Devon Division.

The All-England Ranger Rally was a highlight of the year, and many Devon Rangers enjoyed the pageant in the Albert Hall and the march past the next day when the salute was taken by the President of the Association, HRH the Princess Royal (Princess Mary, sister of King George VI and married to the Earl of Harewood.) This was followed by a moving service in the Albert Hall.

1957 was Centenary Year, celebrating the birth of Robert Baden-Powell in 1857. It was decided that each division and branch would arrange its own activities rather than have a large county event, although there was a joint Scout and Guide Meeting in the Civic Hall, Exeter, in March, followed by a cathedral service.

There was a World Camp in Windsor Park, at which two of the groups (each group consisted of seven different nationalities) were run by the two Devon County Camp Advisers, helped by five Guiders, two Cadets and fifteen Guide delegates.

On the day of the Camp Finale, Devon Guiders and Guides from nearly every division travelled by coach to Windsor and stayed till after the campfire, arriving home in the early hours, thrilled and inspired by the sight of 24,000 Guides in uniform.

During the camp, Devon's 'Brick', the county's contribution to the Chief Guide's birthday gift, was presented to her by one of the Guides who was helping there. The county had raised £282. 5s. 6d. so far, with money still coming in. Another gift from the county was a sampler, beautifully worked by a member of the Newton Abbot Local Association, which was given to the Guide representative from the island of St Lucia.

Another highlight of this year was an invitation to the Rangers of the county from the Captain of Britannia Royal Naval College, Dartmouth, to a march past, at which he took the salute, and then to see over the college. There was a special service in the college chapel, and colours which had been given to the Dartmouth Sea Ranger Crew were dedicated.

Suzanne Sainsbury (Taffee Waggett) from Plymstock remembers her Guiding days in the 1950s:

Sister Betts, District Nurse for Plympton, was our feared Captain. I can still semaphore a message, lay a trail, tie a bowline, sheepshank, etc, and a granny knot rather than a non-slip easy to undo reef continues to offend me as it did Captain all those years ago. I'll never forget the humiliation of being the one to fail my Health badge because I guessed that a blanket should be washed once a month. Well, I HAD been asked by my mum to tread them in the bath occasionally! I do retain enough first aid to know when to dial 999, even though I no longer carry 4d in my knicker pocket, and hot sweet tea for shock is no longer recommended! My mum was not amused when we rolled home from a happy camp in the canvas-topped van of Charlie Nicholls, Furniture Remover, when she saw that for a dare my fellow Nushadombi Patrol friends had cut off my pony-tail complete with attached elastic band; I thought it was great fun, but I had a ballet exam pending and my new bob was not a classical profile.

I can remember pushing and struggling with an enormous wicker chest of books from Plympton Library to St Vincent's Home in St Maurice, then back with the 'returns', plus jam jars which we sold for 1d each for our funds. The memory of Captain's hysterical screams when she found the sheep-head skeleton in her sleeping bag haunts me yet. Digging and using the 'lats' wasn't much fun, and decision-making is put in focus when one is starving and ants have invaded the sandwiches. B-P's rule that clothes should be placed neatly in the order in which they would be put on in an emergency in the dark was a useful tip I still practice, as well as making sure the kettle has water in overnight and candles and matches are to hand in case of a power cut. Playing stalking games, singing songs, swimming, climbing, death-sliding at Bickleigh with the Royal Marines – such fun, and new experiences together to take us through life. A particular highlight was the Company walking over to Elburton for the opening by Prince Philip of the King George VI Memorial Playing Fields. I was the first in the Guard of Honour as the jeep hove into view. The blond Adonis jumped down and approached – his smile was directed only at ME. . . .

Chapter 4: THE 1960s

1960 was Jubilee Year – fifty years since Guiding started – and great celebrations were held throughout the country, including a service of thanksgiving in St Paul's Cathedral, attended by representatives from Devon. The Chief Guide came to Devon Guides' annual meeting and a service in the cathedral – both events were packed, and, in the words of the County Commissioner, Shelagh Eastley, Lady Baden-Powell was "a joy and encouragement to us all". At the annual meeting Lady Baden-Powell presented fourteen awards for outstanding service to the movement – four Beavers, five Medals of Merit and five Oak Leaves.

Another highlight in the year was the visit by Princess Margaret and her husband, Antony Armstrong-Jones (they were married that year) to name the new Sea Ranger Training Ship, the *Golden Hinde*, at Dartmouth. Sea Ranger numbers remained high at 179, with only forty-seven Land Rangers – who were very keen and were specialising in overnight hiking, the art of self-defence and firefighting.

Several districts were raising money towards their new Headquarters, and the county raised £1,460 for World Refugee Year.

In 1961, as last year, numbers had increased again, not only among the girls, but there were six more Commissioners and seventy-four more Guiders, and help was growing from Local Associations, Parents' Associations and Trefoil Guilds. Cooperation between Scouts and Guides and Rangers and Rovers in the county was reported as 'growing rapidly' and there was now full participation in the Duke of Edinburgh Award Scheme. Camping was flourishing, a regular Whitsun Training Camp for North and East Devon now being held at Knightshayes with the permission and encouragement of Sir John and Lady Amory. South and West Devon's training camp, previously held at Hemerdon, was this year held at Ashburton, by invitation of Miss Windeatt.

A new venture for Rangers this year was a weekend camping and training at the Outward Bound School at Holne Park, Ashburton. Forty-two of them, from twelve units, backpacked on the moor, canoed on the Dart, went on the 'low ropes', and had to face a seemingly impossible challenge.

In the autumn the Training Van from Headquarters in London visited North Devon, Tiverton, Okehampton, Tavistock, Totnes and Ashburton Divisions and finished in Exeter for the County Training Day. This van enabled training to reach remote country areas and to take charts, books, etc., as well as practical training. Also this year there was a South West Area Commissioners' Conference in Torquay attended by many from Devon (this was before the English regions had been formed).

In 1962, Guide numbers in Devon had increased again (to over 9,000) and as usual there was a plea for more Guiders. Camping numbers were also up. The Clinton Shield competition was an important part of the Guide year, and the finals were always out of doors, partly organised by Scouters and Scouts.

One of the many good turns done by units over the years was picking primroses from the hedges and sending them by post to hospitals locally and in London. This practice was eventually stopped when it was generally considered that wild flowers, even the apparently common ones, should be left to seed.

A new Headquarters was opened in Ashburton by the new County Commissioner, Miss Betty Bindloss. Known as The Golden Fleece, the house dates from the thirteenth century and included a large room for Guide and Brownie meetings and other rooms for Rangers, Trefoil Guild, etc., and a kitchen.

Plymouth had an exciting year, with Guides lining the route when Queen Elizabeth the Queen Mother opened the new Tamar

Road Bridge, and the Queen opened the new Civic Centre. Then, following much money-raising, the foundation stone of Plymouth East Division's new Headquarters near Mutley Plain was laid by Mrs Ledger, a former Plymouth Division Commissioner. This was officially opened in 1963 by none other than the Guide President, HRH the Princess Royal. The Lord Lieutenant of Devon, Lord Roborough, was present, as were the Guide County President, the Honourable Mrs John Mildmay-White and many others. First Class and Queen's Guides formed a guard of honour and Guides of Plymouth East and West took part in the march past. 'They looked splendid, marching to the music played by the Royal Marines Band!' reported Division Commissioner Rosamond Stevens. Hundreds of Brownies were also present, and the Princess spent more than an hour in the building and talked to many people. The Lord Mayor gave a lunch for the VIPs and representative Guiders in the Guildhall. (The Headquarters, which has been improved over the years, has since been called the Rosamond Stevens Hall.)

Fundraising for the Freedom from Hunger Campaign, led by Unity Harley, Guider and Commissioner in South Brent, raised over £1,000. Several delegates went to an inspiring National Conference for Local Associations in the Albert Hall.

The handicapped Guides at Dame Hannah Rogers School in Ivybridge camped by day at a farm nearby; the camp was staffed by Plymouth Sea Rangers, who were also helping the girls at the RN swimming baths each week. A County Rover/Ranger Committee was formed this year, and the Senior Branch was invited to help at next year's Scout International Camp at Torquay. Exeter Division regularly joined the Scouts for their St George's Day Parade; in 1962 there were 2,000 Scouts and Guides at the cathedral service following the parade. Good turns abounded as usual: Exmouth Division reported:

> During last winter's severe weather, Guides went shopping and did housework for the sick and housebound, and one of the Cadets continued with this help every Saturday morning right through the summer.

By 1964 numbers were up again to 9,389. Encouragement of Patrol camping was given by a Guide Association Discoverers' Challenge, and a Challenge Camp was held at Knightshayes (in terrible weather!) at which fifty-four Devon Patrols were joined by others from Cornwall and Somerset.

Twenty-four Senior Branch members helped Guiders run the Headquarters mess at the International Scout Camp at Torquay, and Devon Guides hosted 110 American Girl Scouts, who visited the Torquay camp in relays.

A Guider who wished to remain anonymous gave £2,000 to form a trust fund to be administered from CHQ, the income to be used to help delegates attend international gatherings, or for any other educational or training purposes which would help forward the Guide Movement in Devon.

Coca-Cola sponsored a dressmaking competition, and Torquay hosted the county final, which was won by the 4th Newton Abbot Guides, Teignmouth Rangers being second. Exeter Rangers and Rovers held a conference at the youth hostel and had many joint activities. Exmouth reported joint campfires and parades, etc., with the Scouts, and the Sea Rangers attended the county Sea Scout weekend at Lympstone. In Plymouth East Miss Cross ran a drama group, producing very popular pantomimes with Scouts, Guides, Scouters and Guiders all taking part.

A Plymouth West company met at 4 a.m. for a breakfast hike, and found a dog missing from Plymouth Zoo! Cornwood Brownies gave a party for children from a Dr Barnado's home. The Whitsun Training Camp was held for the first time on National Trust land, at Saltram House near Plymouth: 'The Curator and the tenant farmer were most helpful.' In North Devon a Brownie Pack opened at the RAF Camp at Chivenor.

During 1965 Princess Margaret became president of the Girl Guides Association, following the death of the Princess Royal.

Guider trainings now often consisted of successful Guiders sharing with others ideas, projects, etc., that had worked well with their units. Among good turns that were reported, in Axminster Division elderly people had their shopping done for them, and a Guide took on the milking when a farmer was ill.

A new programme was recommended by a CHQ Working Party in 1966, to be fully implemented in 1968, so 1967 was to be used for training for the programme. Meanwhile, numbers in Devon were now over 10,000; the Guide Movement was so well thought of that leadership training was grant-aided by Devon County and Plymouth City and Exeter City Education Departments, and the staff in the County and City Youth Departments gave personal help at specialist courses. The Devon Girl Guides Association was an active member of the Standing Conference for Voluntary Youth Organisations in Devon and was represented on this useful body by Elizabeth Weir, who was Chairman of Training for many years and a great supporter of and help at Taw Bottom.

Lustleigh (near Bovey Tracey) Guides were given a wood by their Guider, for camping and wide games. They cleared and planted it, and could invite any village child to share their activities. Widecombe-in-the-Moor made history for a few years by the formation of a joint Brownie and Cub Pack, with two Brownie Guiders and two Cub Leaders. They kept their own ceremonies and tests, but played games together – British bulldog being a firm favourite with the Cubs! Lynton Guides found a cottage on Exmoor which they were allowed to use for winter 'camps'.

> Memorable events include tramping many miles with map and compass, negotiating bogs, making hot soup after a snowstorm up on the moor, washing in the icy stream by lantern light, and the comfort of hot coffee before dropping into incredibly soft, warm beds!

Tiverton Division held a rally at Knightshayes, which included an exciting adventure course prepared by the Scouts, including a whizz across a small quarry on an aerial runway while trying to solve a murder mystery planned by the Rangers. Plymouth East were having problems with their Headquarters building – it was leaking badly, the builder was bankrupt and the architect no longer insured! So to raise money to repair it they ran a shop for a week in disused premises awaiting demolition at Drake Circus. They sold second-hand goods of all kinds and were flooded out with goods and eager buyers! People enjoyed the friendly atmosphere of the shop, and £280 was made.

A team of nine Guides from Kingsbridge and one 'passenger' (who was not allowed to put foot to ground) took part in the BBC South-West Tip to Top Competition, the challenge being to travel from Kingsbridge to Hessary Tor near Princetown by three modes of un-motorised transport via Ivybridge and Cadover. They started on bicycles, towing a rubber dinghy on a trailer, then went to Cadover by pony and cart and finally over Dartmoor on ponies, arriving, after heavy rain, in thick fog. They won the under-sixteen section prize – a silver salver – for the most ingenious methods of travel.

Nora Lee, Guider of the 1st Kingsbridge Company, was presented with the Star of Merit, awarded by CHQ for the great courage she showed in facing disablement after a terrible accident in Kentucky. She had her car fitted with hand controls so that she could carry on with her Guiding as well as teaching at West Alvington School. (After retiring from active Guiding she became a staunch Trefoil Guild member, still driving at a great age.)

The County Training Team was particularly strong at this time. Chaired by Rosalie Hacon, the committee welcomed Miss Elizabeth Hartley, Deputy Chief Commissioner for England, who had recently come to live in the Tavistock area and who was a most inspirational person. Another new member was Miss Valerie Dampney, and Miss Hope Rattey and Miss Beryl Paul were welcomed to the Training Team.

In 1967 The Hon. Mrs John Mildmay-White JP, who had been County President since 1954, resigned due to ill health. Before her marriage to Mr White, the Hon. Helen Mildmay, daughter of Lord and Lady Mildmay of Flete (in South-West Devon) was involved in Guiding from its early days (her mother had been Division Commissioner for Totnes), and greatly encouraged adults and children alike even in her retirement. Lady Amory, of Knighthayes, who 'knows Guiding from the inside', became the new County President.

The highlight of 1967 was the visit of the World Chief Guide, Olave, Lady Baden-Powell, to Torquay on 4 November. '1000

Guides in the morning and 700 adults in the afternoon had the unforgettable experience of being held spell-bound by someone who has the power so to enthuse and re-enthuse people of every age, that they realise as perhaps they have never realised before, the value and the possibilities for good of the Movement of which they are members,' said County Commissioner Betty Bindloss of the occasion.

There was a get-together for Guides aged thirteen to fifteen – two from each district – to spread the word that Rangering is fun. The number of Ranger units was growing, and there were new Ranger Guide service units with new uniforms. Sea Rangers were still flourishing (see Chapter 10). Hope Rattey, Torquay Division Commissioner, was congratulated on producing the 100th edition of the *Torquay Tattler*, a monthly newsletter for the three districts, 'helping to give a feeling of unity to a big section of Guiding in Devon'.

The year was spent training and preparing for the new programme coming next year, which, Guiders were told, would give greater freedom and flexibility generally. Districts and units were working hard to earn the money to buy the new handbooks.

The Patrol Leaders of Lynton had an exciting winter weekend when Miss Pat Pilditch (Guider, District Commissioner and retiring Division Commissioner for North Devon) took over a chalet at Lee Bay.

> They awoke on Saturday to find the beach, rocks and countryside covered in snow and icicles, and spent the weekend largely doing winter sports.

Pat, who lived and worked at Lee Abbey, was a stalwart of Guiding in the area for many years.

Plymouth East said goodbye to Miss Rosamond Stevens, who had been Division Commissioner for the whole of Plymouth, then for Plymouth East; it was through her determination that their Headquarters was built. The annual Thinking Day gathering at 7.30 a.m. on Plymouth Hoe had been started by Valerie Dampney in 1950; in 1967 300 Guides met on the Hoe for a short service and hoisted the world flag, then 200 returned to Abbey Hall, where the 12th Plymouth Company provided breakfast. Plymouth West Guiders and Rangers provided for the first time a crèche for Guiders' children at the County Training Camp.

Special Report for 1967

NORTH DEVON GOES SOUTH TO SEE 'THE CHIEF'

Saturday, November 4th, 6.45 a.m., a clear, dark morning – Lynton asleep apart from a few Leaders and Seconds who could be seen creeping out of their homes to pick up the Utilibrake which was to take them to Barnstaple on the first stage of the journey to Torquay. At 7.45 a.m., the coach, which had started from Combe Martin, reached Barnstaple already partly filled with Guides; then on to Torquay via Exeter, picking up others from the scattered towns and villages of North Devon. A second coach came from Appledore, across to Bideford, skirted Winkleigh, and down to Torquay, collecting up its complement as it went. And so nearly 80 Guides came south to meet the World Chief Guide, Lady Baden-Powell – 'Our Chief'!

Shortly after 10 a.m. we arrived in pouring rain, along with a cavalcade of others. Guides scampered across the car park from all directions to the shelter of the Spa Ballroom entrance. The vestibule and cloak-rooms were a milling mass of humanity, picnic bags and wet macs, somehow miraculously controlled by Torquay Guiders. The ballroom gradually filled – Queen's Guides and recruits, old uniform and new, Guides from the cities and towns of Devon, from the fishing villages, farms and hamlets. Miss Hettie Smith welcomed us, and as soon as we were squatting on the floor in the space allocated, we found we were learning new songs, one to welcome our Chief (our own special Devon version) and another to say goodbye. Then, after several false alarms, the Chief arrived, dressed in the blue uniform of the World Bureau, accompanied by the County Commissioner, Miss Bindloss, and others.

The Chief told us something of her own childhood in South Devon, and went on to stress the importance in life of what she called 'the three H's' – Heads, Hands and Hearts – which should be used and trained for our own enjoyment and the welfare of other people. She also told us about her 'Runties' – those little groups scattered about the world, struggling hard to do their

Guiding under such great difficulties of poverty, illiteracy, war, lack of transport, and so on. She then joined us in a sing-around accompanied by an impromptu orchestra.

The time came to leave for lunch with the Mayor, and amidst cheers and singing the Chief went on her way, and we left too. Back to our waiting coaches, lunch eaten on the way to Exeter (some provident maidens at the back were observed to have changed into slacks), Christmas shopping in the pouring rain in Exeter: and so back over flooded roads to all corners of North Devon, after a day which will never be forgotten, to see a wonderful Chief who will always be remembered for her friendship and fun.

1968 was described by Betty Bindloss as the year of transition. The new handbooks arrived in March, but unfortunately, due to misunderstandings at CHQ over the number of books the publishers would produce on the day of publication, not enough books arrived for every girl to have one, and the various celebrations round the county had to make do with one token book! Others followed in due course. The following is taken from the 1968 annual report *Guiding in Devon*:

THE LAUNCH

Many and varied were the events arranged for the launching of the new handbooks in Devon, and it is significant how willingly Mayors and Chairmen of Local Authorities and other civic dignitaries co-operated in the ceremonies.

At Exeter over a thousand Brownies, Guides, Rangers and Guiders watched as a helicopter from the Royal Marines came down where they gathered on the playing field of Exeter School, by kind permission of Mr Hone, the Headmaster. Out stepped Colonel Parsons and his Aide-de-campe, in their dress uniform, carrying parcels containing copies of the new Handbooks. Alderman Whitmarch, Chairman of Devon County Council, then addressed the gathering and presented the books to representatives from the different Districts.

Plymouth East Division assembled in the Drill Hall at the Royal Naval Barracks, with the Royal Marine Band in attendance, and with the Commodore, R.N., to present the Handbooks, while Plymouth West Division enjoyed a grand 'get-together' at Bishop

Vaughan's Secondary School at Crownhill, for the presentation of the new Handbooks by Mrs Lloyd-Jones, wife of Plymouth's Town Clerk. This was followed by a District Challenge, and by Camp-fire and other ceremonies.

Ashburton had a series of events beginning on the 18th March with a big meeting when the Portreeve cut the string of the first parcel of books. A diary of these events was duplicated and sent out with the Parish Magazine, and a local baker made biscuits in the shape of a trefoil which were on sale during the period. There was also a 'window spotting' competition. Teignmouth Sea Scouts brought the new books in to The Point by launch. Shaldon Brownies received them, after which they were carried by a chain of Brownies, Guides and Rangers to Teignmouth Grammar School, where they were presented by the Chairman of Teignmouth U.D.C.

The presentation at Sidmouth took place in the grounds of the Council Offices, watched by parents and friends. The Guide Companies marched into horseshoe formation and the Packs assembled on the lawn. Members of S.R.S. Scorcher had built a 'Space Rocket' from which the Handbooks were handed to the Chairman of the Council who presented them to Guides and Brownies.

Exmouth East and West had small 'get-togethers', P.Ls. and Sixers receiving books from 'old friends' of the Division, while at Budleigh Salterton ceremony in the Public Hall, the first presentation was made to the eldest Guide and the youngest Brownie by the Chairman of the Council, after which Guides and Brownies gave a display to parents and friends on the new 8-point Programme. A short camp fire and a prayer for the success of the new programme ended the evening.

Honiton's books were presented at a special meeting by the Mayor. Tiverton, Lynton and Tavistock also linked their distribution with Annual or other public meetings. Okehampton and Holsworthy District Commissioner and Guiders made a tour of the rural area, in a decorated car, distributing the books to outlying towns and villages. North Devon, another rural and scattered Division had articles on the new programme in the *North Devon Journal* and *Bideford Gazette*, Barnstaple had a display in a shop window, and Bideford displayed the new uniforms etc., and showed an Animation film at their A.G.M. Ivybridge District delivered books by pony phaeton at Dame Hannah Rogers School, and other Companies held a camp-fire at which the new books were presented by the Editor of the *South Devon Times*. Torquay's ceremony was at the Town Hall, attended by the Mayor and Mayoress and Deputy Mayor in full regalia, while Paignton had a sailing boat, mounted on a float, with sails set, and decorated to simulate waves, towed through the town by Guides and Rangers, led by a band to the appointed spot, where the Council Chamber handed out books.

These are some, but by no means all, of the celebrations marking the introduction of great and forward-looking changes in methods of training in the Movement.

Commissioners and Guiders attended trainings in large numbers to learn how to put the new programme into practice.

There were severe floods, particularly in East Devon, in July, and Rangers and Guides helped people made homeless.

By 1969 Betty Bindloss and her sister Dorothy had generously given Bowerman's Cottage at Manaton to the county, to become Devon's 'County Guide House' and an adventure centre on Dartmoor. Planning permission had been obtained to extend it by building on two rooms and a toilet annexe and making a parking space, and units were challenged to raise money for it to be ready for use in 1970. Money poured in, including generous donations from the County President, Lady Amory, and from Mr Rattey (father of Hope), and by December over £3,000 had been raised, and a grant from the Ministry of Education and Science applied for. It was vested in a trust deed at CHQ and a small management committee was formed. Building work started in October, and gifts of furniture, etc., were received. (See Chapter 12).

The Chief Guide celebrated her eightieth birthday in 1969, and to mark it Devon raised £130 for the Olave Baden-Powell Memorial Fund, which gives bursaries to Guide members travelling to overseas camps and gatherings. One representative from each of the thirteen divisions joined 715 other Guides and Rangers at Windsor for a weekend of sightseeing and a sing-song attended by the Chief Guide. They marched to the band of the Irish Guards to a special service in St George's Chapel – and very smart they were! Another smart occasion was when

Plymouth and Torbay Rangers formed guards of honour for the Queen Mother when she visited Torbay in the Royal Yacht *Britannia* to open the new YMCA Youth Club.

At the AGM in March an 'Any Questions' session was held, with Elizabeth Hartley in the chair and the Bishop of Crediton (the Right Reverend Wilfrid Westall), Miss P. Gilbert and Mr Waterforde-Young forming the panel. Instead of the usual trainings in the morning, a well-designed exhibition on the new Eight-Point Programme was staged by Guiders from every division. Inspiringly designed by Angela Graham, Assistant County Commissioner and Chairman of Training, it was so successful that it was put on again in October at Torre Abbey, Torquay, where it was seen by many packs and companies, by the general public and by Commissioners from South West England at their Training Conference.

The County Youth Service organised the usual Canoe Course at Thorverton, attended by twenty-five Rangers. They also ran a camping canoe expedition in July, thoroughly enjoyed by ten Plymouth Sea Rangers, who trained for endurance during the previous weeks. They set out from the Barbican, carrying some equipment in the canoes, the rest being in the safety boat with Miss Beryl Fyfe, the County Boat Adviser, and canoed to Earth Island (National Trust) on the St Germans river. They camped overnight, but because of the falling tide they had to strike camp in the dark and leave at 5 a.m. However, 'It was a unique experience to be canoeing on this lovely river whilst the dawn came up.' They cooked breakfast at Weir Quay near Saltash Bridge, and returned down the Tamar to Drake's Island, where they spent the rest of the day relaxing on the beach in the sun. They covered twenty-eight miles, a good achievement in twenty-four hours.

Chapter 5: THE 1970s

1970 was Diamond Jubilee Year – sixty years since Guiding started. There were many celebrations: six young Guiders and three older ones from Devon had the thrill of attending a Buckingham Palace Garden Party. Twenty-eight Devon Guides went to a special service in Westminster Abbey and fourteen to Westminster Cathedral. Some Rangers and older Guides went to a Theatre Workshop and then took part in a Diamond Jubilee Spectacular at Wembley Stadium, and a special train was chartered to take 447 Guides, Guiders and Trefoil members from Devon to watch this marvellous production. Devon held its own services of thanksgiving and dedication at four centres (because there would be too many for the cathedral), at Barnstaple, Exeter, Plymouth and Torquay. Brownies held their own special service.

The whole county, apart from Brownies, came together for 'County Day' at Powderham Castle. As Angela Graham wrote in the annual report, 'Some 5,000 poured into the Castle grounds, and the rain poured down on them!' The Royal Marines provided some exciting activities and there was a big campfire sing-song at the end of the day, but the very large numbers with no wet-weather shelter meant that the day was not an unqualified success.

The theme for Jubilee Year was 'Three Cheers', the idea being to give service by cheering up a person, a place and themselves. Among many examples of cheering a place, the 1st Stokenham Brownies, who met in a log cabin in a wood in Brown Owl's garden, made a path by clearing brambles and nettles and planted wild flowers and sixty trees. The Pack, the Guide company and the Sea Ranger crew spent many working meetings clearing the site and lighting bonfires, on which they grilled sausages. This venture was also a contribution to European Conservation Year. Another example was the clearing of a ton of litter from Slapton beach by Kingsbridge District.

Bowerman's Cottage was completed in March after teams of volunteers had spent many weekends decorating and fitting out. It was proving to be very popular and was greatly appreciated by those who used it. (See Chapter 12)

Brownie Sea Day was an unforgettable experience for 1,200 Brownies from Plymouth, Plym, Tavistock and Okehampton Divisions. Elizabeth Hartley quoted in the annual report the comment by Commander Cliffe, who hosted the day, "There is no-one like a Brownie for cutting the Navy down to size." The Brownies made no response when told they were going to sea, they would visit the dockyard and they would watch a gun-team rehearsal for the Royal Tournament, but when told there would be swings and roundabouts they roared their approval. She went on to describe how there was a kind of Never-Never Land happiness in the air, with so many little girls enjoying themselves in so many different ways, thanks to the kindness of the naval personnel. No Brownies were lost and no litter was left behind.

A Jubilee Camp was held on Dartmoor, at Prince Hall Farm near Princetown, for Tavistock/Okehampton and Plym Divisions. Mrs Joan Round, Plym Division Commissioner who was a Certified Trainer and County Press and Publicity Officer, was in charge, and about 400 Guides camped in twenty groups of their own units. For a base they used Devon County Education Committee's Outdoor Pursuits Centre next to the camping fields, and its qualified instructors and the 22nd Army Youth Team provided a wide range of activities on and off the site, including a night walk on the moor. Two campfires for everyone were led by the very gifted County Arts Adviser, Miss Margaret Brotheridge. Although hard work for the organisers, the camp was a great success, especially as all the handicapped Guides from Dame Hannah Rogers School attended and took part in many activities, including the night walk, when they were pushed in their wheelchairs by willing Rangers and Guiders.

Plymouth East's early morning Thinking Day ceremony on the Hoe included a trip for ninety-one Guides, etc., in a minesweeper to throw garlands and bottles with messages over the side.

The County's Service project was to raise £800 for the Royal Commonwealth Society for the Blind for eye camps in India. A total of £2,200 was raised, and at a presentation ceremony at CHQ, attended among others by a Guide from the School for the Partially Sighted in Exeter, it was announced that this would pay for sixteen eye camps, through which 600 people would have their sight restored.

In October a farewell tea party and then a buffet supper were held for Betty Bindloss, who was retiring as County Commissioner. She was congratulated on her new appointment as the first Region Chief Commissioner for South West England. (See page 377.)

In the annual report for 1970 there was an anonymous piece, 'DIAMOND JUBILEE RANDOM MEMORIES'; it is a moving summary of the year:

> I remember hazy sunshine and new warmth, and a feeling of acute anticipation as the day of the first celebration dawned. I remember the single voices of girl readers floating down from the Minstrels' Gallery in the old Cathedral, and the figure of our County Commissioner, dwarfed by the building's vast dimensions, leading us in re-dedication.
>
> I remember little groups of Brownies, in brilliant May sunshine, collecting in the villages along the route to another Church, the brimstone butterflies in the hedges like scraps of their Brownie ties – and I remember, too, a sudden rush of unpremeditated tears. I remember the damp mists rolling away with the turning tide, and afternoon sunshine glinting down onto hundreds of blue-clad figures moving freely among the trees – and a lone heron flying on heavy, silent wings over them all.
>
> I remember the sudden silence on a school playing field after a miraculously ordered exodus of six hundred Brownies, and the tired but deeply contented faces of the few Guiders still remaining. I remember, too, the face of one Guide, inspired and moved beyond words, at the conclusion of the Wembley Spectacle.
>
> I remember a train thundering through the warm September

night, perfect companionship and fellowship, and a hearty left-hand shake on the station at three o'clock in the morning! And I remember a faint echo of Wembley in a Parish Church just before Christmas, in soft candle-light, a choir of Guides humming the Theme Tune to haunt, with a myriad of memories, those of us who had heard it before: "Music, when soft voices die, vibrates in the memory. . . ."

1971: Angela Graham was now the County Commissioner, and in her summary in the annual report she mentions the vast amount of fundraising done for good causes – for example, Yelverton District sent £50 to the Dartmoor Rescue Group; Honiton District sent £34 to children in Vietnam; Sidmouth District sent £61 to a hospital in Nepal; and Clyst St Mary Guides sang carols for two hours outside St David's Station, Exeter, and collected £10 for Shelter; the five Packs of Brixham Brownies, through jumble sales, a pantomime, etc., raised £250 to buy a guide dog called Guider and were on their way towards another, called Brownie. She also mentioned some of the many acts of service being carried out around the county – for instance, North Tawton Brownies provided refreshments for 300 people at a bazaar; Dawlish Brownies collected and refurbished old uniforms to send to an underprivileged Pack in Bristol to enable them to go on Pack Holiday; Exeter Guides tidied up the County Showground each day of the show, and distributed appeal leaflets for Help the Aged to every house in Exeter; Brixham Sea Rangers took part in a sponsored struggle on the River Dart in aid of the Multiple Sclerosis Appeal, making their own craft and after seven hours being one of the few teams to complete the course.

Kathleen Thomas, Commonwealth and International Adviser for Devon, reported a marked interest in international Guiding. A Guide represented South West England at an International Camp in Sweden and two Rangers went to an international gathering in France. For the first time a weekend for potential candidates for international events was held at Bowerman's, with representatives from the divisions and the Lone Ranger Company. 'The experiment proved most worthwhile as we were able to get to know each other in a way which is quite impossible at a short interview,' wrote Kathleen. They enjoyed a programme of international interest and walking on Dartmoor.

Laurie Pearson, Guider of the 1st Dartmouth Company, took her Guides to camp at Netherurd, the Scottish Guide Training Centre near Peebles. This involved much fundraising and camp practice, and being a great success was the first of many camps and holidays in the UK and overseas that the Dartmouth Guides enjoyed under Laurie's enterprising and inspirational leadership.

The National Festival of Song took place in 1972. The county finals in Exeter in January were ably organised by the County Arts Adviser, Margaret Brotheridge; eleven divisions had entered, with 350 Rangers, Guides and Brownies going to the finals. The Brownies went first, with varied programmes and high standards; some accompanied themselves on guitars, percussion, recorders, etc. The 3rd Crediton Pack (Tiverton Division) under Guider Mrs Muriel Foden were first, with Totnes second and Honiton third. Then there were the solos, duets, trios and quartets, and again the standard was high. The winning solo entry was a Ranger, Jane Gosling, from Honiton Division; Alison Clear and Julia Miller from Exeter won the duet section, and three sisters – Wendy, Diana and Shirley Collins from Oakford (Tiverton Division) – won the trio section. Plymouth West won the quartet section. The Guide programmes were so varied that it was difficult to judge, but in the end the winners were Plympton District Guides, led by Mrs Jefferies, who then formed Devon's entry for the Radio Heats in Bristol. They didn't get into the regional final, but the Oakford trio were asked to sing as entertainment between the heats – an honour for Devon.

Another international weekend was held at Bowerman's; last year's enabled two girls to represent the Region at an International Camp in Sweden and two in Romania. A Devon Guider, Marilyn Goldsbrough, was one of eight representing England at a Scout and Guide Conference in Paris. Fifteen units were taking part in the Duke of Edinburgh Award Scheme through Guiding.

Sail training on big sailing ships was encouraged for older girls, not necessarily Sea Rangers, and this year the Northcott Foundation sponsored a cruise on the Sail Training Ship the

Malcolm Miller; girls were interviewed by a small committee, and a Torquay Sea Ranger was the first to benefit from what became an annual sponsorship for many years. Others had a cruise on the Ocean Youth Club boat, the *Scott Bader*, which was based in Plymouth. These 'cruises' are not like today's holiday cruises – they are hard work and you learn to work as a team to sail these beautiful ships. (See page 345.)

An unusual piece of service was given by Walkhampton Guides to a large group of refugees from Uganda. Their Guider, Anneliese Barrell, who was also involved through her work with handicapped children, tells this remarkable story:

In the autumn of 1972 the disued Plasterdown Army Camp on Dartmoor between Whitchurch and Horrabridge became the refugee camp for those Ugandan Asians expelled from Uganda by President Idi Amin. They had been forced onto planes by armed militia at Entebbe Airport and arrived in the cold snowy Dartmoor weather in the early hours of the morning. They were cold, bewildered, tired and hungry. At Plasterdown they were met by warmth and friendship by the local WRVS members, local clergy, parishioners and local government officers.

A few weeks earlier local Guides from Tavistock, Walkhampton and Plymouth had spent weekends preparing beds and rooms for the refugees. They found some of the requests rather strange as cultural differences had to be explained. I well remember how our backs felt having made up nearly 400 beds!

When the first busloads of refugees arrived on the night of 17th October they were taken for a hot drink and something to eat while their meagre luggage was unloaded and strewn over the floor of a large hut. Sequins spilt out of bundles wrapped in saris, bags of personal belongings were everywhere. Each person could only bring what they could carry and only the equivalent of £50. Extreme hardship for many; these were professional people – doctors, solicitors, teachers, as well as dressmakers, barbers, cooks, etc. The atmosphere was one of frightened anticipation, but everyone was relieved to be safe and determined to make the best of the situation.

I was asked by Miss Elizabeth Hartley, the then Deputy Chief Commissioner for England, who lived in Dousland, if I would bring some of the Walkhampton Guides to help play with the children in the camp. I later went to CHQ in London to enquire about Guiding in Uganda and how best we could help the children. Elizabeth and I had a hut set aside for recreation and I requested that bars be removed from the windows and that the heat be sufficient. We arrived on the second evening with a car full of toys and activities for all ages, boys and girls, including blown-up balloons, and we put all this in a side room which still had barred windows. The children arrived and the parents crowded around the entrances, fearful of what their children were up to when all of a sudden the balloons in the side room burst. Elizabeth and I were in uniform; the parents screamed, thinking we were military and were firing at the children. What a lesson to us! We soon reassured everyone and proceeded to have great fun together. The refugees soon organised themselves and tried to make life as normal as possible.

Our involvement with the girls continued until the next summer. We invited them to our meetings and homes and were very sorry to see them go, but very pleased that they moved on to a better life in other parts of the country; many had relatives and friends in the UK. To thank all those who had helped them, the refugees gave a party at the Festival of Diwali. I remember the ladies cooking Indian delicacies and decorating the rather drab hut with bed sheets and coloured toilet paper. They sang and danced for us and despite the situation they were in it was an extremely happy occasion.

During the settling in time I was responsible for logging the refugees through the camp medical centre. Each one was medically checked, and we even had a baby born within the first few weeks. It was a very busy time and steep learning curve for many. I know that the Guides gained much from the friendships they made with the Asian girls; we shared skills and experiences. The one thing that sticks in my memory is the sheer determination amongst the Asians not to let this dreadful, terrifying, ordeal ruin the rest of their lives. They never complained. They were an inspiration to us all.

The two Plymouth divisions took alternate Saturdays to occupy the Asian children at Plasterdown, including knitting instructions. 'At least we taught them to cast on and knit, but we never got around to casting off!' And in East Devon, the Asians in the Honiton camp were also given neighbourly help.

In July the Queen came to Dartmouth to take the salute at the Lord High Admiral's Parade at the Royal Naval College.

A hundred Brownies, Guides, Rangers and Guiders lined up in front of the crowds – then it suddenly rained and they were all drenched. The Queen came over and spoke to some of the Guides, and the Duke of Edinburgh made them laugh by telling them they were in the height of fashion – the wet look!

In 1973 the County Training Team were busy teaching Guiders how to use the new Study Papers, which were considered helpful. Joan Round had now retired as a trainer, and Elizabeth Bowden and Anneliese Barrell had joined the team.

There were the usual, often unusual, number of good turns round the county: Axminster Division watched a film on the work of the RNIB before setting out on the Dartmoor Pilgrimage, when they raised £134 for blind people with additional handicaps. Holsworthy District had a seven-mile sponsored walk through woods and lanes round Shebbear and raised £300 for the Sennen lifeboat; to thank them the RNLI gave them boat trips in Plymouth Sound. A very cheerful Torquay Guide in a wheelchair regularly visited and helped at an old people's home. The 45th Exeter Guides gave a Christmas dinner to twenty elderly folk, with whom they had kept in touch. Honiton Guides were responsible for selling the catalogues at the Honiton Show. Exeter Division had a publicity campaign, with Guides and Brownies demonstrating activities on the Cathedral Green. Exeter University Scout and Guide Club gave a party to interest fellow students – ten students were in fact helping with Guide units. Ilfracombe District presented the town council with a book with the names of all the Guiders over the last sixty years. Dartmouth Guides collected 158 gifts for the mentally handicapped at Starcross Hospital. Several units raised money for famine relief in Ethiopia.

There was of course a lot of fun. Two Bideford Rangers went on the joint Venture Scout/Ranger Guide cruise to Gibraltar for a folk festival in St Michael's Caves. Kingsbridge District held 'Crazy Sports' – filling a barrel with leaking buckets, blindfold potato races, and passing kindling across a swimming pool before lighting a fire and cooking sausages.

Since the Song Festival in 1972 there was a great demand

for trainings for campfires and singing evenings, which kept the County Arts Adviser, Margaret Brotheridge, and her team busy. Fifteen Guiders attended a Region Drama Conference in Taunton.

Devon Conservation Forum and the Standing Conference of Voluntary Youth Organisations in Devon held an 'Eyesore Pinpointing' competition, which was won by the 2nd South Brent Guides. They found a broken iron fence along one side of the children's playing field, sketched it, mapped it with grid references and suggested remedial action – which was then done by the parish. A Bideford Guider, Miss Phyllis Durant, had the honour of being made the ninety-ninth and last Freeman of the Borough of Bideford – an honour too for the Guides.

A sad happening in 1973, initiated in London, was the ending of the Sea Ranger Branch. (See page 199.)

1974 was Brownie Diamond Jubilee Year. The following report was written by Miss Jean Blathwayt (Division Commissioner for Exmouth), who, together with her sister Barbara, gave many years of good Guiding for the county:

> It is difficult to get a complete picture of what was going on in the County this year among its 6,000 or so Brownie population. . . . The biggest happening was the Brownie Food Market project, thought up by a small committee appointed by the County Executive. These markets were to take place at the same time, on the same day, all over the County. . . . Most units were more than willing to participate. The money raised from these markets was earmarked for the mentally handicapped in Devon, and out of this idea grew another one, contrived chiefly by Miss Lorna Harvey and M. D. Howes, the Voluntary Help Co-ordinator of the Royal Western Counties Hospitals, to raise enough money to buy a minibus for the patients of the Hawkmoor Unit for the mentally handicapped.
>
> And so something memorable was brought to its exciting climax on Saturday September 28th when Mrs. Graham drove the big white brand-new minibus, packed full to bursting with excited Brownies, down to the car park outside the main hall at Hawkmoor Hospital. The hall was full of Brownies and Guiders and friends and patients, all waiting expectantly, and among the specially invited and welcomed guests were Miss Bindloss, our Regional

Chief Commissioner, our Assistant County Commissioner, County Secretary, County Treasurer, and representatives from the Royal Western Counties Hospitals. A Brownie from Ashburton handed over a cheque for £2,000, after having told the assembled company in clear, lucid tones, what it was all about. Then it was tea for all. . . . Mrs Graham called our project "Operation V.C.", standing for Vision and Communication – an apt summing up of a big, concerted effort in the Devon Brownie World, which had produced such a happy and satisfactory result.

1974 was the 150th anniversary of the foundation of the RNLI, and the Guide Friendship Fund aimed to raise £5,000 to buy an Atlantic-class inshore lifeboat. In fact £15,000 was raised, and the lifeboat, named *Guide Friendship*, was launched at Aberdovey in November. Plymouth was the venue in July for the first international lifeboat exhibition. Devon Guides raised at least £500 for the RNLI this year.

The Young Leaders scheme was now well established, under Mavis Budden, the County Leadership Adviser; Young Leaders were girls aged sixteen plus who helped in units and were training to be Guiders (they were originally called Cadets). This year, as well as trainings in the arts and general activities, there were two residential weekends at Bowerman's. At the first, organised by the East Devon Youth Officer, the girls were challenged to programme and carry out an expedition from Bowerman's to Pixie's Holt (Dartmeet), where they had to pitch camp for the night. The return journey included rock climbing, for which they had been prepared by going through the assault course at Pixie's Holt. There were seventy Young Leaders in the county by now.

Angela Graham initiated a tape-recording competition for Guides and Rangers separately, the subject being 'The Sound of a Season'. It was won by the 1st Yealmpton Guides, with Ilfracombe second and Salcombe third.

1975 was World Conference Year, opened in Brighton by the president, Princess Margaret. Several Devon units took up the World Conference Challenges, which taught the girls about the family of Guiding round the world. The county event was a Guide 'It's a Knockout Competition', which was great fun for all fourteen Divisions that took part. Organised by the young Outdoor Activities Adviser Miss Chris Tozer, with the help of Rangers, at Kingsteignton School, it was won by Plymouth East, who thus gained the Clinton Shield for this year. In North Devon, Brownie Revels were held at Crow Point beach, the theme being pirates – they had a sandcastle competition and searched the sand dunes for Captain Hook. Holsworthy District held a sponsored seven-mile walk and raised £300 for refugees in Vietnam and Cambodia. Walkhampton Guides won a Coca-Cola award for European Architectural Heritage Year for their work on clearing common land at Huckworthy Bridge, and Hatherleigh Guides took part in a de-ivying project, also for Heritage Year.

Dolton Brownies sold gallons of soup at Dolton Carnival and won first prize for a haybox soup kitchen in a pram. Crediton Guides cooked 300 hot dogs, which they sold in two hours at the Council of Churches Bonfire Night, in aid of Tapes for the Housebound. Poltimore Guides collected firewood for an old-age pensioner.

Exeter Division Commissioners and Young Leaders worked on a service project on an old housing estate to find out why so few girls were joining the Guides or Brownies. Division Commissioner Mrs Margaret Branch described what they did:

> We ran a Day Camp, inviting 36 eleven year old girls from the school on the estate. We had six Patrols with a Young Leader acting as a Patrol Leader; each Patrol had a tent and we organised a typical day in camp with ordinary Guide activities, such as tracking, a scavenge, crazy sports, outdoor cooking and camp fire singing of the more raucous variety. The Young Leaders also talked to the girls in their tents and showed them the Guide Handbooks and asked them their views on the Guide Movement. The most notable feature was that the girls needed much more supervision than a Guide Company. They quarrelled, hurt each other, and took more than their fair share of food. There were many little scratches and grazes needing sympathy more than first aid. In fact many of the children needed a lot of attention; they wanted physical contact and just someone they could hang on to all day. In talking about Guides, they thought it was fun, but only one or two said they wanted to join a unit. They did not want to

commit themselves to anything; they preferred a club which they could attend when they felt like it and where 'Pop' and crisps were provided.

We had a follow-up Halloween Party with 100% attendance. . . . They made the decorations, masks and cakes. The food disappeared inordinately quickly, but we soon discovered they were hoarding it in their laps. The usual Halloween games were thoroughly enjoyed and a ghost story produced piercing screams. However, we felt that with all our other commitments we could not keep up the project on a regular basis. In discussion afterwards, the Young Leaders felt that we should be flexible up to a point to suit the girls' needs, but that the pattern of Guiding must remain. We have shown them what it is about and that we would welcome them. They have to decide themselves whether they want to make that commitment.

Looking at the impact we have made, only one of the Project girls joined Guides at first, but perhaps we did make an impression on the neighbourhood because the numbers in the existing Guide Company suddenly increased from 12 to 20. In October we happened to start a new Guide Company just outside the estate and more girls from the estate joined, three of them Project girls. If we produce one good Guide from among them, perhaps it will have been worthwhile, but many girls got a glimpse of the happiness which Guiding generates.

Margaret Brotheridge, the County Arts Adviser, was working hard to spread the enjoyment of all the arts, which was an integrated part of the Eight-Point Programme; she reported on a successful eisteddfod, where Guides competed in music, mime, choral speaking, singing and craftwork.

Plymouth and Torbay both have singing groups, which are proving to be very popular and relaxing. Guides have tried their hands at bell ringing and sword dancing and . . . a Company has formed a folk group and have entertained disabled centres with their songs and country dancing.

With regard to handicrafts, she reported:

Many lovely gifts were made for the delegates to the World Camp as well as supplying stalls at bazaars and coffee mornings with fund raising articles.

When the South West Region was formed, many counties divided, making two or three Guide counties. Dorset, Devon and Cornwall remained whole. But in 1976 discussions took place as to whether Devon should be divided. Angela Graham reported:

> It seemed that practical reasons in favour of dividing just predominated, but that the sentiments of most people were in favour of continuing as one County. Therefore it has been agreed not to divide so long as there is someone to undertake the job of Commissioner for this, much the largest County in the South West Region both in area and Guide population.

Because of inequalities in the way the population of Devon is distributed, dividing is not really feasible, and fortunately there has always been someone willing to travel the length and breadth of Devon as County Commissioner.

The most exciting and original event of 1976 was the Elizabethan Sheep Shearing Festival – a week-long arts workshop held in Honiton School. The County Arts Adviser, Margaret Brotheridge, whose expertise and enthusiasm were behind the project, reported:

> On 9th April sixty-three Guides started to descend on Honiton with all their paraphernalia and the trainers arrived from Manchester, Cheshire, Birmingham, Somerset and Hampshire. . . . The main hurdle was catering for 100 at every meal. Supper time came, hatches flew up, doors opened wide and in came the hungry herd. After every scrap was eaten . . . the kitchen team settled down to what everyone called a week of fantastic food.
>
> The Guides had sorted themselves out into their working groups of Music, Drama, Dance and Craft and each group was to contribute items for an Elizabethan Sheep Shearing Festival – sheep shearing because of the rural character of Devon and Elizabethan because there were so many famous Devonians in the reign of Elizabeth I. There was no script except for an extract from Shakespeare, so the dialogue and action were all to evolve during the course of the Workshop. During the group sessions many ideas came from the Guides. Pat Poyner, who was responsible for the drama, worked on the Shakespeare portion and the main theme of the Festival, also the report of a sailor seeing Drake on Plymouth Hoe and the knighting of Drake by Elizabeth I. Ruth Hemp in her dance sessions worked out an amusing sheep

shearing dance, the sad story of the Flemish Weavers, and a most effective scene of lace-making. Hettie Smith had fun in the music sessions teaching various Elizabethan songs, helping the Guides to compose pipe music for the festival dance. . . . Guides in the craft group were engaged in Elizabethan crafts including candle-making, tapestry work, spinning and banner making; also they provided all the props that were required. . . . Margaret Roberts and Audrey Mayell were in charge of costume and everyone brought bits of material to be cut up and run up into whatever was needed. Shrieks of laughter came from the costume rooms as Guides and Guiders tried on mob caps, baggy trousers, beards and jackets.

During the interest sessions we had a chance to see various crafts that would have been carried on in Elizabethan times: spinning and weaving, Honiton lace-making which was introduced into Devon in the Elizabethan age, archery, flower arranging and Honiton Pottery was visited as they made our souvenirs of mugs and dishes. . . . Groups visited Stockland Hill Radio Station, Axminster Carpet Factory, Cricket St. Thomas Wildlife Park and twenty went horse riding. On Palm Sunday we attended various churches in the morning and held a Songs of Praise in the evening. One of the most thrilling events was the banquet. Everyone dressed suitably for the occasion and sat down to roast turkey with all the trimmings. . . .

The climax of the week was the final performance to an invited audience of about 200. The atmosphere was of infectious happiness and many of the guests remarked on this during tea afterwards. . . . The week proved that although Guiding has changed in many ways yet the Promise and Laws continue to bind us together.

Valerie Dampney, the County Programme and Training Adviser, added:

The Arts week at Honiton was an unqualified success and showed how a few days together can weld Guiders and Guides from all parts of Devon into a happy working group to produce a performance of great quality.

The summer of 1976 was hot and dry and over 1,000 Guides in the county camped – a record. Problems were fire risk and hard ground! Plymouth East Rangers and Guides had become part of a Youth Emergency Team along with other organisations in Plymouth and took part in a mock emergency staged during the year at a disused railway line – a train carrying a dangerous load became derailed; people were injured and had to be evacuated. Rangers worked in a Headquarters taking telephone and radio messages; some Guides were casualties and others worked in a Rest Centre. A Plymouth West Company camping on Dartmoor had the thrill of climbing Sheepstor to see the sunrise and have breakfast at dawn. Jane Kelsey, a Guide in St Budeaux West District, made local headlines when she rescued a three-year-old boy from the River Tamar.

Bideford Guides had a float in the local carnival depicting Guiding in the Common Market. Winkleigh Brownies were the mainstay of the parish church choir, and Aylesbeare Guides rang the church bells for their District Thinking Day service.

1977 was the Queen's Silver Jubilee and the Rangers' Diamond Jubilee. The Queen visited Devon, and had a reunion with her former Sea Ranger skipper, Sylvia Clarke (see Chapter 12). County Commissioner Angela Graham and her husband were invited to a reception on board the Royal Yacht *Britannia* in Plymouth Sound and Exeter Ranger Joan Ross was fortunate to accompany them.

Ranger celebrations took many forms and kept Chris Tozer busy; she was Ranger Consultant for the county as well as Outdoor Activities Adviser, and Angela Graham in the annual report gave her a special word of thanks for coordinating the various county and national events so well. One of the main events was a Ranger weekend at Ravenswood School, Stoodleigh, near Tiverton, in April, described by a South Brent Ranger, Bertha Harley, whose mother, Unity, was Division Commissioner for Totnes:

> Ravenswood School turned out to be a vast Tudor mansion surrounded by a large garden with views of the beautiful rolling countryside of the Exe valley, ideal for the activities of around 75 Rangers. The weather too was ideal for the 'night adventure'. On the first night a full moon watched us as we used our imaginations to transport us from Rangers in Devon

to aeroplane passengers crashed in the Holy Land and treating casualties, improvising shelters with fertiliser bags and fire lighting. Then we went through an assault course (by now it was 10.30 p.m.) – through a dangerous jungle with only a rope trail to lead us – a sheer cliff of wood to scramble up – a mine field of tin cans to crawl under and a tunnel of rubber tyres all at the dead of night!

On Saturday we spent the day doing our chosen activities which included gliding, archery, hand-bell ringing, fly-fishing and keep fit. In addition Rangers worked furiously at all hours knitting – I won't forget the sight of all the Rangers in my dormitory sitting up doing their knitting in bed, last thing at night; not unlike patients in a hospital geriatric ward! (The completed blanket went to Help the Aged.) I think the highlight of the weekend was the formal dinner with guests which included both roast turkey and the County Commissioner, followed by what could be called a Variety Show. We played Kim's Game with the drama group miming all the objects, country dancing with wild abandon and sobered up with the Plymouth Rangers' very good singing, followed by prayers and Taps.

On Sunday morning we all trooped off to Stoodleigh church which had been beautifully decorated by the flower arranging group. The Palm Sunday service was very moving; the greater part of it was chosen and led by the Rangers and a guitar group accompanied some hymns. To round off the morning we had an energetic mini-knockout. Blindfolded, one poor team member after another had to dribble a football across the lawn which proved hilarious to watch. Then our team linked together with rope scrambled over five tree stumps in three minutes. After lunch, Diane, an Exeter Ranger, gave us a very interesting slide show of her visit to Our Cabana in Mexico.

This weekend was thoroughly worthwhile and extremely enjoyable and our thanks to the Guiders who put so much energy and time into making it such a complete success. It's amazing what you can do in a weekend!

For several years the Rotary Clubs of Devon ran Public Speaking Competitions for young people in teams of three – one to introduce the speaker, one to speak and the third to thank the speaker. In 1977 a team of three Guides from Kilmington in Axminster Division won the under-thirteen competition, the subject being the history of Guiding.

A Ranger service project was to collect litter in seventy-seven minutes, and one and three-quarters tons were collected! Another piece of service was clearing Wray Cleave woodlands near Moretonhampstead and many Ranger units spent days working there.

The Queen's Silver Jubilee was celebrated in many different ways round the county – for example, Brownies from Plymouth East and West, Tavistock and Saltash had a Sea Day at HMS *Drake*, and Exeter Guides and Scouts held a two-day exhibition in St George's Hall with an entertainment in the evening. The county celebrated by holding a Devon Durbar on the (old) County Showground. The idea, based on Indian durbars, came from Unity Harley. Each division took a period of history from cavemen to the year 2000. About 3,000 Guides and Guiders took part, parading in the excellent costumes they had made – slaves, queens, chambermaids, soldiers and farmers – and a dragon consisting of twenty pairs of green legs under a shell of brown hessian. A Torbay Guide wrote:

> Our Division were cave men (and women of course!) dressed in furry bikinis and sacking! Armed with clubs, cudgels and animal skins we waited until it was our turn to display our dress. . . . All the Guides dressed to represent the ages from prehistory times to 2001 paraded round the arena to a commentary about each display. On seeing the other costumes we were impressed by the care and work put into designing and making them.

There was a commando course provided by the marines and a Patrol challenge and finally a campfire sing-song led by Margaret Brotheridge. "We would like to say a big thank you to all concerned for a smashing Jubilee Durbar." Angela Graham, who was dressed as Britannia holding a trident in a chariot, wrote:

> The parade was a wonderful spectacle, enhanced as it was by Mrs Chanter's clever commentary delivered entertainingly by Mr. Geoffrey Philpotts the Scout County Commissioner.

A sad occurrence this year was the death of Olave, Lady Baden-Powell, aged eighty-eight. Twenty-eight services of thanksgiving for her life were held in Devon. At the service in Ashburton Division the church pulpit was decorated with Olave Baden-Powell roses.

There was heavy snow in the February of 1978 and many Thinking Day meetings had to be cancelled.

In Taw and Torridge Division the newly formed Torrington Rangers helped deliver milk by sledge and meals on foot; they also helped clear Lydford Gorge of snow damage. In the spring Silverton Brownies raised money and planted a small grove of trees in the grounds of the new school. Lympstone Guides helped the Devon Family History Society with recording gravestone markings. Lone Guides and Rangers were flourishing under the enthusiastic guidance of Miss Greta Gray, a stalwart and very experienced Guider who shared her remote home at Oakford, near Tiverton, with Mrs Kathleen Thomas. Twelve Lones had a successful Easter get-together at Bowerman's, and some of them camped with active units in the summer. Two Lones – Sara Haskin and Wendy Bootherstone – gained their Queen's Guide Award. Cooperation with the Scouts continued – in Axminster Division a joint Scout and Guide Patrol Leaders' weekend was held at the Lyme Regis Adventure Centre, and forty Devon Rangers took part in 'Raven', a South West Region joint Venture Ranger camp in Taunton.

In North Devon Division Guides decorated a Cheshire Home for Christmas and gave Christmas parcels to old folk in Ilfracombe, Woolacombe and Lynton Districts and shopped for them on Saturdays in Braunton. Their hard-working Division Commissioner of many years' service, Miss Phyl Fowler, retired this year, and Mrs Kay Thorpe took over. There was great sadness, locally and round the county, at the news that a Guide in the 1st Westhill Company, near Aylesbeare, Genette Tate, had disappeared while doing her paper round. The mystery of what happened to her has never been solved.

There was a new challenge to Devon Guides in May when the Devon County Show organisers asked for Guides to act as runners and messengers at the show and to stand as markers in the ring. The Guides who took part were well turned out and extremely reliable and willing, and earned high praise from all the show officials. The following year the Guides were offered camping facilities on the showground, and this service to the community has continued every year since, thanks not only to the Guides who take part, but in large measure to the dedicated Guiders who organise a new team each year and look after them.

Many Rangers were taking part in the Duke of Edinburgh Award Scheme, and some of them met the Duke himself when he visited Devon and saw the displays they had made to illustrate what they were doing for the award. A new outdoor activity was deer spotting, which involved getting up very early and joining a 'meet' of the local branch of the British Deer Society at the crack of dawn. In addition to the meet in Ashclyst Forest near Exeter, a group of Guiders and Rangers went to the red deer rut on Exmoor – "a marvellous experience". Some Plymouth units went deer spotting in woods near Plymouth.

Special Report for 1970

BOATING

Two Sea Rangers from Plymouth and Topsham were chosen by the County to cruise in the *Malcolm Miller* and the *Winston Churchill* this year and thoroughly enjoyed the experience in spite of very windy weather. One Plymouth Sea Ranger was awarded the Plymouth Outward Bound Scholarship and had a very interesting time climbing and canoeing in Wales.

Sea Rangers from Topsham and Plymouth enjoyed two weekend cruises in October aboard the Ocean Youth Club boat *Pelican*, based at Plymouth, but in spite of a few queasy moments all are keen to go again.

A weekend training was also spent at Drake's Island Adventure Centre in October, canoeing, sailing and climbing. Rangers from Plymouth and Weston-Super-Mare attended.

The usual regattas were held at Totnes and Salcombe again this year. The County Regatta was again held on Sunday, but for a whole day, starting with a Service in the Chapel at Britannia Royal Naval College, Dartmouth. The weather was the worst in the history of County Regattas, in spite of deluging rain at times,

70 Rangers, parents and friends attended. A record number of crews were there, from Dartmouth, Brixham, Paignton, Topsham, Torquay, Plymouth, Kingsbridge and Salcombe. After the Service everyone had a picnic lunch at Sandquay, where, fortunately, indoor accommodation had been provided. At 1.45 p.m. the rain was still heavy, so it was decided to have at least the Princess Elizabeth Cup Race. However, as soon as the crews and spectators emerged, the rain miraculously stopped, and it just remained fine for the duration of the Regatta! We were very sorry to miss Captain Franks this year owing to illness, but extremely grateful to Mr. John Dampney from Plymouth who came and organised the starting of the races at short notice. We were also delighted to have Mrs. Franks with us all day in spite of the damp conditions, and she also presented the prizes.

RESULTS: Princess Elizabeth Cup . . . S.R.S. *Orpheus*, Topsham County Cup for Overall points . . . S.R.S. *Research*, Dartmouth Burgee for Overall points (2nd place) . . . S.R.S. *Churchill*, Brixham

BERYL FYFE
County Boating Adviser

Special Report for 1971

OUR 'ADVENTURE BY LAND' CERTIFICATE

Five of us, having decided to try for our 'Adventure by Land' Certificate, were given instruction during Ranger meetings on mapping and compass, first aid, the right equipment to take, etc, and we had a practice weekend near Chagford.

The date of the test was fixed and we planned our menus, checked our kit, and booked beds at Gidleigh Youth Hostel. Saturday came, and off we set. At Chagford we were met at the bus by the Tester, who is a Warden of Dartmoor National Park; he dropped our kit for us at the Hostel, and after we had eaten our packed lunch the test started.

A pleasant surprise awaited us – the Warden was being helped that weekend by Group Scout Service teams (ex Rover Scouts) from Southampton and St. Austell, and while we waited to be tested individually on mapping, compass etc., we worked with them pulling down outhouses around a derelict cottage and making huge bonfires of the rubbish. Later, when we had finished the test, we joined the Scouts in an unsuccessful attempt to remove a large boulder from the bed of a stream which was being diverted by this obstruction from its natural course. All our united efforts were in vain, however, and after these exertions, we went back to the Hostel to cook our supper, and then SLEEP.

Next morning the Tester arrived early to collect us from the Hostel and we were taken to Meldon Valley to see the dam which is under construction and will be finished this year. We walked through the valley, which will soon be flooded, each carrying a fully packed rucksack and putting into practice some more of our mapping, having been given the task of leading the Service Groups!

Mr Boyes, the Tester, is a member of the Okehampton Dartmoor Rescue Team and is training his dog 'Tor' in rescue work. During the course of our walk we watched him being trained in obedience tests. Finally, we were taken to the Headquarters of the Rescue Team in Okehampton and shown the rescue equipment in use, including the new McKinnis Stretcher. After having our equipment and packed rucksacks inspected and our first aid equipment examined, we went to the bus stop to make our way home after a very strenuous but thoroughly enjoyable weekend.

We were all very pleased and relieved to hear about a week later that we had gained our Certificate.

FIVE EXETER RANGER GUIDES

Special Report for 1973

A VISIT TO BUCKINGHAM PALACE

The Duke of Edinburgh's Gold Award Reception was held on 28th November. I spent the previous night at the Guide club with my mother who was one of my guests, the other being Miss Lowry, the Lone Adviser for Devon.

We had to be in position in the Palace by 3 p.m., so at 2.30 we made our way there from Guide Headquarters, and were directed to the Ballroom where the guests sat on tiered seats and the Candidates were divided into groups, there being 790 Candidates. At 3.30 Prince Philip came in and went to each group in turn, talking informally and asking questions about our exploits. He handed the certificates to the Marshal in charge of each group, who handed them out to us.

The Ballroom is beautiful, with two thrones at one end and a Musicians' gallery and organ at the other. The musicians played throughout the reception – including, "Behold the Lord High Executioner"!

When eventually we left the Palace we were greeted by driving snow which made the walk back to Headquarters distinctly chilly! But it was a wonderful day, and I hope this account may inspire others to have a go at this very worthwhile scheme. I enjoyed doing it, and I made many friends and found new interests.

FELICITY GARDINER
Assistant Guider, 4th Devon Lone Guides

Chapter 6: THE END OF 1978 TO 1982

There was a record number of Queen's Guide Awards in 1978 – twenty-nine, including Heather Taylor in the Visually Handicapped Company in Exeter; she was the first in this company to get the award.

In October 1978 Angela Graham retired after eight years as County Commissioner and Lady Amory retired as County President. A farewell party was held at Exeter School: 'It was a unique gathering, drawing together well loved Guide personalities who have given generously of themselves in the past. . . . Together with them were the Guiders of today which included the young fresh faces of those who are coming to be the replacements of the future," wrote Mrs Elaine Whidborne in the annual report. Angela, who was taking over as County President, paid tribute to Lady Amory, thanking her for all the help and support she had given to herself and to Devon Guiding generally. Rosemary Howell, who had been, together with Mrs Vivien Chanter, Assistant County Commissioner, took over as County Commissioner, and spoke with humour and affection of all that was owed to Angela Graham for her eight years of leadership. At the party a Laurel Award was presented to Miss Lorna Harvey, a Brownie Guider of long standing in Ashburton, who was as popular with adults as she was with the Brownies.

1979 was the International Year of the Child, and many activities and imaginative fundraising events took place round the county. The money raised was to go to the Royal Commonwealth Society for the Blind and help Devon Guides to link with Branch

Associations in Fiji and Grenada, and units also raised money for other good causes. One unusual event, the brainchild of PR Adviser Elaine Whidborne, was the Guide presentation of 'Pause for Thought' on local radio's *Morning Sou'West* on five consecutive mornings in August; this was an opportunity to put over to the general public something of what the Guide Promise, and in particular 'duty to God', means in Guiding. A Ranger, a Guide and a Brownie from Plymouth East and West made their promises during this programme. Great interest was shown in this project at the County Commissioners' Conference when Rosemary was asked to speak about it.

The thirty Guides who were helping at the Devon County Show in May had the thrill of meeting Prince Charles when he visited the show; they were praised for their efficiency and hard work. Exeter Division had a Backwoodsman Day, when ninety Guides all lit a fire and tried out rope ladders and bridges and made one-man shelters. Two South Brent Rangers accompanied handicapped children on the Ten Tors Expedition, putting up tents and cooking for them. Chittlehampton Guides organised a party for under-fives in the village. The Axminster Division Scout and Guide Patrol Leaders' training at Lyme Regis Adventure Centre was held for the eleventh consecutive year.

South West Region held a Scouter/Guider Training Conference at Exeter University; the Saturday evening entertainment was a very amusing talk in Devon dialect by Anthony Beard, 'The Wag from Widecombe'.

The county finances were now in a strong state; appointed by Angela Graham in 1972, the treasurer was a retired bank manager, Mr Bill Wyatt, who immediately used his professional skills to invest and manage the considerable sums of money in the Guide coffers. (Previously the finances had been managed adequately but unadventurously by retired Guide personnel.) In 1972 the annual turnover was just under £11,000; by 1979 it was nearly £35,000. Bill liked women. With a twinkle in his eye, he always got on well with the county executive! The County Team had also been strengthened by Angela's appointment of Mrs Hilda Mitchelmore as County Secretary. An experienced and enthusiastic Guider in

Exeter, Hilda was assistant bursar at Exeter School and brought her business expertise to her county appointment. She was an enormous help and a good friend to Rosemary Howell and the County Commissioners who followed her.

Mrs Vivien Chanter retired as Assistant County Commissioner and was replaced by Mrs Loveday Fergusson, who had been District Commissioner for Newton Abbot. Miss Phyl Fowler, recently retired Division Commissioner for North Devon, was presented with the Laurel Award, and another occasion for congratulation was the appointment of Devon's gifted Arts Adviser Margaret Brotheridge as Visual Arts Consultant at CHQ.

A connection with Fiji was gaining momentum, and Mrs Kathleen Thomas, the County Commonwealth and International Adviser, explained in the annual report for 1979 what was happening:

At the Commonwealth and International Advisers' Conference in Durham three years ago, it was proposed that counties adopted one of the Branch Associations and made contact in various ways with its members. Devon was allocated Fiji and then because we are a large county, was asked to adopt Grenada also. The Branch Associations are administered by our national Headquarters and are usually very small. In 1978 a conference for the Branch Associations' Chief Commissioners was held at Foxlease. This was the same year Fiji celebrated its 50th anniversary and no representative was able to attend this conference. However, we were happy to welcome Mrs. Archer, the Commissioner for Grenada.

We were very fortunate in making immediate contact with Fiji as its Equipment Secretary was visiting her daughter in Plymouth. She was able to take back with her a tape of camp fire songs made by Plymouth Guides. She also . . . appealed for new handbooks as the Association was changing over to the eight-point system. This appeal was met with a wonderful response and some 60 Brownie and Guide handbooks were sent. Fiji is a small Association with approximately 11,000 Brownies, Guides and Rangers. There are four Divisions with an average of five Districts in each. The Association is very poor and its main problem is finding sufficient leaders, and some Guide and Ranger units run themselves.

We are looking forward to welcoming two of Fiji's members at the Interlink Camp to be held at Foxlease at the end of July and having the girls in the County as our guests before and after the camp. Every Ranger, Guide, Brownie and Guider in Devon is being asked to contribute 10p to help towards the cost of bringing the girls over. This is a very positive way of helping a very poor Association and a splendid opportunity of spreading friendship. We hope that the two visitors – a young Guider and a Guide – will take back an encouraging picture of Guiding in this country and ideas they can use.

We have had less success over our contact with Grenada and it is not certain if any of its members will be able to attend Interlink. Sadly, the country is in political turmoil and letters are not getting through. However, we are hoping that eventually we shall establish a good link with Grenada as we have with Fiji.

(In the event, two girls did come from Grenada and were given hospitality by Cornwall.)

By 1980 the county had raised well over £3,000 to bring the four girls over for the Interlink Camp; the Amory Charitable Trust had also made a generous donation. To keep the link going, the county was planning to send two Guiders to Fiji to take and bring back ideas to help Guiding there and back home.

Interlink '80 – the South West Region Camp at Foxlease, to which each county invited Guides from the Branch Association country with which they had linked – was a great success. The Camp Commandant was Mrs Joan Richards, who had been County Camp Adviser for North and East Devon for many years and was now South West Region's Outdoor Activities Adviser. She describes it:

A Camp with a difference. After much work and planning it all came together at Foxlease in July when 400 Guides, Rangers and Guiders including 46 visitors from 18 other countries joined together to live, work and play for a week. The theme of the camp was English Crafts and Activities, ranging from archery to pottery. The Guides were housed in ten camp sites, each with its own craft name, e.g. Potters, Foresters, Wheelwrights etc. Each had a lovely gateway.

The opening ceremony was performed by President of South

West England Mrs Betty Clay, the daughter of the Founder and Chief Guide . . . and away went 400 balloons. . . . The days were full of activity such as hiking, orienteering, swimming, trampolining, fencing, dance, kite making and lots of music and singing. During the week the New Hebrides became independent, and as we had a Guider from that country a very moving ceremony took place late at night by flare torchlight, when the flag of Vanuatu was raised. At our closing ceremony in the evening twilight the flags of our visitors were taken down by English campers and given back to our visitors to take back to their countries. Only the World Flag was hoisted on the main flagpole by a colour party of handicapped Guides, each in a wheelchair. This one flag reminded us that what we had shared was Guiding. A very successful camp which developed into one of great happiness and friendship, and an experience that none of us will ever forget.

After the camp two Guides from Modbury took the young Fijian Guide, Sala, home with them and reported that she entered into everything with enthusiasm. Devon's Lone Guides and Rangers had played an active part in the Fiji project; they raised £53 for the fund, and met the girls at Heathrow, visiting Hampton Court, Windsor Castle and Stonehenge on the way to Devon. Sereana Rakalo, the Fijian Ranger, spent three days with a Lone Ranger, who took her to Castle Drogo, Plymouth and a country fair – but the highlight was a Devon cream tea!

After two years of planning, the main excitement in Devon Guiding in 1980 was the Crediton Jamboree – the large international Scout and Guide camp held on Lord's Meadow, Crediton, in August, as part of the town's celebrations for the 1,300th anniversary of St Boniface, who went from Crediton to become 'the Apostle of Europe'. Thanks to the enthusiasm and persuasiveness of the very efficient and charismatic Scout County Commissioner, Geoffrey Philpott, the Scouts were keen to include Guides for the first time, and one of the Guide County Commissioner's main worries was that there should be enough Portaloos on-site for the 6,300 young people who camped! They came from twenty-two other countries as well as from over Britain – a truly international event. Guide and Scout families all over Devon had overseas Guides and Scouts to stay before the jamboree.

The project which caught the interest of the national press was the building of Anglo-Saxon huts. With foresight, seventy-six Guides from Totnes Division arranged a hut-building practice day beforehand on the camp field at Lukesland, and were taught thatching and hurdle-making by professionals. At the jamboree the first prize for the hut building went to a team from Witheridge (North Devon) with their guests from Como in Italy. The individual camps all made elaborate gateways, and Hatherleigh and North Tawton Guides won a certificate and £10 for their gateway made of macramé. Other activities included making and paddling coracles, making helmets and shields and swords, and on the day the Devon Cubs visited there were water and flour battles between Celtic and Saxon Cubs! There were activities for disabled Scouts and Guides in wheelchairs, and canoeing and water sports on the lakes of Shobrooke Park. There was a large and very popular market, and a very efficient hospital, and a day the townsfolk could visit; they were impressed by the orderliness of the camp and the good behaviour of the young.

On the Sunday morning after the Scouts and Guides' own service, 820 Patrol Leaders marched with their County Commissioners at their head to Crediton Parish Church, to renew their promises led by the Chief Scout, Sir William Gladstone. He was one of the VIP visitors to the camp, together with Mrs Sheila Walker, Guide Chief Commissioner, and Mrs Betty Clay and her husband and grandson. (Betty Clay, being the daughter of the founder, was always particularly popular with overseas Scouts, to whom any connection with the Baden-Powell family was significant.)

Prebendary Everard Samson, senior chaplain to Devon Scouts and to the jamboree, known to the Scouts as Sam, wrote a report for the *Scout Council Bulletin* in which he paid warm tribute to the 500 Venture Scouts and Rangers, Scouters and Guiders who made up the camp staff. 'They carried out their duties with such politeness and cheerfulness to see . . . that [the camp] ran smoothly and everyone's needs were met.' He also praised the 'wonderful Service Team with their Directors who not only worked so hard by day and by night but who paid the same as everyone else for doing it'.

'Sam' also mentioned something that he found very moving.

> The Guides from Bangor in Northern Ireland and the Guides from
> Eire asked that they might be allowed to build a hut together,
> sleep in it together and fly their flags over it. Here was a splendid
> example of that spirit of brotherhood which our Founder strove so
> hard to promote.

He went on to mention the discipline and good manners seen at
the camp, and said:

> The great gatherings of the Jamboree, the Opening and Closing
> Ceremonies and the Scouts and Guides Own were truly wonderful
> sights . . . with the blue of the Guide uniforms providing vivid
> splashes of colour amongst the rather sombre uniforms of the
> boys and men. . . . This was a jamboree which will be talked
> about for many a long day and will set a standard which will be
> hard to beat in future.

Following the jamboree, the Service Team had a reunion camp at
Caddihoe, and returned to Crediton to plant trees on the site. The
Scout and Guide County Commissioners also planted a tree, an
oak, in Crediton Churchyard, with a commemorative plaque. (It is
growing well, on the north side of the church.)

1981 was the International Year for Disabled People (IYDP),
and Devon Guides gave a huge amount of positive service for
disabled people as well as raising over £8,000 for IYDP funds.
Sidmouth District Rangers, Guiders and Brownies held a Day
Camp for disabled people, and many activities were enjoyed in
spite of the rain (this was a very wet summer and many camps
were affected). A new Guide unit opened in St Budeaux East
District involving physically handicapped and able-bodied girls,
who worked for Friend of the Deaf badges and helped at Hartley
House for the Deaf's summer fair. Combe Martin Guides travelled
to Instow every Sunday through the summer to help at the Andrew
Home for the Blind. Holcombe Rangers baked and sold cakes in
aid of a Kidney Appeal and Riding for the Disabled.

There was a recruitment drive county-wide for new Guiders,
with shop-window displays and articles in local papers – the

journalist Sarah Foot wrote a good piece in the *Western Morning News*, and Mavis Budden did a talk on *Morning Sou'West*. A kind friend of Guiding, Mr Gregory from Umberleigh, made a film of Devon Guiding to be used for publicity purposes. All this produced about thirty new Guiders who stayed, and some good publicity. Exeter Division gained eight new Guiders and two unit helpers. Exeter also managed to raise £5,000 in a week towards their new Headquarters.

This year saw the introduction of Health and First-Aid Certificates as part of camp training – the idea of Devon's Joan Richards, South West Region's Outdoor Activities Adviser. A survival weekend for Ashburton Division Guides was held in May at the Cabin, Maidencombe, near Torquay; this cabin on the clifftop with some rough land around it belonged to Mrs Foky Bradshaw, a very energetic and inspirational Guider who had moved to Devon from Surrey after her husband died, and who was now Division Commissioner for Ashburton and had taken over as Young Leadership Adviser from Mavis Budden. She went on to become Adviser for Boating and then Outdoor Activities. Her cabin was very basic, but weekends there were great fun and on this survival weekend, in wind and rain, the girls made shelters and slept in them, cooked without utensils and ate off shells and tinfoil – and they all gained their Backwoodsman badges.

Hillwalking was being encouraged with Walking Safely trainings, and Coombe District Rangers entered two teams in BOOTS, a mini Ten Tors Expedition organised by Plymouth Scouts; they finished the courses for ten and fifteen miles. Ranger numbers in the county were still growing and the various events for them through the year were well attended. There was a 'Dabble Day' in Exeter, and a lightweight camp/hillwalking weekend at the Throwleigh Adventure Centre. The highlight of the year was the Devon Moot, a Venture Scout/Ranger Guide camp for four counties, this year held at the County Showground, Exeter; 179 Rangers from fifteen units joined this exciting weekend. A tremendous storm with a force-9 gale did a lot of damage, but the campers rose to the challenge magnificently.

As a follow-up to the link with Fiji, the Guide county paid for two Guiders to visit Fiji and do some training there. Kathleen Thomas, the Commonwealth and International Adviser, who had worked so hard to establish this link, wrote:

> My visit to Fiji accompanied by Christine Tozer has been one of the most memorable of my Guiding life. The welcome we received and the hospitality given is a tribute to the County for its imaginative and positive approach to the idea behind the linking up with small Commonwealth countries.

(See page 356 for Chris Tozer's account.) The Fijian Chief Commissioner, Mrs June Barnes, and her deputy, Mrs Senimili Dyer, enjoyed a visit to Devon, staying with the County Commissioner.

As every year, a number of girls were selected for overseas camps, and many units went abroad. Following the jamboree, a group from Plymouth and another from Crediton visited Denmark, where they were given wonderful hospitality by their new friends.

In 1982, nationally the Guides, together with the Keep Britain Tidy Group and Lloyds Bank, launched Adopt and Cherish, a scheme whereby girls adopted a piece of land to look after and were responsible for its upkeep for three years. Several units took part and did well, taking on places like churchyards or a corner of a village. Bickington Guides (Taw and Torridge Division) adopted the car park and cleared out a vast amount of rubbish and intended to plant bulbs and bedding plants. The Swallow Patrol of the 1st Ivybridge Guides won second prize – £150 – in a national competition to design 'The House of the Year'.

1982 was the year that the land at Taw Bottom was bought (see Chapter 11) and fundraising was going on apace; Barbara Lillicrap's sponsored knit the previous November made over £8,000 and resulted in 400 blankets being given to Oxfam and the Save the Children Fund. Lynton Guides and Brownies were first in the South West Region for their Adopt and Cherish project of clearing a storm-damaged wooded hillside. They were presented by Lloyds Bank in London with a certificate and cheque for £200. The 3rd Southway (Plymouth) Guides were also the first in the Region for their continuing 'Cherish' project.

One of the highlights of this year was the Festival of Song and Dance in Exeter Cathedral, another inspired event planned and compèred by Margaret Brotheridge. Two years of rehearsals and much hard work by many people resulted in a first-class and exhilarating performance. Here are the thoughts of a member of the audience:

October 28th was a beautiful golden day. . . . Our ancient Cathedral standing mellow in the green Close. Into this setting came 2,000 members and friends of Devon Guides – the participants and spectators of our Festival of Song and Dance. The audience from the afternoon performance seemed only to have one comment: 'Wasn't it WONDERFUL?' they said. For the performers it was 'One down successfully and one to go.' Seats booked long ago were filled a second time that day. The choir and the musicians took their places. . . . The National Anthem soared to the fan-vaulted roof and we were under way. A world of song – in the nave all the world seemed to be singing – singing of joy, of wandering, of coming home and most of all hope; young voices, clear and resolute. Interspersed with the singing came the dancing – a touching mixture of grace and vigour and a kind of understated discipline especially when it came to the magnificent maypole dance.

Lynton Rangers, Guides and Brownies with their District Commissioner Mrs Cantello came.

The Blessing given by the Dean; with 'Go well and safely' still in our ears, we did as the Dean had bidden us, 'Go forth with the sound of melody and a song in our hearts.' The project raised the magnificent sum of £1,600 for the Cathedral, which was presented to the Chairman of the Preservation Trust after Sung Eucharist one Sunday in Advent.

For Axminster Division the highlight of the year was a joint event organised with the RNLI – the Launching of 1,000 Lights. Over 15,000 people came to see the first-time launching of candlelit miniature boats on the River Axe – an amazing sight! There were many stalls set up on the day which benefited the RNLI, the division and the county campsite. Mr Ronald Keech, husband of Division Commissioner Mrs Cynthia Keech, was later presented with a Thanks badge for making 1,000 wooden frames for the boats, testing them and acting as marshal.

Mrs Margaret Branch retired after ten years as Division Commissioner for Exeter; a division camp was held at Caddihoe with an American Indian theme to say thank you for all she had done for the division. Three hundred people attended the camp, with eight sub-camps run on ordinary Guiding lines, with cooking on wood fires. Ten Rangers formed a Service Team, mainly helping with the exciting activities which included backwoodsman challenges in the forest and a variety of American Indian crafts. 'One camp had a collection of scalps hanging up (old wigs from a jumble sale) to deter strangers.' Margaret Branch reported:

> We included 24 Guides from Belfast, who made a tremendous impact on the camp with their entertaining ability. Tears were shed all round when they departed at midnight on their long journey back to their unhappy city. The BBC Children in Need Appeal paid their fares, and apart from giving these girls a glimpse of Devon and a very happy holiday, the troubles of Belfast became more real to the Exeter Guides, and perhaps we now feel more involved in finding a solution to the problems there. We hope to keep the strong ties which were formed with these Guides.

One of Margaret Branch's achievements had been to find Belmont Lodge and start negotiations for a lease and alterations to make it a Division Headquarters. This was finally brought about by Mrs Beryl Hitchcock, who now became Division Commissioner.

Knitting for the Needy was going on apace: Chagford Guides were given the use of a café for their sponsored knit – they put up a tent, had a campfire and knitted all morning. In North Devon, the Brownies at Chivenor RAF Station did their knitting while being watched by the Duke of Kent, who was visiting. There were some unusual good turns: Ilfracombe District again delivered Christmas cards free for retired and handicapped people. Rangers from Exeter North-East District organised a rota for two of them to visit a fourteen-year-old schoolgirl while on dialysis.

A Feniton Patrol won second prize in the Tandemania competition organised by the Graduate Scout and Guide Group – one activity was cooking a caveman meal in a cave in Beer.

Ashburton Division Rangers used radio equipment in camp which David Hood (Scout Assistant County Commissioner) had put together for Scouts and Guides to use. Young Leaders enjoyed two residential trainings (fourteen at each) at the Cabin, Maidencombe, where they experienced serious training mixed with excitement which included radio communications; they had a wide game where each team had a radio and, for example, had to rescue three small Guides from the bottom of the cliffs.

Chapter 7: 1983–6

1983 was the year that Devon welcomed the Chief Commissioner, Lady Baden-Powell, for a very full three-day visit to the county. The granddaughter-in-law of the late Chief Guide, she delighted everyone she met, with her informal and deeply interested manner. She was welcomed at Exeter St David's Station by fifty girls from Tiverton Division and shook hands with them all, and later met girls and adults from Barnstaple, Plymouth, Plympton, Exeter, Wembury, Torquay and Honiton. It was also the year that the new county campsite at Taw Bottom was officially opened and blessed (see Chapter 11).

It was a year of terrible weather and it wasn't only the Taw Bottom opening camp that suffered. Dawlish and Starcross Guides were camping at Beer when a torrential storm hit them and the field was struck by lightning: 'Patrol Leaders turned up trumps helping to sort out the chaos, wearing bikinis to keep their clothes dry.' Joan Richards, Outdoor Assistant Adviser for Camping for North and East Devon, described the Guides' involvement at the County Show:

> Mud, mud and yet more mud played a very large part . . . particularly in the feature 'Devon County Life', the corner of the Showground this year was featuring youth groups and the part they play. Devon Guides were asked to participate, (a) by setting up a standing camp and display tent, and (b) by groups performing in the arena twice daily. Groups of 12 Guides and their Guiders came from all parts of Devon . . . to perform items relating to the Guide programme, including tent pitching, fire

lighting, cooking, dancing, and an egg and bacon race between patrols, run on the lines of the gun carriage races . . . at the Royal Tournament. As well as performing, they also cooked lunch or high tea in the standing camp. In spite of the most awful weather, which turned the site into a sea of knee-deep mud, everyone kept very cheerful, and went on with a will to entertain the public. Not one item was cancelled – all honour to the Guides and their Guiders who worked so hard to put on something worthwhile.

The Devon Junior Council was formed in 1983, coordinated by Margaret Branch. It consisted of young Guiders, Young Leaders and Rangers, with representatives from each division aged sixteen to twenty-four. The aims were (1) To encourage further the participation of young members of the Girl Guides Association in the affairs of Devon Girl Guides. (2) To provide a forum for the debate of issues of concern, nationally, regionally and at county level. (3) To be available to assist the County Executive Committee and give the opinions of its age group to this committee. They met three times during the year, on two separate days and a weekend of discussion and activity; their discussions were mainly on Guiding subjects – for example, the image of Guiding, and the promise and law, which they felt were basic to the Guide movement and should not be watered down in any way.

Mrs Hilary Hatherley, the County Arts Adviser, reported on Arts to See in '83, which involved all sixteen counties of South West England and which culminated in a

glorious May day when Guides, Brownies and Rangers from all over the Region packed Salisbury Cathedral for the final performance. Songs and dances from all over the Region were performed with great enthusiasm at a very high standard, with three units representing Devon – Brownies from Brixham and Plymouth, Guides from Seaton and a Guide choir from Modbury. The walls and aisles of the Cathedral were overflowing with visual arts including banners, model villages, collages, flower arrangements and pictures which all made the Cathedral look very colourful and full of life. Outside in the Close, in beautiful sunshine, more Brownies and Guides danced and performed for the enjoyment of visitors and the public.

Earlier in the year the Queen came to Exeter Cathedral to distribute the Maundy money and a Teignmouth Ranger had the honour of representing Devon Girl Guides in the congregation. The 27th Exeter Brownies (who were attached to the cathedral) formed a guard of honour for the Queen as she entered, and gave her posies, and she spoke to them all.

Unusual venues were often chosen for promise ceremonies: Torrington Rangers chose to be invested in a helicopter at RAF Chivenor, as they felt that the Search and Rescue Squadron set such a marvellous example of community service. The ceremony was made even more remarkable when the alarm bells went and the helicopter had to be evacuated for use. The last Ranger was hustled down the steps, just in time, with their Division Commissioner. When the crew returned they heard first-hand of the successful rescue of a small boy, trapped by the tide.

1984 was the seventieth anniversary of the Brownies, and all over the country Brownies celebrated with a National Tea-making Challenge, and some very ingenious tea parties took place around Devon. In Exmouth one unit served tea in a police cell. Newton Poppleford Brownies gave a party for the over-sixties and made 827 cups of tea in a fortnight. The Trinity URC Brownies in Plymouth East made tea up Smeaton's Tower on the Hoe. Mutley (Plymouth) Brownies served tea to senior citizens as they left the post office after collecting their pensions: 'The surprise and joy on the faces of these unsuspecting people was wonderful to see.' St Budeaux West Brownies served tea to the Bishop of Plymouth in a police cell. The 16th Devonport Brownies made tea in the ferryman's 'Wendy House' at Torpoint and each time the ferry came in the Brownies took trays of tea to passengers in cars and buses on the ferry. The 1st Dartmouth Brownies held an important tea party in the Guildhall, attended by the Mayor of Dartmouth and the High Sheriff of Devon.

The Adopt and Cherish scheme came to an end with the 3rd Southway Guides (Plymouth West) winning through to the regional finals and being presented with £100 from Lloyds Bank, and in the national finals another £50; they had not only worked hard on the Notre Dame School garden, but had also kept a logbook with details and photos. Torrington Rangers had cleared and cultivated the area around the recently restored little chapel near the River Torridge that had been used by lepers in the Middle Ages, and they kept it well tended.

The old Queen's Guide syllabus had now been replaced by a more challenging one for girls in the Senior Section, and Commissioners were now responsible for steering the girls who attempted it. Mrs Sheila Wooldridge, Division Commissioner for Tiverton, had a Ranger and a Young Leader who were embarking on the new Queen's Guide Award.

> Their activities range from regular Guiding to studies in Indian culture, the EEC, matters of local concern and the more traditional cooking and needlecraft skills – all being fitted in with their A level studies.

Three Young Leaders in Culm Valley District were highly commended for their talk about International Guiding at the Rotary Club Public Speaking Competition.

Annual meetings for Devon Girl Guides were normally held in schools around the county, but in 1984 it was held in Plympton St Mary Church because Plymouth Argyle were playing at home that day and traffic would have made it impossible to use the school that had been booked. At this meeting the Countess of Morley was welcomed as the first Patron of Devon Guides; she took a great interest in Guiding and supported it in many ways and was a great ambassador for it, especially in her role as wife of the Lord Lieutenant. The new Region Chief Commissioner, Mrs Jean Eburne, was also welcomed. The young speaker, Dr Ishbel Hartley, who had been Chairman of the National Junior Council, spoke of the pressures on young people today and how Guiding can help.

Guides could now become Young Leaders at fifteen; numbers were increasing and eleven gained their certificates in 1984. Foky Bradshaw, their County Adviser, was now giving residential trainings in Axminster, Plymouth and North Devon as well as at her Cabin near Torquay. Foky, who was also Ashburton Division Commissioner, was presented with the Laurel Award at

Dartmoor '84 Division Camp, which she ran at the Dartmoor Training Centre at Prince Hall – 233 Guides attended this very enjoyable camp, together with twenty-six Guides from Belfast who 'delighted everyone with their ability to entertain'. This connection with Northern Ireland was kept going for some years, with exchanges taking place in both directions.

Another award this year was the Star of Merit to a Plymouth Ranger, Rachel Stoddard, for displaying great courage and fortitude under suffering after losing the sight of an eye in an accident.

Exeter Division Rangers celebrated their silver jubilee, the unit having been run for the whole of the twenty-five years by Mrs Hilda Mitchelmore (who was now also the County Secretary). Fifty ex-Rangers returned for the jubilee evening, one-third of whom still had connections with Guiding.

Devon had two members in the National Scout and Guide Orchestra. There was a national singing competition – Encore '84 – and Devon's County Music Consultant, Mrs Rita Sandifer from North Devon, helped run it. Two units, from Feniton and Chagford, competed in the regional final, and although unsuccessful they had a good day out in Salisbury.

There were several changes in county staff at this time. To quote the County Commissioner's introduction in the 1984/5 annual report:

Miss Chris Tozer has retired from her strenuous job as County Outdoor Activity Adviser in order to take over the same job for South West Region – so we will still have the benefit of her imaginative zeal and expertise. Mrs. Unity Harley has retired as Ranger Coordinator, having overseen and encouraged a welcome growth in both numbers and activities in our senior section, and she has taken over as Adviser for Lone Guides and Rangers from Miss Greta Gray, to whom we have said a fond farewell after many years of organising the Lones with enthusiasm and efficiency. Mrs. Sheila Bromidge, whose encouragement and advice has helped many Guiders with their camping, has retired as County Camp Adviser for South and West Devon. . . . We welcome Miss Valerie Dampney as a second Assistant County Commissioner, Mrs. Pat Coward as Outdoor Activity Adviser and her Assistant Mrs. Brenda Gunby, Mrs. Laurie Pearson as County Camp Adviser for South and West Devon, Mrs. Anne Hewson as Ranger Coordinator and Mrs. Margaret Branch as Press and PR Adviser.

This illustrates the amazing versatility and tenacity of Guiders and Commissioners, who take on one big job in the county after another, quite often when running a unit as well. It has ever been thus, and still is.

> 1985 – the 75th anniversary of the Girl Guides – will be a year of very special memories for all of us, young and old alike. . . . With the coming of the Light of Guiding from Buckingham Palace to every unit in towns and villages throughout Devon; with the parties and their special birthday cakes; with the many camps (where participants refused to be daunted by the rain) and special projects; with the inspiring services in Salisbury and Exeter Cathedrals and in churches and chapels, we have looked back in thanksgiving. We have tried to involve as many as possible of those now elderly folk to whom we owe a debt of gratitude for handing to us the torch of Guiding, and we have re-dedicated ourselves to carry it on to the future.

This was how the County Commissioner summed up the year in the annual report.

The editor of the report, Margaret Branch, summarised the coming of the light to Devon as follows:

> Princess Margaret started the ceremony in the forecourt of Buckingham Palace, handing over lights to Region Commissioners. Mrs. Jean Eburne, Region Commissioner for S.W. England, brought the light (by train) to Exeter station at 9 a.m. on Tuesday 25th June and handed it over to Mrs. Rosemary Howell, County Commissioner. She in turn passed it on to Mrs. Loveday Fergusson on the station platform before joining Mrs. Eburne and they both continued on the train to Plymouth. In the meantime on Exeter station Mrs. Fergusson, Assistant County Commissioner, ceremonially handed over the light to seven Division Commissioners who had gathered there from the eastern side of the county. They were accompanied by Rangers,

Guides and Brownies. Everyone concerned in this ceremony then travelled by decorated bus to Exeter Guide Headquarters, the lanterns being kept burning while breakfast of sausages and baked beans was served to 60 people.

Meanwhile on Plymouth station Guides and Brownies were lined up, each holding a large letter which they turned over simultaneously as the train arrived, so that the Commissioners were welcomed by seeing the words 'Girl Guides 75 years'. . . . The light was then passed onto the six Division Commissioners from the west of the county, accompanied by Rangers, Guides and Brownies. The Station Manager had provided a room so that everyone could meet together for morning coffee. The Lady Mayoress, Mrs. Joan Mills, was present and welcomed the travelling party to Plymouth.

During the afternoon the two Division Commissioners from north Devon travelled by train from Barnstaple to Exeter. Their lights, which had been kept alight all day, were presented to them by the County Commissioner, this time on Exeter Central Station, and the Commissioners with their escorts of Rangers, Guides and Brownies were welcomed to a picnic in Northernhay Gardens, before being sent off on their way back to north Devon. The train made a special stop at Eggesford station so that the light could be handed over to the South Molton contingent there.

In the Divisions there were many ways of distributing the light to the various gatherings, mainly to District parties which took place between the Tuesday and the Saturday; but there seems to have been an opportunity for nearly every Ranger, Guide and Brownie as well as Guiders and Trefoil Guild members to receive their own light, the flame having been passed from Division to District Commissioner and from Guider to Guide.

Ashburton Division chartered a steam train on the Dart Valley Railway which runs from Buckfastleigh to Totnes. Hundreds of Guides travelled on the train which made a special stop at the small station of Staverton to deliver the light to the neighbouring Division of Totnes. Other unusual methods of transport were by Rangers riding motor bikes, using roller skates and by a ten-legged race in Braunton; by open-topped bus from Exmouth to Bicton; by decorated pick-up truck in Torbay. In Plymouth Rangers ran in groups carrying the light around the city. In Exeter lights were taken from their Headquarters simultaneously to all the District parties, one by cart-horse to an outlying village, by pantomime horse, by vintage coach and by trek cart. Sidmouth District used a 1910 vintage car and drove it along the sea front.

Honiton Guides . . . polished up a fire engine, which travelled through the town bearing the light, giving the appearance that it was being pulled by Guides.

There were parties everywhere, with friends old and new. There were cakes, candles, promises renewed, gas-filled balloons released with good wishes, and many moving ceremonies.

Axminster Division met around a camp-fire, each Guide lighting her own candle, turning a dreary damp evening into one glowing with warmth and friendship. . . . South Brent and Braunton Districts each had parties on estuaries, some Rangers arriving by boat. Candles in paper boats floated out to sea. A beach party for Ilfracombe District was held on Combe Martin beach – a camp fire was already burning when the light arrived and it was handed to each Guide and Brownie along the water's edge. Totnes had a party with rafts. . . . There were parties on the sea front at Torbay and Exmouth. Ottery St. Mary and Plym received the light in camp, and Holsworthy Guides were engaged in a day of fun and challenges when their light arrived. Other Districts had themes, 'A Mid-Summer Night's Dream' for Tiverton in Knightshayes gardens; a circus party with clowns in Brixham. Money raised for charity was combined with the light ceremonial at Tavistock and at the Medieval Fair at Yelverton and a Street Fair in Honiton.

Fremington Church was the meeting place for their District as soon as the light arrived in North Devon on Tuesday evening. A District orchestra accompanied hymns and the singing of 'All join hands'. Bicton Church, where the first Guide unit in Devon was registered, was the venue for a service for Exmouth Division. The Axminster Division service was held in Colyton Church, and afterwards Guides congregated around a floral Guide badge which had been grown in the local park. At a service in Buckfast Abbey for Ashburton Division, as well as the ceremony of the light their new Division standard was dedicated.

There was a very successful county camp organised brilliantly by Chris Tozer at Bicton Arena, called BADGER camp (Bicton Arena Devon Guides Encampment Rally). Gillian Coley, a Guider in Ottery St Mary District and a member of the Junior Council described it:

What a wonderful way to celebrate 75 years of Guiding. Thirty or so different camps; about 900 campers including Guides from Ireland, Sweden, Jamaica and Denmark; and so many different activities, from Morris dancing to canoeing, the Maori stick game to orienteering, brass rubbings to walkie-talkies, all packed into a week at Bicton Arena, East Budleigh. Guide companies from all over Devon came and pitched camp on 28th July in good weather. . . . On the first afternoon we had our opening ceremony, performed by Lord and Lady Clinton, who very kindly allowed us the use of the arena, and our County Commissioner. . . . The display at the ceremony was wonderful. Each company paraded their Colours into the area, and the 'Welcome to Badger' display was very well done.

The second day was Rally Day and we were joined by about 1,500 Guides. The Devon Junior Council . . . prepared a quiz booklet and many Guides took part. The Rally Day was . . . rounded off by a 2,000 strong Conga all around the camps finishing up in the arena where we sat down exhausted – it was lovely weather – and had a camp fire. Another happening which caused us to rush into the arena was the presence of a paraglider with a camera. As many Guides, Young Leaders, Rangers and Guiders as could formed the shape of the 75 Logo on the grass and sat there three deep until we were sure that the paraglider had used up his film. That is something I shall always remember.

One afternoon we had the pleasure of watching the Sharkiah Folk Troop, Egyptian musicians and dancers who had come from the Sidmouth Folk Festival especially to perform for us. The Guides joined in as they danced. The evening of Wednesday was fun with a fancy dress parade followed by an open air Barn Dance. The costumes were very good and varied; dustbin liners were very much in evidence. Saturday brought the inter-camp competition . . . a mini-marathon . . . volley ball and five-a-side football matches.

I had a really enjoyable time at Badger Camp – as I feel sure did everyone else. Thanks must go to EVERYONE involved.

'A trip to London' was described by Hilda Mitchelmore, County Secretary and Exeter Guider:

Devon County Guides chartered a train to London during the October half term week, and the final figure for Guides travelling was 670. As we all streamed into the Underground at Paddington some poor man walking in the opposite direction was heard to exclaim, 'How many more of them?'

Each District or Unit had planned their own day, and among their activities were a trip up the Thames to Tower Bridge, walking to see Big Ben, the Houses of Parliament, Horse Guards and Downing Street. Some of the Guides from Exeter were fortunate to be outside No. 10 when the Prime Minister came out, and she came across and spoke to them. Some Guides fed pigeons in Trafalgar Square, some visited Olave House, others went to Madam Tussauds, CHQ, the Commonwealth Institute and of course to see the Guards at Buckingham Palace.

Back at Paddington, waiting for a train in the usual Guide manner, singing started up and echoed around the station. A large percentage of the children had never visited London and quite a lot had not travelled by train before. Although we did not set out to make a profit, £147 was passed over to swell the total for the County Good Turn for 1985. Our thanks must go to British Rail and Mr. Little at St David's who were extremely helpful and very efficient in coping with us.

There was an arts-and-crafts competition, which had entries from all the divisions; the standard of work was extremely high, particularly in the collage entries and the dressed dolls. This formed an exhibition in Exeter Library and some items were then displayed round the county, receiving a great deal of interest and compliments from the general public.

The Junior Council, now coordinated by the inspiring Guider and trainer Miss Elizabeth Smith, had considered during the year such subjects as handicapped people in Guiding and helping unemployed young people, and had a talk by a member of the Religious Consultative Council. Della Salway finished her term of office as chairman, and was now a Guide representative on the British Youth Council, one of ten in the country, so a great honour. Susan Twigg was the new chairman. Hilary Jones, who was on the National Junior Council, attended a weekend at Broneirion, the Guide Training Centre in Wales, on 'The Promise in the Real World', and had been pressing for trainings for Guiders on drug abuse. Some of the ideas that came from that weekend had already been implemented.

Music in all its forms was flourishing under the guidance of Mrs Rita Sandifer from Woolacombe, the gifted and energetic Music Consultant to the Arts Adviser. She trained the choir and instrumentalists for an inspiring thanksgiving service in Exeter Cathedral, which was arranged by North Devon and Taw and Torridge Divisions in June. In August twelve Guides and five Guiders took part in the BBC *Songs of Praise* in Ilfracombe. Two coachloads of Guides went to the Albert Hall Spectacular, 'a kaleidoscope of light and sound whirling us through 75 years of Guiding'. A Young Leader from Tiverton, Angela Blackwell, was allocated one of the CHQ violins and played in the Scout and Guide orchestra. In December fifteen Devon Guides had the thrill of singing carols round the Christmas tree in Trafalgar Square.

In 1986 Rita held a Music Weekend in Woolacombe, and in October a Music, Dance and Drama Workshop in Sidmouth for older Guides and Guiders, which finished with an excellent concert.

There was another joint Scout/Guide jamboree in 1986, at Mount Edgcumbe in Cornwall, just across the Tamar from Plymouth. The site was chosen to commemorate a Scout jamboree held there and visited by Lord Baden-Powell fifty years before. Once again Geoffrey Philpotts, the Scout County Commissioner, was the Camp Chief. Six thousand Scouts and Guides from Finland, Norway, Denmark, the USA, the Netherlands, West Germany, Switzerland, Tunisia, Belgium and South Africa as well as England, Scotland, Wales and Northern Ireland made this a really international event.

Mrs Foky Bradshaw, who was in charge of boating for the county as well as 'Co-ordinator for Young Leaders', described the jamboree from a Guider's point of view. Her job was to feed the Fal Camp Chief, Mrs Patricia Coward, for three days and teach rowing for five days. The first evening she helped the Finns – who arrived at midnight, their bus having broken down – to find their kit and bed down in the reception marquee.

The following evening the wind developed into a gale and the rain poured. I never knew if it was a Force 8, 9 or 10. Tents around us ripped up from stem to stern, lat poles split, metal ridge poles bent to right angles and frame tent poles collapsed. One frame tent I noticed went up a foot into the air and down again at regular intervals. One patrol of Guides were holding hands and dancing around in a circle – perhaps the patrol leader thought that it was safer than in the tent. There was no Jamboree opening on the Saturday and on Sunday only a short Service in the rain.

During the week the weather improved and the 6,000 enjoyed a great variety of interesting activities, some in marquees, some out of doors, and of course the water activities, canoeing, rowing and sailing at Barn Pool, where sometimes it was warm in the sun. Handicapped Scouts and Guides joined in. I shall never forget the smiling face on the spastic lad as he came down the abseiling frame; where else would he get a chance to do that? The Red Arrows display was terribly exciting. . . . Looking back on it, I know I never want to camp in a Force Something gale again, but I do remember laughing a lot and of course, as always we have made more friends.

Special Report for 1983

COUNTY CAMP SITE – TAW BOTTOM

Saturday, 7th May 1983, saw the launching of the County Camp Site. A never to be forgotten day, largely due to the weather. My memory will always be that of a sea of happy faces, not to mention the mud. Our Division Badge Secretary, aged 81, who planted a tree, remarked to me only this week, 'It was such fun, wasn't it?' This to me is the essence of Guiding, the wet camps are the ones which stand out in my memory as they always cause such laughter and a sense of belonging to a truly friendly organisation.

Those who camped there during the summer had the most wonderful weather and had very happy camps.

Brenda Gunby's account in September "Star" put it all in a nutshell:

I quote: "Thinking of trying a new camp site next year? Not many can boast the following:

Superbly situated – mid Devon, sheltered, peaceful

countryside. Easy access. Plenty of wood available, water on site, sluice for lats (no pit to dig). Ideal for pioneering and backwoods activities, hiking or pony riding over the moors nearby.

Friendly local shops, milk delivered. Places of interest: local Church and pottery, working water mill museum, quaint villages, all within easy walking distance.

Too good to be true? No, the description fits the new Devon County Camp Site, Taw Bottom, South Tawton. We have just returned from a most enjoyable week's camp there. We highly recommend the site and will certainly go again."

Obviously many Guiders are looking forward to going there in 1984 as the bookings have started coming in, so if you decide to make a booking don't delay too long.

BARBARA LILLICRAP
Camp Adviser for Taw Bottom and Chairman of Fund Raising Committee

Special Reports for 1984

RAINBOW '84

Rainbow '84 was the name given to a special camp held at Taw Bottom in August 1984, at the request of and with the help of the W.R.V.S. It was a week to remember for 16 under-privileged girls, most of whom were experiencing camp for the first time, when they were taught to live under canvas, the Guide way. They were looked after by three staff known to the children as Mrs. G., Buzz and Thumper, as well as by some of the Junior Council and eight Rangers/Young Leaders, including myself.

We took the role of Patrol Leaders, with two patrol leaders and four children to each patrol. There were four patrols, blue, red, yellow and green, with each patrol having a separate tent. Just as in a Guide camp there was inspection each day, and there was great competition between the four patrols to win it and become the proud holders of the 'Rainbow Man' for the day.

During the week the children participated in numerous different activities, including craft when they made macramé owls, natural pictures, and they even made their own woggles.

The Junior Council organised various treasure hunts and

trails around the camp site, and we entertained them with camp fires, teaching them new songs and actions to go with them.

A backwoodsman's day was arranged where we spent a day rotating around four bases or activities. The four bases were kite-making, clay pot making, natural shelter building and rope ladder making. For lunch each patrol had to build its own camp fire and cook its own lunch on it, and to the children's surprise the results were quite tasty.

We took them all on a visit to a museum in the nearby village of Sticklepath, where they saw how waterwheels were used to work a forge. They went on an afternoon's hike across the moor, and they also went swimming in Okehampton, as well as shopping there.

By the end of the week, not only had we worn the children out, but ourselves too, although everyone involved had enjoyed themselves. It was certainly a camp to remember and an experience I, for one, will not forget.

TINA FORD
1st Paignton Ranger

This camp was organised each year by Brenda Gunby, Guider in Wembury, who was Assistant Outdoor Activities Adviser.

The name was changed to Spectrum when the pre-Brownie branch was named Rainbows.

A TRIP TO SANGAM

"Share the joy . . ."
"Share the friendship . . ."

Sangam – meaning joining together – an experience that will be with me forever.

Sangam is a World Centre for Girl Guides in India and I was very lucky to be one of the three Guiders from England to attend the first joint service session there, with members of the Scout Movement. There were participants from Australia, Sri Lanka, India and Finland, two volunteers from Norway and England and the Guider-in-charge from Denmark and Australia.

We spent a very busy ten days working together and sharing our new experience in India. The main project was to strip and paint 20 outside window frames; a task that was new and challenging. We also cleared a lot of ground and planted some new shrubs.

For three days we had 24 Indian children, aged 12–16 staying for a holiday camp at Sangam. We taught the children many crafts, games and songs from different countries and some children enjoyed a morning in the swimming pool for the first time. The children all came from the Convent of St. Mary's Children's Home in the nearby town of Poona. One thing they enjoyed very much was cooking bread twists on the camp fire.

During the session we visited a Leprosy Rehabilitation Centre, the Convent of St. Mary's Children's Home and an Indian colony which included a middle class home, the school and local shop – all of which were a shocking but interesting experience and one that makes such things as striking miners and the unemployment problem seem so small.

We also had some time to do a little bit of shopping for souvenirs and saris, and visited the Aga Khan's Palace.

In the evenings we had country sharing, Indian dancing, campfire and also attended a young Musician's concert in aid of the Convent of St. Mary.

I should like to thank everyone in Devon for their help towards my trip, and would be delighted to share my experience with the aid of a slide show.

NICOLA DURMAN
Asst. Ranger Guider, S.E. Exeter

OLYMPUS '84

Sally Newman, a Guide from Axminster Division had the rare experience of attending an International Camp on Mount Olympus. They arrived at the site in a very remote area, having travelled up a terrifying mountain road. There were 2,700 Guides in the camp, mostly Greek, only 200 from 18 foreign countries including Japan, South Africa and Egypt.

Sally travelled in a party of 22 Guides from UK. During the camp, apart from joining in an incredible range of activities from journalism to ecology to Greek Dancing, they spent some time doing community service in a local mountain village.

One evening the whole village turned out for a dance festival, a memorable occasion. Water was in short supply in the camp and had to be very carefully rationed, the standard of hygiene not reaching levels customary in England.

The theme of the camp was 'Cherish Friendship' and one day was set aside for discussions, talking about the use of technology in their lives, preserving nature and finally what Camp Olympus had meant to them. It was about peace; finding that young people from all these countries felt the same way about the world as they do. It made them wonder why the world is such an inharmonious place.

The Camp Song:

> Up here on Mount Olympus, in the heart of nature
> Beyond frontiers, in a big friendly crowd
> We open up new ways to high goals
> All of us having the same ideals and one hope
> For peace and love to spread throughout the world.

70TH ANNIVERSARY OF BROWNIES

North Devon and Taw and Torridge Divisions

'Let's have a party.' 'No, let's work for it,' so the idea emerged of having sponsored activities to raise money towards the Brownie House at Taw Bottom. The event was dogged with problems from the start; the venue had to be changed, then the date; experts could not come on the revised date; the programme had to be altered and altered again.

The day dawned, or should it be poured, coaches came from all directions from Witheridge to Hartland, Lynton to Dolton and all the intermediate towns and villages, arriving from 9 a.m. onwards. Splashing through puddles, dashing through drips we were soaked before we started. Ah! Well we are here. Brownies were everywhere, with the chatter of excited voices. 'Where do I put my wellies?' 'Who wants the candles?' 'Which is the box for crafts?'

One large circle round the sports hall, three deep, with yellow spots, red dots, blue squares, gold stars, 'Have we got enough?' At last all stations are filled and action starts, cycle proficiency, safety in the home, peg doll dressing, a zany dressing up race, netball shooting. Shrieks and screams, the Brownies are squirming under fly sheets and squashing space hoppers. Change over and start all over again.

Lunchtime came and blessed rest for all, when the Disco, due at 2.30, arrives. Who was willing to run events in the Hall while Disco equipment is being tested? The Brownies seemed unruffled, it was the poor Guiders' ears which suffered. The Disco is in full swing and the Brownies are all happy.

Then came the final event. The enormous white and yellow birthday cake is assembled in the top section of the hall, looking very impressive. Seventy candles adorning the top with a central candle dominating them all. This is one which Mrs. Fergusson, the Assistant County Commissioner will light. The candles are all lit, words spoken, 'Happy Birthday' sung. The unremitting rain could not dampen the enthusiasm as it cascaded onto, and in some places, through the roof above. It was only when we stopped singing that we could hear the tattoo above us. An assortment of songs were sung, then thanks all round and Brownie Bells.

5.30 p.m. and at last it is all over. Home.

The telephone rings, it is the Press. 'We are very sorry but we have lost the film of all the photographs we took at the Brownie Party.'

Who said, 'When is the next one?'

ELIZABETH BOWDEN
Division Commissioner, Taw and Torridge

Special Report for 1985

SOUTH WEST REGION THANKSGIVING SERVICE IN SALISBURY CATHEDRAL

Beryl Hitchcock, Dorothy Carpenter and I had the great honour of carrying the County Standard as part of a spectacular procession of over 130 flags and standards, in Salisbury Cathedral.

The sun shone over the Cathedral and as the Green became full of Guiders and surprised tourists we began to get caught up in the wonderful atmosphere. As the Service began our procession moved through the nave – the Union Flag, the World Flag, Ranger Flags, Division Standards, County Standards, each followed by its County Commissioner, the S.W. Region standard with Mrs.

Jean Eburne, and lastly the St. George of England standard and the Chief Commissioner the Lady Patience Baden-Powell.

During a very simple but moving ceremony we were thrilled to hear of some of the Chief Guide's experiences related to us by her daughter, the Hon. Mrs Betty Clay. After the renewal of our Promise led by the Region Chief Commissioner we collected our colours. It was a very emotional moment for us all as the flags and standards were dipped for the National Anthem.

If ever you get the opportunity to attend something like this do make the effort to go – it gives your Guiding spirit a tremendous boost and is an unforgettable experience.

JANE HAYDON
D.C. Exwick District

Chapter 8: 1987–99

During 1987 Mavis Budden took over as County Commissioner from Rosemary Howell, and in her annual report she paid tribute to Rosemary:

> Her wise, enthusiastic, friendly and sympathetic leadership was appreciated by us all, while the high standards she expected both from herself and her County Executive Committee kept Guiding values secure in Devon. . . . We are very pleased that she has agreed to remain Chairman of the Camp Site Committee and to accept responsibility for 'Walking Safely'.

Other changes in county staff included Patricia Coward, who had given sterling services as Outdoor Activities Adviser, leaving Devon to become warden, with her husband, Brian, of South-East England's campsite. She was about to become County Commonwealth and International Adviser; Kathleen Thomas, who had done this job brilliantly for a number of years, agreed to stay on until Sheila Wooldridge could take over. The retiring Ranger Adviser, Anne Hewson, was warmly thanked for developing the potential of the Ranger programme, promoting the Ranger Council, encouraging overseas visits and working well with the Venture Scouts. Ann Veale was taking over from her. Ann Perry was also thanked for her smooth running of the Duke of Edinburgh Award Scheme, and Hilda Mitchelmore welcomed in her place.

The new Rainbow Section for five-to-seven-and-a-half-year-olds was now established with new units springing up throughout the county, and Ann Perry was welcomed as the Rainbow Consultant.

There was a small reorganisation of the county – Tiverton Division, being large and scattered, was divided into two – Tiverton and Mid Devon Divisions, and several new districts were formed.

North Devon Division had the unusual occurrence of two Star of Merit Awards, which are presented by the Guide Association to girls who have shown great courage and cheerfulness in the face of severe illness or accident. One went to Lisa Davies, a Young Leader in Braunton, who was very severely injured in a car accident, and the other to a Brownie from Bratton Fleming, Michelle Godfrey, who had been in a serious fire accident while living in Avon. Mavis Budden commented:

> There are others, too, who have coped with serious illness with equal fortitude and whose constant practice of the Guide Law has been a real inspiration to those around them.

Exmouth Division Commissioner, Mary Tuckett, reported with sadness the death of an Otterton Guide, Emma Sawdon, after a major operation.

> Emma's sister Zoe, a member of the Otterton Brownie Pack, found great comfort in the weekly Unit meetings and was assured by all the Brownies that 'we will be your sister'. Recently the youngest girl Holly has joined the Brownies to keep up the tradition started so enthusiastically by Emma. The Division gave two trophies in her memory. . . . The Otterton Guides each gave a week's pocket money to buy a World Flag to use in camp and it was flown for the first time at a weekend camp in October in Caddihoe, when Emma's family, together with friends and Guiders, watched as Zoe, escorted by two Guides, raised the flag in a moving torchlight ceremony.

Rangers once again did an excellent job in providing the Service Team for the Spectrum camp at Taw Bottom to give socially deprived children a holiday. The Ranger unit in Ashburton District held an investiture ceremony on the nuclear-powered submarine

HMS *Sovereign*, and Newton Abbot South Ranger Unit held one in a Hong Kong junk at the Exeter Maritime Museum. A Ranger from Exeter North-East District, Jennifer Morris, attended the first jamboree held in Nepal. She wrote:

> One of my most vivid memories of Nepal lies in the faces of the people. Everywhere we were greeted by smiles. . . . What have they got to be so happy about? They live in real poverty. . . . Most of them live in two rooms with a large family, their houses do not have any water supply and there are open drains in the streets. . . .
>
> The Jamboree award was gained by taking part in service projects, tree climbing, jungle trails, etc. The Nepalese Guides pushed themselves really hard to do these strange activities as to return home without gaining the award would have been a disgrace. . . .
>
> We think of Nepal as a backward nation needing development, but there is much we can learn from her people.

The Totnes Division Commissioner reported:

> We were very proud of the South Brent Rangers who on their way to visit the camp (at Holbeton) were first on the scene of a cycling accident and were able to render first aid and comfort to two men – one of whom needed 40 stitches in a facial wound.

Cadover Division had a very successful recruiting drive, with the encouragement of the County PR Adviser, Margaret Branch. Division Commissioner Anne Hewson reported:

> It started with a manned display outside the local supermarkets (in Ivybridge), followed by 14 Open Evenings run by Units. They were visited by the Team (Commissioners and Guiders who talked about Guiding). Guiders and Units did their hostessing marvellously . . . 14 adults were recruited . . . over 200 Badge Testers were found.

Sheila Wooldridge reported from Tiverton Division:

> Sarah Bartlett received her Queen's Guide Award at a luncheon given by the Chief Constable in March. She strove with

commendable courage and determination, while in very poor health, to complete the necessary clauses and face the County Panel. . . . Now a new treatment has given her fresh hope and strength, initially to spend some time working in a Cheshire Home and eventually to return to her medical studies.

(Author's note: Sarah qualified as a doctor and in 2017 was working as a GP in Somerset.)

Joy Slocombe, the very popular and energetic Division Commissioner for North Devon, who also ran the award-winning Ilfracombe Museum, retired this year. Joy had managed to get a Brownie unit going in Slade, a community outside Ilfracombe that had its problems. Joy's successor, Ann Linscott, reported that Slade hosted the Brownie Revels for the district, 'And many girls AND boys joined the maypole dancing – all good for public relations.'

Brenda Gunby reported from Plym Division:

> Everyone in the Division was very saddened by the sudden death of Mrs Joan Round who was an active member of the Local Association and Trefoil Guild. Joan had been a Unit Guider, Camp Adviser, District and Division Commissioner as well as County Secretary and will be missed by her many friends in Guiding.

County fundraising over the past two years had been for a study bedroom in the proposed new World Centre in London (called the Olave Centre). Devon raised £10,000, some of which came from the County Sponsored Knit, which also raised money for Taw Bottom, and which produced many colourful blankets for Oxfam and Save the Children. (The foundation stone for the new World Centre was laid by Betty Clay in 1989 and opened in 1990. Called Pax Lodge, it is a lovely welcoming building in the leafy surroundings of Hampstead in North London.)

In 1988 the South West Region challenge, Integrate in '88, encouraged units to look at many aspects of disability. Ashburton Division Commissioner Betty Hinchliff wrote:

> They were encouraged to experience disability by spending time in a wheelchair, using one arm only and doing things blindfold.

They were encouraged to give service, both by practical help and by raising money, but more importantly to get to know some disabled people so that they could become aware, not only of their disabilities, but also how much they could actually do.

She also wrote about Grace Travell:

A Guide in Chudleigh with considerable physical handicaps, and the whole community, including Guides, organised a sponsored walk to raise money for a special word processor which will make communication much easier for her.

Mary Jones wrote that in Axminster Division one Guide unit used the challenge to visit and measure entrances to local shops and public places like banks and seaside facilities for the accessibility of wheelchairs. The results were then printed in a booklet and the local council asked all the tourist information offices, hotels and surgeries to display it for the use of local residents and tourists. Beryl Paul reported from Totnes Division that

One disabled lady said her life had been changed now that Brownies smile and chat to her when they see her in the village. Salcombe Guides were practising the Manual Language on a bus when they were answered in sign language by a passenger for whom this was the only means of communicating.

There were again many camps at Taw Bottom, including the Junior Council's camp for disadvantaged girls, brilliantly run by Brenda Gunby and her team. Because of the new Rainbow Section in Guiding, the name of this camp was changed to Spectrum.

There were also the County Training Camp, Ranger lightweight camps, Guide camps and Brownie Revels at Taw Bottom, and it became base camp for a very successful Scout and Guide Expedition Week organised by David Hood (Scout Assistant County Commissioner) and Foky Bradshaw (Guide Outdoor Activities Adviser) for assessing members for the Duke of Edinburgh Gold Award and the Queen's Guide Enterprise. 'This was a splendid example of Scout and Guide co-operation,' wrote Mavis Budden.

The Shaldon boating weekends were as popular as ever, and a new canoe joined the fleet. Mavis and Ted Budden had given the county a Mirror dinghy, which was kept at Torquay, together with a sloop, so sailing was possible. Seven Rangers and Young Leaders sailed on the *Sir Winston Churchhill*, the *Malcolm Miller*, and the *Lord Nelson* and the Ocean Youth Club ships and returned with glowing accounts of their adventures.

The Torbay Division Commissioner, Valerie Stephens, reported on the visit of the Queen and Duke of Edinburgh to Torbay in July for the William and Mary Tercentenary celebrations:

> Many Brownies were able to give the Queen posies, and several Guides and Rangers spoke to the Duke at a reception held in connection with his Award scheme.

The Totnes Division Commissioner, Beryl Paul, reported that the 1st Dartmouth Brownies celebrated their sixtieth birthday:

> To commemorate this they were invited to participate in the Britannia Royal Naval College Parade, marching with the Cadets to the Royal Marine Band – a red letter day indeed.

She also reported that Salcombe Guides and Rangers had a rowing camp:

> They rowed from Salcombe to Frogmore Creek, about 6 miles, to the home of their District Treasurer, camped the night in her garden and rowed home the next day.

Brenda Gunby reported from Plym Division that for the fifth consecutive year the Elburton Guides and Brownies won their class in the Plymouth in Bloom competition for maintaining the trefoil-shaped garden in the centre of the village.

Thinking Day saw the launch of South West Region's Action International Challenge, 'Heads, Hearts and Hands'. Devon supported it by purchasing 900 booklets. Guiders reported that even if their units did not enter the challenge, the booklet was packed with ideas which would help to promote World Guiding in an enjoyable way.

Several county personnel had retired this year and were warmly thanked, including Rita Sandifer, Foky Bradshaw, Margaret Branch, Unity Harley, Anne Veale, Elizabeth Bowden and Audrey Downward. Special tribute was paid to Valerie Dampney, Assistant County Commissioner, and to Hope Rattey, Division Commissioner, who had now retired after giving outstanding service to the county for many years and whose influence had contributed to the high standards of Guiding in Devon. Betty Bindloss had also recently retired as warden of Bowerman's. 'I should like to thank her, from Devon, both for providing us with Bowerman's and for the many years she has looked after the cottage and its visitors making everyone feel so welcome and at home,' wrote Mavis Budden.

Elizabeth Smith was welcomed as Assistant County Commissioner and Programme and Training Adviser, having been an excellent and thought-provoking trainer for some years. Chris Tozer was congratulated on being presented with the national Laurel Award.

In 1989 there were celebrations for the centenary of the birth of Olave, Lady Baden-Powell and the seventy-fifth birthday of the Brownies. One of the highlights of the year was the performance in Exeter Cathedral of *We Follow a Star*, described by Mavis Budden, the County Commissioner, as a most inspiring day for performers and audience alike and a truly worthy climax to the many months of hard work and preparation. The event raised £2,000 for the Cathedral Music Foundation Trust; some of this was used to buy medallions for the head choristers of the cathedral, presented at a special Evensong. Inscribed, 'Presented by Devon Girl Guides 1989', these medallions are, as the Dean said, "very valuable and significant additions to the life and dignity of the choir".

Brownies celebrated in many enterprising ways: Ashburton Division Brownies sang seventy-five songs for charity, planted seventy-five plants in a school garden and served seventy-five cups of tea.

Individual Guides, Rangers and Young Leaders took part in International Camps in Denmark, Sweden, Holland, Austria,

Kenya, India and Ethiopia, thanks partly to the county's International Fund; and the importance of the home visits before and after the camps has always been recognised.

There was good weather for camping this year, and several Division camps were held: Mid Devon Division camped at Wembworthy Field Centre, with an American Indian theme, and Brownies on Pack Holiday shared activities with the Guides, making totem poles and sailing paper canoes as well as paddling their own real canoe.

Tributes were paid to Joan Richards, who retired after many years of outstanding service to the county as Guider, Commissioner, trainer and Camp Adviser for North and East Devon. Elizabeth Bowden, one of the County Training Team and a previous Division Commissioner for Taw and Torridge, also retired this year.

Money raised for charities took many forms as always: two Exeter Guiders were sponsored to come through customs at Heathrow on their way home from Our Chalet wearing a pantomime-horse costume!

Two Devon Guiders took a Region group on a Sailing Camp in Sweden; this was particularly challenging as it included 'less able' boys and girls as well as groups from several European countries.

A recruitment campaign for more Guiders was continuing, and eleven new Guiders were reported in Taw and Torridge Division. The new more casual uniform designed by Jeff Banks was 'accepted quite enthusiastically and is popping up throughout the Division,' Exeter Guiders reported.

Modern technology was appearing. Local radio in Sidmouth linked Guides and Brownies with others in different parts of the country; Jamboree of the Air set up a station in Ivybridge Methodist Hall, giving opportunities to speak to people in Ireland, Sweden and Holland, which resulted in Brownies and Guides taking the Radio Communication badge; and in a village in Mid Devon Division Brownies shared the Scouts' Jamboree of the Air week and eight gained the Radio Communication badge. "It was brilliant speaking to Buenos Aires," said one girl.

Opportunities for international travel were increasing, thanks to the hard work and commitment of Devon's Commonwealth and International Adviser, Sheila Wooldridge. Sheila reported:

> The Youth Exchange Forum is a national group within the Education Service which encourages exchanges within Europe. I have been a member of the Devon Forum from the start and find that the Girl Guides Association is held in very high esteem. Our expertise in foreign travel is being used by the Forum and at a training day in February we are contributing market stalls and workshops.

A Devon Ranger/Youth Leader, Fiona Hampton, was one of five chosen to represent the Girl Guides Association for the first time in the USSR. With girls from other countries they spent four weeks at Camp Artek in the Crimea, the camp being run by the Youth Pioneer Organisation of the USSR.

> Our days were long and busy but great fun. . . . After the chores we went to the beach close by. . . . There were sporting activities, Olympic Games and competitions between camps: one challenge was to climb a 545m mountain at 5.45 am. Every night there was a concert or a disco. The local area was very beautiful. We visited the Botanical Gardens, the Palace where the Yalta Agreement was signed and other things. Although things seemed cheap to us they are not for them and shops are in short supply of everything. Our diet consisted of potatoes, meat or fish and tomatoes. . . . I would like to thank the Soviet people for their incredible hospitality.

The main event of 1990 was Pirates International Camp. Wonderfully organised and run by Foky Bradshaw, with the help of Laurie Pearson, Sheila Wooldridge and many more hardworking Guiders, it was a highly successful result of three years of planning. Mavis Budden wrote in the annual report:

> Many friendships . . . were forged and who can say what future benefits will be derived from the increasing awareness of other cultures by our girls and vice versa?

Camp Chief Foky Bradshaw (previously County Outdoor

Activities Adviser and Division Commissioner for Ashburton) described the opening:

> Guides and Guiders from 17 countries, in their colourful uniforms, with their flags held high entered the main ring at Westpoint, Clyst St Mary on the evening of July 28th followed by our 'Pirate' County Commissioner towed in a dinghy by nine Pirates, followed by a team of Guide sailors, to start the long-awaited Devon International Camp – PIRATES 1990. The Camp was opened, the flags unfurled, the day had really come. . . . No longer did it matter that the parties of Pakistanis and Greeks were much larger than expected, that the Kenyans arrived almost unannounced, that the smiling Japanese spoke very little English. They were all there, after an exciting week of home hospitality with our Guides. So many people gave up their beds . . . lent tents, sleeping bags, cutlery, plates, waterproofs (never used) and bags of warm jumpers that went home unopened due to the heat wave. Even the West Indians found it hot!
>
> All through the week bus and minibus loads of jolly Guides sped through the country lanes to swimming pools, riding stables, caves, rocks, the ski slope, rivers and lakes for boating, Kent's Cavern, the Model Village, the Cathedral, the Town Hall, the Rifle Shooting Range and Dartmoor for walks. Meanwhile back at camp Guides practised camping skills, enjoyed a great variety of Craft, Dancing, Akido, Grass Ski-ing, queued for the shops, information and made new friends.
>
> On the boiling hot Wednesday 600 excited Brownie Pirates joined us for a jolly day. The next day with the temperature at 99°F the camp filled up with extra Guides for Rally Day and 'It's a Knockout' organised by our valiant Junior Council. The evening Camp Fires were enjoyable and we were privileged to be entertained by our visitors and some of our own Guides in bright costumes with dance, song and skits.

Helen Falla, a Guide at Pirates, wrote a report, ending:

> The highlights were the Camp Fires and the colourful display of national dances from all the countries represented. When we struck camp, the tent pegs were as hard to get out as they were to knock in. Thank you to everybody involved in making Pirates a success, especially our Camp Chief Captain Pugwash and to the Guiders in our camp.

The Messenger Service at the County Show, now an annual event, took place in 1990 at the new showground, which presented challenges for the thirty campers from South and West Devon, thirty-six day girls from Exeter, and Guiders led by Marion Farley. There was much praise for the girls' work and the initiative they showed. The practice of a Guide display was revived, and camping and outdoor cooking was portrayed in the Special Features Arena and Brownies demonstrated some of their activities. Devon Guides had been asked to organise the ten-minute closing ceremony, and the show organisers were delighted with Rita Sandifer's programme.

1991 was Devon Year of Youth, and Guiding was well involved. At a Celebration Day at Bicton College, Devon Guides' eight new canoes were shown to HRH Prince Edward; readings and drama were prepared for a special cathedral service; at the County Show art and craftwork from all sections were on display and Guides demonstrated their outdoor cooking skills to crowds of interested visitors; and at the County Youth Day two Young Leaders were selected to join a committee to explore the possibility of a County Youth Council.

Fundraising for charities, both local and national, has always been a part of Guide activity, and in 1991 Devon Guides raised over £6,000 for the St David's House Appeal for the West of England School for Children with Little or No Sight. The money was used to purchase a Turb-bobcat wheelchair and other physiotherapy equipment. Shebbear Guides (in Taw and Torridge Division) came up with an original way to raise money for this appeal; they kidnapped the vicar and would not release him until the ransom had been paid!

1991 was also the seventy-fifth birthday of the Senior Section – Rangers and Young Leaders (the descendants of the cadets). Chris Tozer, an experienced and keen Ranger Guider and Ranger Adviser for the county, described how they celebrated:

> The year started with Units walking, riding, paddling, sailing, etc, to 'Beat the Bounds' of their Divisions. In February a night's sleep at Guide Headquarters was followed by joining Plymouth East Division on the Hoe to see the sun rise on Thinking Day.

The next day a party went to London for the Thinking Day Service in Westminster Abbey and for a celebration called 'Shout', activities for Rangers to do in London.

Many joined in physical activities week at Teign School; abseiling, caving, archery and assault courses were undertaken. A successful fete was held at Foxlease which raised £2,000 to offset Trail '91 expenses. Another early start in May was needed for the Lundy Island trip and lie-ins did not appear on the programme for the activities weekend at Taw Bottom in June. July saw us assembling for an overnight hike, including a vertical rocky descent, in the dark of course. Then in August came the national event, Trail '91; a travelling camp held simultaneously at the seven Training Centres. Some girls visited several centres and others stayed at one centre. Three Fremington Rangers visited Broneiron in Wales, Netherurd in Scotland, Waddow in Lancashire and Glenbrook in the Peak District. 'We made many new friends and tried out many different things. The Trail also gave us an insight into how large the Guiding family is and how much there is to offer if only you look for it.'

One of the September events was Unit based, raising money for Riding for the Disabled; another was the annual Region activities camp at Foxlease, at which everyone was expected to wear very brightly coloured clothes. A coach load attended from Devon. October was another opportunity for individual units to do service by adopting a derelict wall or a piece of land and renovating it. The November Bug Burn and Fireworks took place at Taw Bottom in awful rain and gales, and Rangers, Young Leaders and Venture Scouts showed their skills in keeping their tents standing throughout the night (not a planned activity!). A disco in Tiverton was the final event of the Devon Celebrations.

The 1991 census showed that there were 176 Young Leaders, including those who were also Ranger Guides. Eunice Hodson, County Young Leader Adviser, reported that most divisions now held regular Young Leader meetings, and Guiders said what a great asset they were to the units. Some girls used their Guiding skills to help and encourage in other spheres – for example, helping the Community Health Team at a holiday for handicapped adults. As well as celebrating at many of the events with the Rangers, three Young Leaders were awarded Sail Training Bursaries and five were able to go on international visits.

A Young Leader in Mid Devon Division, Juliet Perry, did a sponsored parachute jump to raise money for her local Guide and Brownie units in Sandford, making £125 for each unit and £63 for the Girl Guide Friendship Fund. This is just one example of enterprises undertaken by Young Leaders that year.

Brenda Gunby, Plym Division Commissioner, reported:

> Rangers have celebrated their 75th year in style. Plymstock West Unit buried a Time Capsule at Saltram House, containing uniform, a tape, photos, newspapers and items of interest that they wrote. They plan to unearth it in 25 years time for the Rangers' Centenary.

Brownies had been asking to be allowed to camp for many years, and after much thought and discussion and planning, 1991 was the year it started. Several counties offered to run pilot camps and Laurie Pearson, County Outdoor Activities Adviser, reported on the Devon pilot camp at Taw Bottom (see page 145).

In some ways 1991 was not an easy year. Mavis Budden wrote:

> Guiding has not escaped the economic recession. Cuts in grants have inevitably affected our financial situation at county level. The end of free school lettings will affect some units at a time when parents are finding it increasingly difficult to help in meeting the new costs. We have been most fortunate that our recently retired County Treasurer, Mr Bill Wyatt, managed our affairs so well during his nineteen years with us that we do have good reserves to tide us over. I should like to record our sincere thanks to Mr Wyatt while at the same time welcome our new Treasurer, Alan Wooldridge who, I am sure, will look after us equally well.

Alan was the husband of Sheila, the County Commonwealth and International Adviser and Division Commissioner for Mid Devon. Before retiring to Devon, Sheila had been very involved in Guiding with British Guides in Germany when Alan was posted there with the British Army. (See page 365.)

W. F. Wyatt – an obituary by Angela Graham (County President)

Bill Wyatt, who died in December 1992, came to help us on the County Finance Committee shortly after he retired from the Bank he had served for many years. A short time later he became County Treasurer and held that appointment for some eighteen years, having survived working with three successive County Commissioners.

Those bold facts give little indication of the affection in which he was held in the County. His appearances at the A.G.M. afforded an opportunity for all Guiders to make his acquaintance and his speeches (brief or not so brief) invoked a sympathetic and interested response – quite an achievement for the holder of an appointment whose reports can so easily be greeted by yawns. Perhaps this had something to do with the fact that his concern for Guiding always shone through.

Although he could be exasperating (and who is not?), his dedication to Devon Guiding was never in doubt and resulted in a truly sensational up-turn in the County's financial situation; members at all levels benefited from his management and he was never stingy in his response to requests for help for worthwhile projects. The needs of the membership, the core of Guiding, always had priority.

Bill's last years were somewhat saddened by loneliness and ill health which he bore with courage and humour. I think that his involvement with Guiding, the friends he made and the knowledge that he was filling a need, sustained him throughout.

It was good that we were able to give him a memorable party and presentation on his retirement in 1991 when we were able to express our gratitude for his work for Devon Guides.

The following year the Division Commissioner for Exeter, Beryl Hitchcock, took over as County Commissioner. She wrote:

Halfway through 1992 we said goodbye to our much loved and respected County Commissioner Mavis Budden. The warmth of your feelings for Mavis was made so obvious by the attendance at her farewell party in June. Fortunately, Mavis and her very supportive husband Edward are still both involved in Devon Guides.

Elizabeth Smith and Mary Jones were Beryl's assistants. Mary was now the Community Involvement Adviser and would be travelling round the county to represent Guiding on various Community Council Committees and would be looking into Guiding situations in rural areas. Elizabeth was a very experienced and excellent trainer.

Hilda Mitchelmore, who had been an outstanding County Secretary for seventeen years, also retired. Beryl wrote:

> The dedication and time given to Guiding by Hilda can never be repaid, but we all hope the scroll of her Guiding life, so artistically prepared by Margaret Branch and signed by the Commissioners, will be one of Hilda's most valued treasures.

Sylvia Spicer, who assisted Hilda for several years, also retired and was also warmly thanked.

A European Challenge was undertaken by many units. The posters for this were designed by the chairman of the Junior Council, Paulette Gower from Exmouth. These helpful posters were eagerly purchased by counties throughout the Region and were taken overseas by many who visited European countries. An Environmental Challenge was even more popular with units.

Devon hosted a Region Training weekend for Ranger Guiders in Teignmouth, and Rangers joined Venture Scouts on a canoeing expedition to the Gorge du Tarne in the South of France. Three boating weekends were held; these were always very popular and oversubscribed, and the county canoes were much used.

There was a change in Guiding this year. Uniform now became 'Guide wear', with a choice, and there were new 'Guide Handbooks', which were seen as a useful resource for both girls and Guiders. The 'Go' Challenge was now available for older Brownies, and many Ranger units, Young Leaders and young Guiders were taking part in the fifteen-plus pilot scheme. Devon was also piloting a method of training for the Adult Leadership Scheme and group tutoring of Commissioners. There was a second trial at Taw Bottom for Brownies holidaying under canvas, and Rainbow units were starting up all over the county, with bright and cheerful tabards – orange and violet colours were now added.

The international side of Guiding was much in evidence. Mid Devon Division hosted a visit from a one-time Crediton Brownie Guider, who came from the Ascension Islands with six Guides. They tried horse riding for the first time, which was quite a culture shock as there are no horses on Ascension.

A Devon Lone Guider, Corrie Newell, was one of three from the UK to attend a Lones training in Sydney attended by over fifty Lone Guiders from Australia, Tasmania and New Zealand. She wrote:

> It was refreshing to have more Ranger Guiders than any other section at a training, and an eye-opener to discover that there are not only Lone Brownies, but that their equivalents of Rainbows ('Gumnuts' in Australia and 'Pippins' in New Zealand) all have thriving Units meeting by letter.

Home hospitality followed:

> We were shattered by the end of it all, but so inspired with lots of ideas to bring back with us, and with so many new friends.

Fiona Handyside was one of sixteen to join a Scout camp in Poland at a small seaside resort on the Baltic.

> The camp site was very civilised and the Polish Scouts were very friendly. Camp, with its emphasis on friendship and the outdoor life, is as important to Polish Scouts as it is to English Guides, but it is hard for us to grasp how poor the Polish people are.

Sightseeing included Gdansk, and the amazing Cathedral Jasna Gora with its famous icon of the Black Madonna.

> Poland is a deeply religious country. . . . During periods of foreign oppression . . . the church came to be identified with national identity and the struggle for independence. Scouts too are identified with this struggle and this gives them a military feel – the hat is based on the four-cornered hat of Polish soldiers . . . and the Scout Law requests them to be as reliable as Polish Medieval Knights.

A Young Leader gained an Olave Baden-Powell Bursary towards her dream of working for a year with the charity 'Action Plus' in Africa.

To celebrate the tenth anniversary of Taw Bottom, the Junior Council ran a training camp for Guiders with Patrols.

Anneliese Barrell, the Adviser for Members with Disabilities, reported that many more Guiders were now accepting into their units girls with disabilities who might have previously been excluded. She was getting more requests for help and had been 'privileged to eavesdrop on Units busily integrating their disabled members'. Marie Bembridge of the 1st Goodrington Guides was awarded the Guide Association's Star of Merit for showing courage and determination in overcoming her disabilities to progress through the Guide programme.

Devon Guiding decided to raise money for the Children's Hospice South West to be built at Fremington in North Devon. A target of £10,000 was easily reached.

1993 was the Golden Jubilee of the Trefoil Guild and many celebrations took place. June Usherwood, the County Chairman, described some of them:

"Arts to see in '93" set the tone which produced many beautiful items; twelve of which went forward to the Region and Mrs. Joan Knapman's calligraphy reached Swanwick.

The passing of the Baton involved all 26 Guilds and the unorthodox methods of travel between Guilds were quite enterprising! Its journey started in Braunton; police vehicles were used (some transporting Trefoil convicts!), a Red Cross ambulance, vintage cars, a bicycle, a tricycle, boat, ferry and steam train, and a dragon wove its way through the streets of Exeter. It was carried by Hector, Miss Wickens' dog, while the Guild walked in relays; by a fire engine, a 1910 charabanc, a mobile crane, a decorated motorised camper and a fifty-year-old wheeled stretcher. There were Old Uncle Tom Cobleigh and All on an elongated hobby horse and supermarket trolleys decorated and motorised. It finally came to rest, two months later, in Tavistock after Guides had relayed it through the town. What laughter we had and what wonderful hospitality at each interchange!

There was the impressive Region Trefoil Guild Service in

Winchester Cathedral. To see the Cathedral packed with Trefoil members was a moving moment, as was the bank of County Standards at the chancel steps. Our County Commissioner was with us as were Sue, Mary and Dorothy who carried and escorted Devon's Standard in such a dignified way. . . .

Our own Golden AGM included tree planting, a cake and a very attractive red and gold flower arrangement, all organised by Plympton Guild. We were privileged to enjoy an excellent talk by Miss Elizabeth Smith.

A Fun Day was held at the County Camp site: "Something on a plate" produced a wonderful array of delicious food! Members participated in a collage competition, a mini Olympics, and finished off with a rousing camp fire.

Hope and I joined the National Camp at Foxlease. . . . Four members went to Lorne and . . . Eleven of us went to Our Chalet.

Exeter Cathedral was taken over one Saturday afternoon in October by Guiders, Rangers, Guides, Brownies, Rainbows and Trefoil Guild members for a Service of Thanksgiving. To see so many blue and yellow girls in the Close at lunchtime was memorable, and to see the Cathedral packed later in the afternoon made one feel very proud to be part of the thought-provoking and uplifting Service.

The County Fellowship Day was enhanced by an interesting talk by Laurie Pearson on her visit to Sangam. Pat Razey (Plympton) conducted an excellent Service. The following day we had the Trefoil Guild Sunday when most churches had a red and gold flower arrangement, appropriate prayers and in some churches a special Service which united the County.

Guilds individually have been busy planting trees, shrubs, bulbs and flowers; reunions and money-raising events have been held, all with a gold or yellow theme. One Guild even found some gold wallpaper to make a path to the party! What a special year it has been and certainly one to remember. Here's to the next 50 years!

The following year Mavis Budden took over as chairman of the Trefoil Guild; June Usherwood became president in place of Betty Bindloss, who had been a protagonist for the Trefoil Guild as a 'natural progression' in Guiding since she retired as Region Chief Commissioner. Previous chairmen (as recorded in the annual reports since 1973) were Connie Sheerman, Phyl Fowler and Audrey Downward.

Sue Brown, Ranger Adviser, reported that Devon Rangers had taken up new challenges with great enthusiasm and six new units had opened. Five girls reported exciting sailing adventures, 'and when seeing photographs of them at the top of the masts of these tall ships, we realised what an achievement it really was'. One of the highlights of the year was the invitation to five eighteen-year-old Rangers and a Guider to do 'duties' at a Buckingham Palace Garden Party. The group was warmly welcomed and spent a memorable day at the palace. They were thanked by the Master of the Household and felt they had done a worthwhile job which was appreciated. One of them wrote:

> The absolutely beautiful décor of the Grand Hall was amazing. During our briefing we were split into pairs and threes, with Rangers from Wales and Ulster, and given our positions. Some were outside, posted at the gates, others on the doors and some were opening car doors for the ambassadors. For the people positioned on the gates and doors, the job was simply collecting tickets – all 10,000 of them! And my job was simply counting them!
>
> Guests streamed through all three main entrances at the front of the Palace for over an hour and it was raining heavily! However, after being refreshed with tea and cake we were allowed to join the guests. We walked down the steps into the huge garden, past two bandstands and tea tents and mingled with the crowd near the Royal Tea Tent. We managed to spot the Queen, the Queen Mother, Prince Philip, Prince Charles, Princess Margaret, the Duke and Duchess of Kent, and the Duke and Duchess of Gloucester. Seeing so many of the Royal Family really made our day.

The cathedral service in October, with its theme 'Thanksgiving for Guiding' was a great success. Beryl Hitchcock wrote:

> There was a great feeling of togetherness and the performance of colour bearers, readers, musicians and dancers was of an extremely high standard.

Among the VIPs who attended were the Lord Lieutenant, Lord Morley, and Patron of Devon Guides, Lady Morley, the Mayor of Exeter, the County President of the Devon Guides, Mrs Angela Graham, and many other distinguished guests. The County Music Adviser, Mrs Margaret Rickard of Woolfardisworthy in North Devon, reported:

> It has been a busy year working for the Cathedral Service, especially as far as the orchestra was concerned. The girls received many compliments on the good sound they produced as a result of their hard practising. My thanks must go to Rita Sandifer and Sally Molligoda who were a constant source of information and who gave up so much of their time to help me.

Margaret deserved much praise for her part in this wonderful performance. The collection from the service raised over £300 for the Girl Guide Friendship Fund.

The annual report, *Guiding in Devon*, had a new look with the 1993–4 number. The 1947–8 report was blue, smaller than A5 and cost sixpence. In the 1950s and until 1965 it cost one shilling and sixpence and in 1966 two shillings. In 1967 it changed to A5 size with different-colour covers and was printed by Quickprint of Exeter. Editors from 1972 included Elaine Whidborne, Kathleen Gabb (who did a nine-year stint), Margaret Branch (eight years), Mavis Budden and Frances Franklin.

The 1993–4 report changed to A4 size, with a glossy coloured and illustrated cover, and was now printed by Peter Howell and Co. of Plymouth. From 2001 it was printed by Colour Works of Torquay. 2008 was a 'Review', and 2009 and 2010 were much thinner publications entitled *Our "Snapshot" of Devon*.

1994 saw the Brownies celebrating their eightieth birthday, each division finding special ways to celebrate 'A Birthday Party with a Difference'. Kate Harding, the County Brownie Adviser, produced a wonderful pageant for the annual meeting.

This year the new Guide Promise and logo were ratified.

The old promise was:

> I promise that I will do my best
> To do my duty to God,
> To serve the Queen and help other people, and
> To keep the Guide Law.

The new promise:

> I promise that I will do my best
> To love my God,
> To serve the Queen and my Country,
> To help other people and
> To keep the Guide Law.

The new Promise badges were now in use, and the Rainbows had a similar cloth badge surmounted by the Rainbow emblem. The Guide Laws were being reviewed and a decision was expected soon.

Outdoor Activities Adviser Laurie Pearson reported that two canoeing weekends and one canoe/sailing day were now annual fixtures, thanks to Joy and Clive Ashford's hard work. The archery equipment was well used, both at unit meetings and at camp. More Guides were gaining their Camp Permits:

> The experience of planning and running their own camps is so worthwhile and so much enjoyed by the girls themselves. . . . A successful PL's and Seconds Activities Day was held at Taw Bottom where Guides enjoyed pioneering, outdoor cooking, archery, kite making and crafts.

Peggy Douglas, the County Walking Adviser, was busy organising training for the Walking Safely Scheme. Not many Guiders went on to do intermediate training, disappointingly, but the Guikers Club (for Guiders who enjoy walking) had several walks of different levels during the year. Three Guide units entered and completed the Exmoor Challenge Walk.

Wembury Guides took part in Coastwatch UK, a national survey of the whole coastline. Allocated a five-kilometre stretch from Wembury Beach to Heybrook Bay, they had to take nitrate samples, investigate pollution, and record seabirds and numbers of visitors.

In Plymouth East Division, Emmanuel Junior Guides won the 'Into Europe' Challenge, the prize being a trip to Morlaix in Brittany; the 2nd Eggbuckland Brownies came second and had an exciting day at the Sidmouth Folk Festival.

Six Rangers from Taw and Torridge Division joined the Drake and Intrepid Venture Unit – thirty-two Venture Scouts and Rangers – for a coach trip of 1,000 miles to Visigrad in Hungary. They took gifts of activity equipment for the recently restarted Guides and Brownies in Budapest, and enjoyed a variety of activities in temperatures of 90°F, one of the most remarkable being a canoe trip down the Danube. Guider Angela Taylor wrote:

> The Danube is quite wide and busy with barges and river buses. Can you imagine about twenty canoes paddling down river escorted by a safety boat and with young Hungarians, one in each canoe, shouting, "Stop! Go!" those being the only two English words they knew? Quite an experience!

Three hundred girls with a disability were integrated into units this year and many more than usual went to camp or Pack Holiday. Anneliese Barrell, who spent time visiting units to help solve problems of integration, reported that there was now an 'Understanding Disabilities Education Training (UDET) Pack' in the county, which would be helpful.

Sue Brown, County Adviser for the Senior Section, reported that the new programme 'Look Wider' had been launched and celebrated.

> This flexible programme has much to offer all groups and individuals from fourteen to twenty six years of age. . . . Our Sub-Thirty groups also offer help and support to these young women.

Many of them were working on the Duke of Edinburgh Award Scheme, the Queen's Guide Award and the new Chief Commissioner's Challenge.

There was a great response to the WAGGGS Peace Pack Appeal, with nearly 200 packs being donated by Devon Guides. Sheila Wooldridge, International Adviser, explained:

> Working in partnership with the United Nations High Commission for Refugees (UNHCR) all 128 countries (WAGGGS) members were asked to help the 90,000,000 people who have no place to call home. More than half of this number are children who have known little but fear, pain and hunger. They do not go to school and have little or no privacy. So the girls are being asked to put together school supplies and personal items in individual bags to brighten the lives of their sad refugee peers. So far 850,000 Packs have been pledged. The UK Association has pledged 97,600 Packs which will go to countries in the African Continent. Many Units and Districts have been busy collecting the necessary items and packing boxes, and these will be gathered together in Exeter early in March 1995.

In September Devon hosted the Romanian Girls' Choir, who gave 'uplifting and tear-jerking performances throughout the County'. The warm hospitality that the choir received was greatly appreciated and the Chief Adviser for Devon Education wrote to express his thanks for the cooperation and dedicated involvement of the Devon Guides.

County Regattas were still being held and this year it was again at Totnes. Organised by Outdoor Activities Adviser, Laurie Pearson, a new trophy, the Sylvia Clarke Cup for senior canoeing, was presented.

In October there was a Fun Weekend for Guiders at Broadleas, a residential centre on Dartmoor.

> The few who gathered had a great time despite the heavy rain, and appreciated the introduction of rifle shooting to their programme.

Among service projects undertaken across the county, Taw and Torridge Division formed a guard of honour at the laying of the foundation stone at the Children's Hospice in Fremington, and Woolsery Guides were working hard to help with the village-hall roof fund, and cleared footpaths for the Agricultural Show.

Elizabeth Weir retired this year from her position as Youth Liaison. Beryl Hitchcock wrote:

> Elizabeth has been absolutely marvellous as our representative on the Devon County Voluntary Youth Service Committee, offering advice on grant applications and forwarding our needs. She has established an excellent relationship on behalf of Guiding, with both DCVYS and the Youth Council teams.

Beryl also wrote:

> Towards the end of 1994 our much loved President, Angela Graham, retired. Angela has been a most supportive President for 17 years, always giving sound advice and offering practical help.

The new president, who had also been a previous County Commissioner, was Rosemary Howell.

1995 saw more Rainbow units opening and waiting lists for Rainbows and Brownies growing even longer. The Region Octopus Challenge for Rainbows was very popular – the various activities ranged from parties for grannies to making octopus puppets from recycled materials.

As well as working on the Peace Packs, the Refugee badge and other similar projects, the girls raised large sums of money for the Blue Peter Appeal, Bosnia, Somalia, Colombia, Water Aid, etc. 'Teddies for Tragedies' caught the imagination; Muriel Boatright (County Registration Secretary) reported:

> There has been a wonderful response from all over the county to my request for knitted teddies for children. These teddies, in bags, have been sent to Uganda, Zaire, Burundi, Romania, Bosnia and other countries and have brought tremendous pleasure to children who often have never experienced owning anything to play with.

It was a heat-wave summer, and Taw Bottom and Bowerman's Cottage were well used. Bowerman's celebrated its twenty-fifth anniversary with a special reunion at Manaton Village Hall. Tribute was paid to the warden, Doreen Smith, and her husband, Frank, for their hard work in ensuring the continued success and development of the cottage.

Many girls enjoyed 'Swing', the Region camp at Foxlease, at which eight Devon Guiders ran a sub-camp, 'And what a great team they proved to be!' The two boating weekends, at Totnes and Shobrooke, were as usual fully booked, the girls enjoying canoeing, sailing and boardsailing. Three Senior Section girls enjoyed cruises on Sail Training Ships; Laurie Pearson, Outdoor Activities Adviser, commented:

> What a pity that more do not take advantage of this wonderful opportunity of sailing on these beautiful ships.

Beryl Hitchcock reported that Guiding plays an important part in community events, both locally and at county level.

> Guides were once again exceedingly busy at the County Show and their presence was favourably recognised by Show officials. Marion Farley and her team of helpers are to be congratulated on their ability to raise the profile of Guiding in this way. This was Marion's last time as Guider in charge, and we thank her and her husband Mike for all their hard work over the years. In appreciation, during the Show Marion was given a special award by the Show Committee.

Devon took up the Region challenge, Arts Alive in '95. County Arts Adviser, Sue Baird (who was also the County Secretary), wrote:

> The idea was to have a weekend of Guides, Rangers and Young Leaders where they could participate in several Arts Workshops from which would emerge a 'Scratch' show. . . . The Workshops were for Drama, Dancing, Keyboards, Puppets, Junk Instruments, Singing and Instrument Playing. On Sunday afternoon, before an audience of about a hundred (family, friends, Guiders and guests), the show went on. The talent was exceptional as was the enthusiasm and confidence. We enjoyed beautiful music and wonderful comedy acting and dancing. The Guides who brought along their own instruments made up a super orchestra of French horns, clarinets, violins, cello and guitar, backed by the 'resident' piano. It was great fun for everyone involved.

There was a special award outside Guiding for Anneliese Barrell, a long-serving Guider and trainer and for five years County Adviser for Members with Disabilities. Her work as a superintendent physiotherapist gained her the Ann Russell Award for excelling in her field of work with people with learning difficulties. She was warmly congratulated by Devon Guiding.

In 1995 the new version of the Guide Law was introduced. The previous one was:

1. A Guide is loyal and can be trusted.
2. A Guide is helpful.
3. A Guide is polite and considerate.
4. A Guide is friendly and a sister to all Guides.
5. A Guide is kind to animals and respects all living things.
6. A Guide is obedient.
7. A Guide has courage and is cheerful in all difficulties.
8. A Guide makes good use of her time.
9. A Guide takes care of her possessions and those of other people.
10. A Guide is self-controlled in all she thinks, says and does.

The new law:

1. A Guide is honest, reliable and can be trusted.
2. A Guide is helpful and uses her time and ability wisely.
3. A Guide faces challenges and learns from her experiences.
4. A Guide is a good friend and a sister to all Guides.
5. A Guide is polite and considerate.
6. A Guide respects all living things and takes care of the world around her.

Changes to the promise and law have only been made after wide consultation, and although the GGA Executive Committee realise they cannot please everyone, after much deliberation the new wording reflects a general consensus, while remaining true to the founder's original vision.

Rangers celebrated their eightieth birthday in 1996 with a weekend camp at Bicton; activities included an overnight wide game, canoeing, archery and swimming, and a big party when each unit brought a cake and eighty candles were blown out by the Region Ranger Adviser with a pair of bellows. The Region badge for the eightieth anniversary was designed by a Ranger from Ottery St Mary.

Many joint activities took place with Venture Scouts, including an inter-unit pub-game challenge, Madventure, five-a-side football, skittles and volleyball.

Learn to Mix in '96 was a Region challenge to raise awareness of many disabilities; everyone could take part in a series of challenges, and many units enjoyed the experience. Training on asthma awareness was included at the County Training Day (there were 320 members suffering from asthma, according to the census).

Devon launched the *Rainbow Tape and Song Book* this year; it was composed, compiled and presented by the Rainbow Adviser, Margaret Rickard, with help from her husband and two friends. This proved to be very popular and was much sought after by other regions and indeed other countries.

In June six Guides and two Guiders from Plympton represented the Region at the Trooping of the Colour in London, and had a spectacular view. Also from Cadover Division, Sparkwell Rangers cycled from coast to coast from Newcastle to the Lake District, staying at hostels and Waddow.

North Devon Division had an interesting year. One Guide company helped with horse trials and carriage driving at Arlington Court. Another, which camped near London, was invited into Downing Street and met cabinet ministers leaving No. 10. They also visited the Heritage Centre at CHQ and enrolled some Rangers and Guides outside Buckingham Palace.

Brownie and Rainbow units on the base at Chivenor had to close when the RAF moved out in 1995. The Royal Marines moved in, but there were fewer children, and the 1st Braunton Guides also had to close.

South West Region celebrated its twenty-five years of existence with a magnificent service in Salisbury Cathedral.

The 1st Dartmouth Guides celebrated their seventy-fifth

birthday with a two-week visit to Dartmouth, Nova Scotia, sightseeing and camping by a lake. They went to the last day of the World Conference at nearby Wolfville. Laurie Pearson, their enterprising Guider, was also the hard-working County Outdoor Activities Adviser, and to everyone's delight she was presented with the prestigious Region award, the Silver Oak Leaf, at the Region Annual Meeting.

Plym Division Brownies, working for World Culture, buried a time capsule in the vicarage garden, to be reclaimed after fifty years.

> In 2046 these Brownies will be able to show their grandchildren what they did in the 1990s.

Sheila Wooldridge retired this year as International Adviser, and Lorraine Richards took over. Beryl Hitchcock paid tribute to Sheila, who had

> so ably permeated all International aspects of Guiding over so many years. Many young people have gained a tremendous amount of knowledge and experience through Sheila's caring dedication.

Two much loved and respected former Division Commissioners in Plymouth died this year. In Plymouth East, Rosamond Stevens will always be remembered, as the Division Headquarters, the building for which she was responsible, was now named Rosamond Stevens Hall. In Plymouth West, Sylvia Ough was remembered by a large congregation at a service of thanksgiving in Higher St Budeaux Church.

For many years Devon Guides had been corporate members of several organisations. In 1995 they were still members of the Devon Conservation Forum, the Devon Trust for Nature Conservation, and the British Orienteering Federation. In the 1970s they were also members of the British Deer Society, and in the 1980s Young Friends of Exeter Cathedral. By paying a small annual subscription to these organisations the Guide county was helping them in return for help in organising various outdoor events. In 1996 the only corporate membership was with the Devon Conservation Forum.

The highlight of 1997 was Friendship Camp, held in the grounds of Powderham Castle during the wettest week of the year. Chris Tozer, who took over as County Commissioner from Beryl Hitchcock after the camp, wrote:

> Despite the appalling weather, there was a lovely atmosphere and the vast range of activities was unofficially enlarged to include 'keeping dry,' 'mud sliding,' etc. This resulted in the presentation of a new 'Wet Weather Camping' badge to all who attended, as recommended by our Chief Guide, Bridget Towle.

The idea of the camp had been Beryl's, and she and Laurie Pearson (who retired as Outdoor Activities Adviser after the camp) wrote:

> Three years ago we never imagined just how much the name we had chosen for our camp, 'Friendship', would be exactly that. Despite the rain, the friendly and happy atmosphere just grew and grew as the week progressed, starting with the moving Opening Ceremony to the finale, a fantastic firework display. Nothing could dampen the enthusiasm of each and everyone on site – in fact the mud 'gelled' us together even more! Our younger members enjoyed an exciting action-packed week, trying their hands at a wonderful variety of crafts, adventurous activities, a Gang Show and an International Evening where they found energy to disco dance and sing at the top of their voices. . . . The visit of the Chief Guide was another highlight of the week when she was able to meet the girls and our friends from overseas. . . . The hardworking Friendship Team, all the Leaders and the kind people who gave up so much of their time to ensure the girls were able to enjoy this wonderful experience must be congratulated and thanked.

The overseas contingent included Girl Scouts from Canada, the USA and Japan, Guides from Northern Ireland, Rangers from Poland and a Guider from St Lucia. Music was a feature of the camp, organised by Sally Molligoda, Music Assistant to the Arts Adviser. A specially composed 'Friendship Song' was sung at the opening ceremony.

Following the death of Princess Diana, a Brownie Pack in Barnstaple sent three cards of sympathy, to Princes William and

Harry, the Queen and family, and Earl Spencer, and they received replies.

Rainbow Guides celebrated their tenth birthday with many parties and had two special comics published for this year. As well as the *Devon Song Book*, there was now a *South West Region Cookbook*, which included recipes well within the capabilities of the Rainbow age group.

Taw and Torridge Division were very proud that Anne Shadrick, a Bradworthy Guide Guider, was awarded the MBE for service in the community. Despite spending time in a wheelchair she took a full part in her unit's activities (and had recently been hauled up an abseil wall to admire the view!).

Bowerman's Cottage was refurbished; and the Taw Bottom warden, Barbara Lillicrap, chairman, Rosemary Howell, and secretary, Elizabeth Weir, all felt it was time they retired. Laurie Pearson took over as chairman, Anne Veale as secretary, and Betty Hinchliff became warden. Betty and her husband, Brian, were great campers who loved Taw Bottom and looked after it well for a number of years.

Amanda Weldon, a Guider in Ivybridge who was Youth Liaison for the county, reported on 'Community Involvement and Development':

> Plymouth East Division identified and carried out a development project at Mainstone Community Centre in Plymouth. The project went extremely well and involved members of the Division and the Mainstone Youth Club and was completed over two consecutive weekends in September. The park area was cleared of all litter and undergrowth and all apparatus was primed and brightly painted. Three of the walls were whitewashed and the fourth was painted with an animal mural, designed by Jo-Ann Fletcher, a Senior Section member in the Division. The project received a CIDA grant of £750. . . . Donations of equipment and goods were also made by local companies.

During 1998 the fundraising for the charity Hope and Homes for Children, begun last year, reached over £15,000. This year the county charity was the Dartmoor Rescue Group, who had organised talks, sponsored walks, a painting competition, etc., to help with fundraising. Over £13,000 was raised by the county.

A significant event this year was the Commissioners' Conference in October, attended by over forty Commissioners, to consider the development of Devon. Wide consultations would take place during 1999.

Science and technology were now part of the Guide programme, and the County Adviser, Sue Blower, very ably organised a county-wide project, Investigate in '98. Most units took part at all levels, and Beryl Wright, Division Commissioner for Exmouth, wrote:

> We have learnt many amazing things in the scientific field. The girls proudly wear their badges.

Trainings for Guiders, Young Leaders, unit helpers and Commissioners were held regularly as usual, and this year a county residential weekend was held at Foxlease. The Region put on two days called 'A Taste of Foxlease'; many went from Devon to find out what was on offer from the advisers and to take part in various activities.

Devon had sponsored a bedroom at Foxlease for a number of years. Now after wide consultation the sponsorship was changed to a newly built training room.

The Senior Section, led by Amanda Weldon, had a busy year. In October 'Octinight 2' was held at Sparkwell Village Hall, when about twenty Rangers, Young Leaders and young Guiders took part in an overnight activity which included peer education, an international wide game, catapult making and lots of fun. They also took part, with some Scouts, in the annual 'Bush Bashing' at Taw Bottom, clearing paths and ditches of brambles. Useful trainings were held, and some Young Leaders achieved the Chief Guide's Challenge.

There was a county-wide PR exercise around Thinking Day (22 February), when most units were involved in some public activity or display locally, many combining it with fundraising for Hope and Homes for Children. There was a special stand at the County Show, and Exeter Division put on a display at the Central Library and had a spot on BBC Radio Devon.

During the year the Countess of Morley retired as Patron of Devon Guides. Chris Tozer, in thanking her, said, "She is a charming lady, equally at ease with young and old." She hoped still to be invited to activities, and became a vice-president. In her place, Lady Clinton became Patron; her husband is the great-grandson of the Lady Clinton who started Guiding in Devon.

In recognition of her sterling work over many years for members with disabilities, Anneliese Barrell was presented with the Region Silver Oak Leaf Award.

1999 proved once again that, in Chris Tozer's words:

> Guiding in Devon is very strong and healthy. This is due, in the main, to the enthusiastic way in which Unit Guiders lead and support their girls.

This year the division and district boundaries were reviewed, resulting in the creation of new divisions of Tavy, Okehampton and Erme Valley. An innovation was the creation of Thanks Certificates for retiring Guiders. Direct mailing of the monthly county news-sheet was continued, and email addresses were included in the directory. There was now much interest in the Internet, and an IT Adviser was appointed (Sue Blower).

Over the years the county had been left some generous legacies, and the County Commissioner reported how they had been spent. Money left by Joan Richards was used to refurbish the kitchen at Taw Bottom; that left by Hope Rattey was used for improvements to Bowerman's, including making a car park; and Lady Amory's legacy was used to refurbish the County Standard.

International Adviser Lorraine Richards reported:

> Devon has always had a high profile as far as International Guiding is concerned. . . . Devon was asked to host a new pilot scheme which the Guide Association wanted to run in South West Region. Called ICE (International Community Experience), it was held in Mid Devon and 30 girls from around the Region (10 from Devon) spent an enjoyable weekend trying different skills and finding out more about International Guiding.

Six of those Devon girls were offered places for a camp in Denmark, and international experiences took place in Hungary, Russia, Poland, Switzerland, Iceland, Scotland, Pax Lodge and Lundy.

There was a World Camp at Foxlease in a heatwave in August, with the theme 'Peace Vision Power'. Twenty-four girls between twelve and twenty-five and four Leaders represented Devon and had a great time. 'One of the highlights of the camp was the opening ceremony when the free fall paratroopers brought the World Camp flag up to the Chief Guide,' reported one of the delegates from Devon. Another described what the World Camp motto meant to her:

> I left with PEACE of mind that the Guide Association will continue to go from strength to strength with the next generation. I had a VISION of a world communicating, no matter what barriers, and living in harmony. And I took away with me the POWER to return to my own Unit in Devon, knowing that any small difference I make will contribute to a much bigger goal.

Devon's connection with Fiji went back to 1980 and the county again sponsored a Guider from Fiji, Titi, to attend the World Camp. "It was great having Titi camping with us – she showed us how to do one of her country's dances" was one comment.

Rainbows had a busy year working on their 'Be a Busy Body' challenge. Keren Budden, the Rainbow Adviser, reported:

> We have used our feet to Line Dance, our hands to make things, our bodies to play games and our mouths to sing. We have thought about cleaning our teeth and looking after our hearts by eating healthy food.

As usual a great deal of service to the community took place during the year. A new initiative was to invite Young Carers to join Guide camps or holidays, and this was very successful.

Betty Bindloss, a former County Commissioner and the first Chief Commissioner for South West England, died in September aged eighty-nine. Her obituary appears elsewhere, but what was not generally known was that she was a friend of Olave, Lady Baden-Powell, and some of Olave's letters to Betty still exist. The following, typewritten in the Chief Guide's inimitable way, is reproduced by kind permission of Girlguiding South West England:

Hampton Court Palace
East Molesey
Surrey
January 13th 1971

My dear Betty,

I have just got your delightful letter and am so glad that all your plans for your big and important and HISTORIC first meeting of your newly founded "SOUTH WEST REGION" Committee and Commissioners at Foxlease, are going so well.

How EXCITING this is; and I am so very glad to know that all your people are going to RALLY ROUND you so well, and that you have got such a good programme PLANNED already for those busy days to be spent together.

Well now it really WOULD be a joy to me to come to JUST see and meet them all, but NOT TO TAKE PART in all your "business" affairs really, but just to SEE THEM IN PERSON just as their best FRIEND! I really truly am getting a bit "out of date;" and, even surprisingly to myself, I don't feel at ALL like making any speeches ever again!!!

So I would like very much to COME DOWN, as you suggest, on SUNDAY FEBRUARY 14th, JUST FOR LUNCH, hand-shakes with those who like, and then SLIP AWAY AGAIN at 2.15, leaving you to go on with your sessions.

I saw PATIENCE this week, and SHE WOULD BRING ME, and we could be with you say about 12.30 – and I believe that MY BETTY may be here then, & of course she could come too! WHAT fun that will be.

I really AM so glad of this PLAN, as I feel so bad about not having visited Foxlease for SO LONG, and in this way I shall be in touch with THEM, as well as with all of you again at long last! . . .

BEST thoughts to you in all this big undertaking; and hope that your OFFICE in Salisbury is perhaps already beginning to FUNCTION successfully ("teething" and/or growing pains may appear at first!!!)

Yours affectly

[signed] Olave Baden-Powell

Special Reports

KNIGHTSHAYES TREE PLANTING

November 17th 1986

Quite by chance, the County Commissioner discovered that Joyce Lady Amory, who was for many years President of Devon Girl Guides, would be celebrating her 85th birthday in November. To mark the occasion, permission was sought and granted from the National Trust to plant three hornbeam trees in the grounds of Knightshayes Court, Tiverton, where Lady Amory still has her home and where she still takes a keen and practical interest in the renowned garden that she and her late husband Sir John Amory developed together.

The trees were planted by Brownie Donna Wilson, Guide Helen Vickery and Young Leader Tina Sanders, all from Tiverton District. Also present were a representative number of Guiders from Tiverton District, County Commissioner Mrs. Rosemary Howell and Tiverton Division Commissioner Mrs. Sheila Wooldridge.

A plaque marking the trees will be put in place later this year and visitors will find them situated close to the Stable Block which is due to be converted into a new restaurant and shop.

Elaine Greensmith
Tiverton District Commissioner

TEA WITH THE PRINCESS

I was thrilled to be invited to Kensington Palace on Monday 15th December 1986 to be presented with the Queen's Guide Brooch by our President Princess Margaret.

We met first at Guide Headquarters, being welcomed by our Chief Commissioner, Dr. J. Paterson-Brown. I was delighted to meet up with the four other Queen's Guides in South-West Region, whom I had previously met last July when the five of us were entertained by our Region Chief Commissioner.

After a nervous hour of preparation and waiting, we were driven across London to the Palace. We were the first 50 Queen's Guides in the country to be presented to her Royal

Highness individually, photographed with her, and entertained to tea, in her private apartments. It was a wonderful occasion, made special by its friendly informality – both on the part of Princess Margaret and our Chief Commissioner.

AMANDA WELDON

AT THE END OF THE RAINBOW – 1987

. . . weeping girls, not wanting to leave their new found friends, exhausted Rangers and Young Leaders, relieved Guiders – the usual scenes at the end of Rainbow Camp. It was a most worthwhile week for all concerned.

The holiday is organised in conjunction with the W.R.V.S. who select girls and provide funds for their stay. We usually aim for sixteen girls aged between 9 and 12 +. The girls come from all parts of Devon and Cornwall and are recommended for selection by social workers for various reasons such as personal or family deprivation. All we ask is that they want to come to camp.

The camp is held at Taw Bottom, which is the ideal site; tents for sleeping, flush toilet facilities, meals in the new expansion, Q.M. in the kitchen and craft activities in the main hall. There is plenty of space and cover for wide games. The Rangers and Young Leaders and Guiders set up the camp on Sunday, ready for the girls arriving mid-day Monday. There are five Guiders, one in charge, one responsible for health and First Aid, the Q.M. and her assistant and one for activities. The Rangers, twelve if possible, need to be experienced campers, willing workers, have a sense of humour and understanding, patience and tolerance. They will be with the girls most of the time helping with duties and activities.

The girls are organised into groups of four, with two Rangers as their Leaders. They sleep, work and play in their groups.

The daily programme starts at 7.30 a.m. with flagbreak and prayers and finishes at 10 p.m. with lights out. Activities this year included a visit to South Zeal shops and a swim at Okehampton, printing Tee-shirts, Crazy sports, Wide Games and a Craft Day, when volunteer Guiders gave time to demonstrate macramé, hand chimes, quilling and sweet making. Two Scouters set up a pioneering course by the river.

On this day the W.R.V.S. Emergency Team kindly cooked the evening meal. We then joined the Guides camping on Beech Site for a sing-song round a real camp-fire.

The camp ends for the girls on Friday at 4 p.m. Then the strike starts, the end of another Rainbow camp.

Brenda Gunby

THE FIRST NATIONAL JAMBOREE – KATHMANDU, NEPAL 1987

One of my most vivid memories of Nepal lies in the faces of the people. Everywhere we were greeted by smiles. One day, while on a bus, a little girl who spoke no English just sat and smiled at me for the half an hour journey. It really made me think – what have they got to be so happy about? They live in real poverty. (Until going to Nepal and seeing and smelling poverty I did not fully understand it). Most of them live in two rooms with a large family, their houses do not have any water supply and there are open drains in the streets. Here we take it for granted that clean water comes out of the taps, but in Nepal we had to sterilise all the water we used. I realised I would have rice to eat, but that was all right, I quite liked boiled rice. I found that eating it every meal for a fortnight was quite another thing.

The purpose of my visit was to attend the first Nepal Jamboree. Travelling from London to Kathmandu took us 31 hours, but some of the Nepali Guides took longer to get there. Some people had to walk two days to the nearest road and then another two days to Kathmandu. At the Jamboree we slept in straw huts as there were not enough tents in the country to house all the participants. The Jamboree award was gained by taking part in Service projects, tree climbing, jungle trails, etc. The Nepalese Guides pushed themselves really hard to do these strange activities as to return home without gaining the award would have been a disgrace. The theme throughout was world friendship and I spent a week swapping names and addresses. Since my return I have been in contact with the people I met, thus keeping the spirit of the Jamboree alive.

Afterwards I stayed with a rich Nepalese family. The girl Manaslu went to a school run by Roman Catholic nuns and each morning the Hindu girls would pray in the school

140

chapel. Hinduism and Buddhism are quite intermingled and the Nepalese freely worship in each other's temples. It gave one an insight into the meaning of unity between the world religions. Along the streets in Katmandu are many shrines. One of these had a large copper plate next to it. In Nepal it remained there untouched. I realised that while walking in the streets I never felt fearful although I was surrounded by different looking people speaking a strange language. It made me aware of how honest, straightforward and trusting the Nepalese are.

We think of Nepal as a backward nation needing development, but there is much we can learn from her people. As we have raced on to become a modern country we have lost many of the qualities the Nepalese still have and take for granted. I feel very grateful that Guiding afforded me the opportunity to see such a rich culture.

JENNIFER MORRIS
Exeter North-East Ranger Unit

DUKE OF EDINBURGH GOLD AWARD CANADIAN EXCHANGE 1987

Four of us, Rangers from Plymouth, were thrilled to hear that we had been chosen to join a party from Devon for this great adventure. We had to attend two weekends, one at Fort Bovisand and one on Dartmoor for selection and 'shake down'.

On 10th August we flew from Heathrow to Vancouver. Here, the party split up and we were taken to different homes as we tried to find out about the lifestyle of Canadians.

During the week we had an absolutely amazing time; we went white water rafting, salmon fishing and water ski-ing, and one or two of us saw 'Cats' and David Bowie's final concert.

The second week was an exploration in the mountains of Strathcona Park. This was really good as the scenery was so beautiful. Views of the mountains were quite spectacular, especially at sunrise, when we used the rays to thaw out our tents. For four days we walked on mountain ridges, down a glacier shute, in silence beneath a glacier and through jungle-like forests avoiding wasps nests.

During the third week we had a slightly more relaxing time staying at a residential centre for handicapped children, where we helped with the evening entertainment, with swimming and at meal times. We thoroughly enjoyed this and the children were really great fun.

At the end of this week we had to say goodbye to the Canadians which was very sad as we had had so much fun together. For our last night in Canada we took the ferry from Vancouver Island to the mainland where we all met for a celebration meal.

CLARE SCHOFIELD
NATALIE CORNFORTH
ERICA LONG
ANNETTE BASKERVILLE

Special Reports for 1989

WE FOLLOW A STAR

Nearly 400 Brownies, Guides, Rangers, Young Leaders and Guiders gathered together in Exeter Cathedral to present two performances of 'We Follow a Star' in October as part of the centenary celebrations of our World Chief Guide, Olave Baden-Powell.

Eighteen months of planning and preparation was finally rewarded when everyone assembled for the final day. Every Division was represented in the choir of approximately 150 who were led and rehearsed by our musical Guiders around the County under the direction of Rita Sandifer.

The orchestra of 50 girls from all sections of the movement from Brownies upwards were splendid under the direction of Margaret Rickard with help from Sally Molligoda and Josephine Gott. Margaret and her husband wrote the lovely final song 'Let us follow the Star together' which many of us were humming all the way home.

Fourteen out of sixteen Divisions participated in the visual displays and every Division provided banners and Guides dressed in uniforms from overseas. These banners were really superb, bright and colourful as were the uniforms. Devon should now have an excellent selection of overseas material which I hope will be available for other members of the County to borrow when organising international events.

Congratulations should go to all the organisations of each

Division's display, which all blended very well, to the narrator, Jill Coley, a young Guider from Ottery St. Mary and to the costume makers and providers of props. Particular thanks should also go to the Guiders who accompanied the girls on the day, looked after them and kept them occupied during the long waits in between.

The administration was admirably carried out by Hilda Mitchelmore, Shirley Dunford and Sylvia Spicer – we could not have done without them.

I hope that everyone who took part, however small, will have a day of happy memories to cherish.

HILARY HATHERLEY

JUNIOR COUNCIL – 1989

Once again the Junior Council's year has been quite packed for such a small group of people.

We took part in a 'Participation Workshop' organised for all youth clubs; the subject under discussion was the part young people themselves play in their own organisations. Six months later we met again allowing groups to discuss how their activities and organisation had improved and to hear reactions of members to changes suggested.

1989 was the year for our 'How in 89' camp at Taw Bottom. Although we were slightly disappointed at the small number who applied we had a very good weekend making headdresses, clay ovens, rafts and totem poles. On the Saturday evening we held an Indian Pow-Pow with everyone in fancy dress, with Mr. and Mrs. Budden leading the Braves as Chief Sitting Bull and Mini Ha Ha. We should like to take this opportunity to thank everyone who helped and advised us, especially Laurie Pearson for her continued support.

When those who were involved with 'We Follow a Star' production were clearing their throats and tuning up, the Junior Council were desperately trying to keep calm and picking off the ever returning fluff from their hats. We were very fortunate to have been invited to morning coffee with the Chief Commissioner, Dr. June Patterson-Brown on her visit to Exeter. Over coffee and biscuits we discussed the ways in which we ought to be encouraging girls of Ranger age to continue with Guiding and how we can change the Girl Guide image to being an outdoor movement. It was a very relaxed hour and afterwards we wondered why we had been so nervous.

Our project for next year is organising the 'It's a Knock-Out' for the Rally Day at Pirates 1990. Preparations are already underway, but we need more helpers. If you would like to join us contact your nearest Junior Council representative.

HELEN BENNETT

ETHIOPIAN PROJECT – 1989

The Mid-Devon Venture Scouts were carrying out a project in Ethiopia, their task to renovate and equip a clinic in Wayu, Okehampton's twin town. I was invited to go when one of their members dropped out, my function being a secretarial one. Other members of the party included a teacher, a doctor, one civil and one electrical engineer, a photographer and a farm worker.

We arrived in Ethiopia on 15th December at 7.30 a.m. and had to stay in Addis Ababa for five days awaiting permits to travel to Wayu. Finally they arrived and we set off. Wayu is a village of about 3,000 people, a hundred miles from Addis Ababa. On the way we saw the mud technology which a village is developing, the bricks being made of mud and straw and compressed into hollow bricks.

The clinic which we were to renovate was very dirty inside. It had been lime-washed about 12 years ago, so my first job was to lime-wash the four rooms inside the building. The walls were made of mud and straw, built up around a wooden frame. The local people showed us how to repair them, where they had been eaten away by termites. After the mud had dried we lime-washed the outside of the clinic as well.

While some of us were engaged in this way, others were treating patients who came to the clinic. Dr. Guy Fender examined a lady who had been in labour for three days. She had to be taken to the nearest hospital which cost 300 birr (£100): the family managed to raise 150 birr and the ten of us each contributed 15 birr and the lives of the mother and baby were saved. Then there was a little girl of nine who had a large abscess on her neck, so the doctor carried out a minor operation on her. Richard, one of our group, had to help hold her down as there was no anaesthetic. Then the doctor also had to deliver a breach baby.

The airfreight, being all the equipment which the Venture Scouts had prepared for the trip, arrived two days before our departure. We had a very busy day instructing teachers how to use the tools and typewriter. There was also a solar panel which could charge a 12 volt battery and we left quite a lot of medical supplies for the clinic.

Life is so different there; the villagers all live in mud huts, about ten people in each one. The water pipe is about a quarter mile from the clinic and water has to be fetched on foot. As our camp was on this route most of the time there were people passing by and children standing and watching us.

In spite of the difficulties, I enjoyed it and learnt a lot from the experience. I am hoping to return to the village within the next couple of years.

ROSIE COLE
Young Leader

Special Reports for 1991

RAMBLINGS BY A GUIDER ON BROWNIES CAMPING

Yes, it has happened, Brownies have been to camp and what a wonderful experience it was for the Brownies and the leaders alike. It was June so the weather had to be good, not so here in Devon, we experienced one of the wettest Pilot Camps in the Region. The Brownies arrived full of excitement and laughter, the fact that it was raining was a minor detail. Cries of, 'Which tent is mine? Where do we eat? What is this used for? Can we go to bed now?' – filled the air at Taw Bottom, they were keen to get on with the game of camping, there was a lot to be done and explore.

After a good hot meal, and how Brownies can eat!, beds were laid out, all eager to go to bed but it was a long time before sleep overtook them!

Saturday had to be brighter, but the rain still came, even so there was no stopping these young people. The size of the bedding rolls was a problem but with the help of a leader they soon looked expertly done. Tents were checked, the mallet was well used, it took some effort to remove tent pegs afterwards. Colours were very proudly done and then it was time for duties and to start the many planned activities.

Working for the Discoverer Badge, following the Nature Trail,

145

making rafts to be sailed on the river and to complete a Treasure Trail were all participated in with such enthusiasm. It had been another busy day, we had managed to eat our evening meal and wash up in true camping style. Brownies are certainly experts at washing up – Guides please take note.

Sunday we had time to sail the rafts, one or two could have made the open sea. Time to strike camp came all too soon, it was still wet, but there were plenty of eager hands to help. Beads were handed out as a token of achievements, there were votes of thanks and cheers for the leaders. Parents arrived and were bombarded with details of the weekend's happening, tired but happy the Brownies left, Taw Bottom was suddenly quiet.

The leaders were exhausted, but after hearing remarks such as, super, fab, terrific, we want to camp again, it is better than Pack Holiday, it just had to be worth it.

The leaders learnt a lot, our reports have gone to Region, but, Brownie Guiders, be prepared for the future. You could be in for something different and I am sure you will enjoy the experience as much as I did.

LAURIE PEARSON

RANGER TRAIL '91

For Ranger Trail '91 we had two preparatory weekends getting to know each other and working out details for the trip, the idea being to visit as many of the Guide Training Centres in the U.K. as possible.

On 3rd August we met at St. David's station and travelled by train to Caersws in Wales and from there by bus to Broneirion Training Centre, our first stop. That evening we experienced a Tympath (a barn dance) and a midnight Service. Activities were laid on at all the centres but we were impressed by the friendliness of everyone at Broneirion. Many Rangers from all parts of the country now recognise us for our Devon yell.

Then we were on our way to Netherurd near Edinburgh, by train again and there we sampled such dishes as Scotch broth and haggis. The activities here were very enjoyable, mountain biking and dry ski-ing as well as sight-seeing in Edinburgh. Late night Movies kept us up until 12.30 a.m.

Waddow, near Preston, was our next stop. We were made to feel very welcome in our Sub-camp Wades Hill and we learned to Clog Dance during their Northern evening. Again there was a choice of many outdoor activities.

Glenbrook in the Peak District was our last destination. The outdoor activities here were pot-holing as well as climbing on Stannage Edge. The weather was rather dull and wet and to our dismay we were expected to be tucked up in bed by 11 p.m. However, we finished up with a really good Disco which helped us to forget the rain. After a Guides Own Service early on Sunday morning we left Glenbrook and began our long journey home, arriving in Exeter at 7 p.m. where we said our sad goodbyes.

During the week we had made many friends and tried out many different things. The Trail also gave us an insight into how large the Guiding family is and how much there is to offer if only you look for it.

KAREN PEDLAR, KIRSTY MACSPORRAN, MELISSA SQUIRES
1st Fremington Rangers

17TH WORLD SCOUT JAMBOREE IN KOREA 1991

Held at Mount Soraksan National Park, near Seoul from August 8th–15th

I was invited to take part in the S.W. England contingent to the Jamboree as a result of the work I did last year at the Guiding International Training Conference in Cheltenham.

Before the camp our unit, Unit 30 met together for four weekends, learning to work well together as a team. We designed our gateway, learned to eat with chopsticks, formed a musical group, had practice in hostessing and performed a country dance. We learned crafts to take with us and did hard physical activities together. For the fourth weekend we attended a Jamboree being held in Somerset to ensure that we functioned well as a Unit. This camp gave us the opportunity to help handicapped Scouts as well as to raise money for Scouts from the under-developed countries to attend the Jamboree in Korea.

On the 30th July we arrived in Seoul. That same evening we decided to explore the city, a fantastic experience. The streets were completely illuminated and packed with market stalls, selling tourist items. The humidity was extreme, so different from the weather in England. Next day we visited the Ohjon Stadium and

Kyong-bokkung Palace; everything was different and we walked around amazed all day.

Next, we travelled to Japan for home hospitality at Asahikawa in the North Island, Hokkaido. Two of us stayed in the home of a dentist and family and we all slept on the floor on quilts made out of straw.

While staying here our whole Unit went to the top of a mountain to renew our promises and then on coming down enjoyed hot springs, which were very relaxing. We met Girl Scouts from Alaska and visited the zoo with them, joined in local ceremonies, dressing up in 'Happy coats' and I was entertained by my family to a five course meal in a hotel. We also had a few days in Sappore, also in Hokkaido, but this time my family were unable to speak English, so it was a case of sign language and the phrase book.

Eventually we arrived at the Jamboree site at 2 a.m. on Thursday 8th August. A fantastic opening ceremony was staged for the 20,000 Scouts present. There was song and dance and the fireworks were spectacular, words cannot express the feelings and the sheer atmosphere created that evening.

There were many different activities put on for us on the site, including swimming, rock climbing, Challenge Valley, silk screening, speed boating and everyone enjoyed themselves immensely. There was never a dull moment with Sub Camp parties and international evenings. The whole site was alive with people chatting, singing and dancing.

Everyone worked well together and Scouts from all over the world were as one, the motto being 'Many hands, one world'. The memories will remain with me forever. I cannot thank Scouting and Guiding enough for giving me this very special opportunity.

LINDSEY NORRIS

JUBILEE SAIL CAMP – SWEDEN '91

I had the opportunity to attend a Jubilee Sail Camp on the banks of a Swedish fiord near Vastervik, Scouts attended from all over Sweden and from the United States, Japan, Germany, the United Kingdom and Denmark. Wonderful opportunities were on offer – sailing, canoeing, scuba-diving and using amateur radio through which we were able to contact Scouts in Poland, Russia and Japan.

A very special feature of this annual camp is that mentally and physically handicapped young people attend – we call them 'guests'. Their age range is between 12 and 18 years. Each 'Guest' takes part in as many activities as possible as well as days out. Our visits included a day in Vastervik sight-seeing and we had a ride on an old steam train. Most evenings were spent singing at the Café created in an old barn on the camp-site, around the camp fire or at a Disco in the barn.

The camp was followed by home hospitality when I had the opportunity to try local dishes, mainly fish and special cheeses, and to visit Stockholm. As Stockholm is situated on islands we toured the city by boat and on foot. During my 2½ weeks visit I saw so much and took part in many new activities. It is a wonderful feeling to travel anywhere in the world and to know that a member of our organisation will be there.

NICOLA WINSER

THE QUEEN'S GUIDE AWARD

I worked on the Queen's Guide Award for three years, starting in 1987 and was finally assessed in November 1990.

I joined Guides nine years ago and always enjoyed it, especially the out of doors activities and taking Interest Badges. As I achieved more badges I gained in confidence and I wanted to challenge myself further. At school I always had trouble as I am slightly dyslexic, which meant my school work suffered. It was really demoralising when I tried my hardest and I was still bottom of the class. In Guiding it was different: the more I put into it, the more I got out of it: I could actually be successful.

When I left school it was suggested to me that I started work for the Queen's Guide Award which seemed to be the ultimate challenge. There were a lot of people who thought I would not be able to do it, partly because I had applied to go into the Army. That made me even more determined to have a good go at finishing it. In doing so I learned to communicate better with other people: that has certainly helped me to get on with my colleagues in the Army. Written work was very hard for me but there are other ways of communicating, by tapes, videos and displays.

This time last year I was stationed in the Gulf, skills which I learned at Guide camp were put to the test. We had to light fires and erect tents, and as I lived in a tent for four months, even the smallest thing connected with camping came in useful, I found. Map reading skills I learned before going on the Dartmoor expedition, I found I could finish the practice. Although my lifestyle had changed so completely, I found I could finish the award. The one thing I really learned from doing it was that you can achieve anything if you put your mind to it.

I had my local presentation in April 1991 when I returned from the Gulf War, but the greatest thing was to go to London and meet other Queen's Guides. Together we went to Kensington Palace to meet and talk to Princess Margaret and Mrs. Jane Garside, the Chief Commissioner.

SARAH SMITH

Special Report for 1996

1st EXMINSTER GUIDES' TRIP TO IRELAND

For Emma this was not just another Guide Camp in another country; read on to find out why.

I travelled with the 1st Exminster Company to Ennis, County Clare, in Southern Ireland. The Unit has three non-sighted Guides, Kate, Susanna and Charlotte, and my role on the trip was to act as a carer for Kate. About two months before the trip I met the other two carers, Tracey and Sarah, the three v.i.p.'s (visually impaired people!) along with their parents and the Unit Leaders.

On watching Kate at this first meeting I saw how severely her blindness affected her in completing the simplest tasks like holding a cup of tea. I realised then the extra responsibility that the Leaders had taken upon themselves by taking the v.i.p.'s, and that in acting as their carers, Tracey, Sarah and myself would have to share a lot of that responsibility.

When we arrived at the ferry port and had to wait before boarding, the first occasion was provided where the girls were in totally unfamiliar surroundings and wanted a description.

We arrived at our field at lunchtime, tired after our long journey, but cloudy skies warned that the sooner we put the tents up the better. This was the first exercise where I was on a one-to-one basis, and as I have never completely mastered putting up ridge tents myself, I felt for Kate, who was relying on my guidance. It was a relief that despite our tiredness Kate was still enthusiastic and eager to do all she could. The hosting Scout group helped the

Guides and as the last pegs were hammered in I felt pleased that Kate had contributed at least as much as the other girls.

On the evening of the next day we visited the ruins of an old abbey and with a backdrop of clouded evening skies the old graves and the ancient building set a scene that I was disappointed that Kate would not be able to appreciate. However, as we stepped into the shadow of the building Kate sensed the change in light and as we walked among the graves she asked me to read some inscriptions and she felt the stone Celtic crosses of the tombstones; by describing the surroundings and by Kate picking up on the history through the engravings, I think she appreciated the trip from an aspect that I had not really considered – the feel and the atmosphere of the place.

The most important times for me and Kate to build up a relationship were at camp, where Kate relaxed easily and I was more at ease because there were no crowded streets, busy roads, etc.

The Ireland trip was the most valuable opportunity that I have ever been offered, and lucky enough to experience. Kate helped me to understand the challenges she faces every day because of her blindness and, watching the determination that usually overcame any despair and frustration, I have come to admire non-sighted people like Kate who have the courage to put their faith in people like me, and the positiveness to integrate and achieve at the same level as other people their age. I am glad that Kate was able to trust me as her carer and I hope that she enjoyed the ten days as much as I did.

Emma Silverthorne

Chapter 9: 2000–2010

2000 was a year full of celebrations for the new millennium. The big event in Devon was HOPE 2000, and the Millennium Coordinator Sue Brown described it:

On Midsummer Day, June 24th, nearly six thousand members of Devon Guide Association congregated at Westpoint near Exeter for HOPE 2000. The day dawned with the County Commissioner, Chris Tozer, giving an interview on Radio Devon to promote Guiding in Devon. This was then followed by a wonderful day of fun and enjoyment for all who attended. The day's programme included outdoor activities ranging from bouncy castles to archery; indoor activities and crafts which filled the huge indoor arena; an NSPCC Sponsored Hopathon and a Pageant. The County President, Rosemary Howell, planted an Oak tree to commemorate the occasion and history was made when The Millennium Flame was escorted into the Indoor Arena at the Opening Ceremony. It was greeted by the Chief Commissioner for South West Region, Mrs Rosemary Dibben, the County Commissioner and thousands of members and guests. The amazing aura and buzz of the day was brought to a conclusion with campfire singing and lighting of 'The Beacon' by the Millennium Flame, one of thousands of beacons all lit at 8pm on the 24th June 2000 throughout the country.

On 19th February there was a special Thinking Day Service at Exeter University, with the theme 'Let Peace Walk the Earth' – one of many such services held throughout the country on the same day. There was a procession of Colours, with the newly refurbished County Standard and many Division standards (some having been made and dedicated in the last few years).

There were superb performances by girls from all sections and a choir and orchestra accompanying the singing – a truly memorable occasion.

Sue Brown also described the journey of the Region's bus: Guiding on the Move.

As a publicity event to promote Guiding 'The Bus' started in Helston on Sunday 6th August, travelled 1,200 miles, stopped on forty three occasions to pick up and drop off girls and their leaders, and arrived at its final destination in Salisbury on the eighth day. A warm welcome by our President, a cream tea and campfire singing awaited the bus and its passengers from Cornwall and it entered Devon on Sunday Evening at The Betts Centre. At 9.30 am on Monday the bus commenced the next leg of its journey with a rousing 'send off' by the Lord Mayor of Plymouth and Sir Francis Drake on Plymouth Hoe. It then continued through Devon calling at Stover Park, for a pond dipping session with the Mayor of Newton Abbot, Exeter City centre to be welcomed by the Mayor of Exeter and Beryl Hitchcock who was also there to promote Exeter Division's Reach Out Campaign. Travelling on through the East Devon villages it arrived in Honiton for activities and games – followed by another delicious cream tea. On the final leg of its journey into Somerset passengers on board included the Region Trefoil Guild Chairman, June Usherwood, and local Trefoil Guild members who were welcomed at Wellington by the Somerset County Commissioner.

The final large-scale celebration was Gig 2K at the Millennium Dome, for which many Guiding members travelled to London.

South West Region celebrated by commissioning a tapestry made up of a panel from each county and island in the Region. Ruth Hartley and her team did an excellent job producing the Devon panel, which featured Drake's Drum with small topical pictures – for example, Exeter Cathedral, a puffin, Smeaton's Tower, etc., round the drum. The tapestry was officially unveiled in May – twenty feet long by five feet, it hangs in St Ann's Manor, Salisbury, the Region Headquarters.

There were special events for which various Guiding personnel were selected: Amanda Weldon attended a reception given by the Queen, Katie Freeman (Peer Educator) met Members of Parliament at the House of Commons, Katie Rippon attended the Queen Mother's 100th-birthday parade, and Sally Harrison was one of only three representatives from the UK to go to South Africa to work with youngsters on an AIDS and HIV project. Chris Tozer represented Devon at a Millennium Service in St Paul's Cathedral in the presence of the Queen.

As well as the special event in Exeter University's Great Hall, Thinking Day was celebrated in many different ways following a challenge by the County Commissioner. Two hundred girls in Plym Division took part in 'Dawn Raucous' – a sleepover, parade, disco and breakfast all before 9 a.m. Plymouth East and others celebrated Thinking Day on the Hoe at 7.30 a.m., as they had since 1950. The Trefoil Guild planned the service, and Valerie Dampney, who started the tradition, was there. This year they broke with tradition for breakfast, which they had at McDonald's!

Region trainings were held in Devon for the Renewed Guide Programme. Kate Harding, Programme and Training Adviser, reported:

> A major revamp of basic Guide training comes into operation in January 2001, when the new Leadership Qualification will provide volunteers with a modular framework and personal Mentors to guide them through the first six months of their Guiding life. As our county is so large this scheme is being organised on a four quarters basis; each quarter will have its own Co-ordinator and there will be mid-week Section trainings in each area for any Guiders, Unit Helpers or Young Leaders, new or not so new.

The Senior Section provided twenty-five volunteers for the Service Crew at HOPE 2000 and did a superb job. Another Octinight was held in October, at the Betts Guiding Centre in Plympton. Activities included a Ready, Steady, Cook Challenge, a wide game at 2 a.m., a song-and-dance routine at 4 a.m., and other activities and crafts through the night – good fun and a great success!

Good publicity was gained when Winkleigh Brownies were filmed by BBC2 for an item on village life, and the 1st Topsham Brownies were filmed by Carlton TV while on Pack Holiday on Dartmoor.

The popular and demanding Hurdlestone Challenge for 500 Scouts and Guides was now in its tenth year (see page 382). For the first time it was won by a girls' team – Bere Ferrers Guides in Tavy Division.

Many good turns were done by units throughout the county. Southway Brownies in Plymouth West Division all gained their Deaf Awareness badge and had a visit from a 'hearing dog' and talked in sign language with the owners. Ernesettle Brownies and Rainbows cooked 200 buns and took them to a local centre for the homeless.

On the music front, Sally Molligoda reported that a County Singing Circle, meeting twice a year, had been formed. The County Junk Band was used successfully in Exeter and North Devon.

> People are now realising that it's not just uncontrolled banging, but quite musical and challenging for all, from Brownies to adults.

There was also a sad event this year. Chris Foster, Adviser for Members with Disabilities, reported:

> We were very sad to learn of the death of Anne Shadrick MBE, a Guider in Bradworthy who, despite all her own problems, brought so much pleasure to others with her musical abilities and her great sense of fun. Her Guides had a wonderfully varied programme and Anne always took part in everything that they did.

Among many other international visits, Kathryn Gilbert, a Ranger in Plympton, went with a Region group to the 19th World Scout Jamboree Volga 2000 in Russia. "I never imagined that Scouting and Guiding could bring so many people from so many countries together," she said.

Devon County Standard Award was introduced this year. An enamelled brooch of the County Standard, it was to be awarded to unit Guiders or District Commissioners who had given very good and often long service. County personnel were not included. The South West Region Silver Oak Leaf was awarded to June Usherwood, who had done sterling work for the Trefoil Guild as chairman and now president as well as PR representative.

There was a change in County President: Rosemary Howell retired and was warmly thanked for the support and encouragement she had given the County Commissioner. Mavis Budden, who had been County Commissioner from 1987 to 1992 and after that chairman of the Trefoil Guild and editor of the county report, took over as President.

2001 was the year of foot-and-mouth disease. North and West Devon were affected by this dreaded disease in farm animals, but restrictions on movement of people as well as animals meant that the whole of Devon was affected in some way. The annual meeting, due to be held in Barnstaple, was cancelled, Taw Bottom and Bowerman's were closed for many months, the Hurdlestone Challenge was cancelled, and the Devon County Show (with its Guide 'runners') was postponed till August and was then held without animals.

Chris Tozer wrote:

> The impact on some of our rural Guiding communities was huge. In Holsworthy and surrounding areas girls didn't meet for months, yet I am pleased to say they returned with great enthusiasm. Camps, holidays, outings and trips were affected, and Guiders had to use their initiative when bringing excitement into a restricted outdoor programme. . . . But despite all this, Guiding has continued to flourish.

Sandra Collier, Okehampton Division Commissioner, described the impact on her part of Devon:

> This has been an extremely difficult year, yet, in Guiding fashion, with the aid of hardworking Leaders and enthusiastic girls, we survived and our numbers increased!

The disease affected us very badly; Holsworthy District being at the absolute centre of the outbreak. The whole area was knocked for six. Okehampton District suffered badly too. Division and District events were put on hold. Virtually all units had to shut down, many until after Easter, two not opening again until May. Many leaders and girls were directly involved, several losing everything, others being confined to their own homes in a desperate attempt to avoid infection. Eventually everything got back to normal . . . and lots of activities were enjoyed.

Division Commissioner Chris Foster reported that Taw and Torridge Division had been hit hard by the outbreak.

Many families of our members were affected and in some Districts, all Guiding had to be cancelled. However the spirit of Guiding never dies and most activities have now resumed.

In addition to Taw Bottom and Bowerman's, a third property came into the ownership of the county – Pennaton Meadow, just outside South Brent. This had been bought by Cadover Division with the insurance money after a fire destroyed the hut at Cornwood. (This hut had been given by the local landowner for young people to enjoy outdoor activities, and was much used by the Guides. But it was on open land and thus vulnerable and it was decided not to rebuild it after it burnt down.) Pennaton Meadow was not used (for camping, days out, etc.) as much as was originally thought, so Erme Valley and Plympton Divisions (which replaced Cadover) decided to give it to the county. Again it was not much used and the county eventually sold it.

The new Guide programme, with 'Go for It!', was proving popular, and the Baden-Powell Trefoil had now been upgraded to the Baden-Powell Challenge. The high point of this is a challenge weekend. Janet Parsons, who organised the first of these with Tina Caunter at Brixham, reported that they took part in all sorts of activities from raft building and abseiling to lacemaking and watercolour painting.

They found out what Guiding still had to offer them and they mixed with others from around the county as many came along. Some have established true Guiding friendships since the weekend and the majority are also hoping to stay in Guiding and will produce some excellent Leaders of the future.

The Senior Section were finding that the new 'Look Wider' file was a great improvement and made the programme more interesting. A new Queen's Guide syllabus was launched and proved to be very user-friendly. The clauses were Service in Guiding, Outdoor Challenge, Personal Skill Development, Community Action and Residential Experience. The Junior Council was relaunched, with Jane Harding as chairman. They met termly and discussed local and national issues. 'This age group, 16–26 years, is our future. . . . I know they will go from strength to strength,' wrote Chris Tozer.

As always, a great deal of money was raised for others – fifty-eight different charities were helped by Devon Guiding this year, and £14,000 was raised for Devon Air Ambulance.

2002 was the year of the Queen's golden jubilee; it was also the year that the President of Girlguiding, Princess Margaret, and its Patron, Queen Elizabeth the Queen Mother, both died.

The Queen came to Exeter, where many managed to see her, some giving her posies, and a Guider and a Young Leader met her. Fifteen Exeter Young Leaders were given a prime position on the Cathedral Close and the Queen spoke to them. They were later interviewed live for *Spotlight South West*.

There were celebrations throughout the county – carnivals and camps and holidays and street parties with a jubilee theme. Plym Division had a fifty-hour jubilee camp in the grounds of Wembury House; Hatherleigh Brownies led the town's floral dance. Sue Samuel, Tavy Division Commissioner, wrote:

> I shall long remember the faces and sea of hats in Bedford Square (Tavistock) when the girls and adults of Tavistock District danced through the square before going into the town hall for a spectacular tea.

A thousand Brownies from Plymouth East and other divisions met in the Drill Hall at HMS *Drake* for the second 'Brownies All at Sea' event, to celebrate the jubilee. They made crowns, bracelets and Union flags, and did Highland dancing, learnt a dance routine and welcomed the Lord Mayor with red, white and blue spinners. At the end of the day Kate Harding invited Commander Crichton, who had hosted the day so well, to be an Ambassador for Devon Guiding.

A Service Team worked at the County Show as usual, but there were no animals again this year as foot-and-mouth precautions continued. Mary Whichello would be retiring in 2003 after organising and running this camp for many years, and she was warmly thanked.

Sandra Collier, Division Commissioner for Okehampton, was presented at the annual meeting with a Certificate for Perseverance under great difficulties during the foot-and-mouth crisis.

Lydia Chapman, who had been a Brownie and Guide in Plymouth East, had died recently, and a small garden at St Andrew's Minster was dedicated and named after her. During her illness her sister Rebecca had been a great support, and the County Commissioner presented her with a South West Region Letter of Commendation.

Thirty Guides, Rangers and Guiders held a sponsored sleepover in the prehistoric caves of Kent's Cavern in Torquay, the first time for 100 years that anyone had slept there.

> It was great fun, a very unusual experience and a total of £600 was raised for Torquay Museum.

Rainbows were enjoying the outdoors: Kingsbridge Rainbows went crabbing in the estuary and caught 286 crabs!

As part of the new Guide programme, Patrol Leaders' Day at Taw Bottom was changed to an Activity Day at Barton Hall, Torquay, for all girls over nine. Activities included climbing, quad biking, abseiling, fencing, zip wire, etc., and it was a great success.

The Junior Council, relaunched in March 2001, now had thirty members. They were proving useful as runners at county events, such as Training Days and the annual meeting and had representatives on the DELTA Camp Committee and Taw Bottom Committee. Fifteen of them went to the Senior Section Fun Weekend at Foxlease (Zero 2). Chairman Jane Harding reported:

> Maddy (Vice Chair) and I have represented Devon at Region Junior Council. . . . Other counties have been keen to talk to us about how our Junior Council was formed and as a result we have produced a booklet titled 'Guidelines for setting up a JC', which is hopefully now being produced to help other counties get their Junior Councils up and running too. . . . Our meetings have continued to be noisy, fun gatherings with plenty of tea and biscuits! We enjoy discussing all sorts of issues within Guiding, at County, Region and National levels. Most importantly though, we have become a group of friends who enjoy sharing our Guiding lives together. I am thrilled with the enthusiasm shown within DJC and from everyone in the county. However, we would not be where we are today without the guidance and support of Chris Tozer, who I would like to thank both personally and on behalf of all of our members.

A Young Leader from Barnstaple, Kate Rippon, who had spina bifida, was presented with the Star of Merit at the North Devon Scout and Guide Gang Show.

There were some sad farewells. Muriel Boatright, known as Boaty, retired after many years as County Registrations Secretary. She had also given many years of wonderful Guiding service in Plymouth East. A former Assistant County Commissioner, also from Plymouth East, Valerie Dampney, died this year, after a long and very distinguished Guiding career.

Several divisions and districts had started appointing Ambassadors. These included MPs, mayors and other people who believe in Guiding and would promote it. Chris Tozer wrote:

> As a County we have appointed Judi Spiers (Radio Devon), Philip Bujak (Head of Stover School) and Liz Procter (PR Officer for Paignton Zoo). We have several others in the pipeline. Thank you to all Ambassadors for taking on this role. We know you will enjoy it and we will try to keep you informed.

Another new idea was affiliate membership, introduced in 2001.

Mavis Budden, the new president, was the first affiliate member.

Ann Werry, Division Commissioner for Teignbridge (known as Ashburton Division until 1999) reported that groups had been to EuroDisney and Legoland,

> But perhaps the most unusual activity was Ashburton Brownies' involvement in the ancient traditions of their town revolving round the Portlet and Baron Juries, dating back continuously for over 800 years. They dressed as medieval maids for the 'Ale-tasting and Bread-weighing' ceremony and took a prominent part in the Portreeve's Service.

Canoeing was popular, and many units included it as part of their programme, using the facilities at Haven Banks, Exeter. Clive Ashford, the County Canoeing Adviser, organised canoeing days at Tiverton and Exeter, and canoeing activities had been enjoyed at Ilfracombe, Plymouth and Tiverton. Clive was thanked for his enthusiasm and commitment.

The four levels of the Walking Safely Training Scheme had been reorganised into the Walking Scheme, introduced and promoted by Walking Adviser Jane Randles.

There were the usual opportunities to travel abroad, and several Guiders had this privilege. Sue Bullock and Hilary Hughes led a CHQ party to Singapore, Ruth David led a party to Germany, and Jan Pritchard and Lorraine Wills went to Our Cabana in Mexico, thanks to help from Hope Rattey's generous legacy.

Chris Tozer ended her annual report for 2002 with a welcome to the new County Commissioner, Kate Harding, who, she said, had a wealth of knowledge and experience, knew Devon thoroughly, was diligent, organised and had a great belief in the good of Guiding. Kate paid tribute to Chris, who

> did such a tremendous job of upholding standards in all aspects of Guiding, setting up systems and writing helpful procedure notes. In her role as Publications Coordinator, she has now added colour and photographs to our revamped monthly Devon Star newsletter.

Chris Tozer became Publications Coordinator, editing *Devon Star* and, with the help of Frances Franklin, producing the annual report. The *County Directory* of personnel and their appointments was published separately from the report the following year.

Kate appointed two very experienced Guiders as her Assistant County Commissioners – Tessa Ricketts and Tina Caunter.

In 2003, boundaries of the divisions and districts were reviewed; some districts amalgamated and the centre of the county realigned, with Mid Devon Division becoming Crediton District in Tiverton Division. (Mid Devon Division was carved out of Tiverton Division in 1987/8 under the dynamic leadership of Sheila Wooldridge, who became the Commissioner for the new division and Elaine Greensmith took over Tiverton.)

County fundraising for the past year had been for Taw Bottom, to pay for showers and hot water. Oak and Ash sites now had these popular facilities and it was hoped that by the summer of 2004 Beech and Hawthorn sites would have them too. There was a celebration to mark the site's twentieth birthday – a day of activities which included a visit by the local Morris Dancers, and everyone joined in. Kate Harding wrote of Taw Bottom:

> What a wonderful facility this campsite is, nestling on the banks of the River Taw at the centre of our county.

She went on:

> It was with sadness we heard of the death, this year, of one of our founder members of the Taw Bottom project, Miss Barbara Lillicrap. She so loved it at Taw Bottom and spent many hours working and camping there.

A Rowan tree was planted there in her memory.

The highlight of the year was DELTA, the County Camp held at Foxlease in the summer, brilliantly organised and run by Chris Tozer, Ann Werry and their team. (See special report by Chris Tozer, page 182)

'Surprise Yourself' – this was the challenge set by the Chief Guide at the start of 2003 – to develop the unit programme, to try something different and to extend one's horizons in a surprising way. Many units were meeting the challenge.

In the Guide section 'Go For It!' is still a wonderful resource and new ones are being produced to maintain the Guides' interest and help them explore new topics [reported Rosemary Farley, Guide Adviser]. I was lucky enough to take part with some of my Guides in the Scizmic Science Go For It! at the Plymouth Aquarium.

Brownies were enjoying a new programme – the Brownie Adventure. Rainbows were busy doing things for their local communities, one unit taking part in the Marathon Challenge for Children with Leukaemia by a 'Skipathon' and by putting on twenty-six items of clothing!

Many Senior Section and young Guiders were now working on the Queen's Guide Award, taking part in Community Action projects and attending Queen's Guide residential events in Britain and abroad. One Young Leader attended 'Innovate', the Senior Section Forum held in Scotland. Others had the adventure, challenge and fun of sailing on tall ships.

The Trefoil Guild celebrated its diamond jubilee in 2003 with many joyful events, including an inspiring South West Region Service of Celebration and Thanksgiving in Salisbury Cathedral, and Devon Guilds had a lovely day together in July at Powderham Castle. Chairman Anneliese Barrell paid tribute to June Usherwood, who was retiring as president:

> June has given so much and has serviced Trefoil Guild so well, she takes with her our thanks, love and very best wishes.

She welcomed Beryl Hitchcock as the new president. The Guild also said goodbye to Ruth Howell, 'our hardworking, long suffering and ever friendly and helpful County Secretary'. Sheila Bromidge was welcomed as her successor.

In Exeter Division Rainbows joined in the annual Scout and Guide St George's Day procession and cathedral service for the first time. Guides again worked with the Scouts in the Gang Show, and had been invited to use their excellent new Headquarters, which has room for archery and has a climbing wall.

Division Commissioner for Honiton, Grace Essex, reported an unusual event:

There are times in the Guiding year when you know it is the best possible thing to be doing! One of these happened to Guides, Brownies and their families in Sidmouth this year. It was Good Friday, it was 7.30 am and we were all up on top of high cliffs looking down at the sea on a beautifully calm day. We were taking part in our Good Friday hike and we still had breakfast together to look forward to.

Sue Piercy, Division Commissioner for North Devon, reported:

The beaches have been popular this long and hot summer, with BBQs, sports, sculptures, pool dipping, rounders, field study evenings and more . . . and all for free!

A Guide Guider in Torquay, Emma Bullock (the daughter of Division Commissioner Sue) spent four months in the summer working as a programme volunteer at Our Cabana in Mexico. Gemma Dunnett also went on a CHQ trip to Mexico and as well as experiencing the local culture, museums and pyramids she met and worked with local children.

At the County Show Mary Whichello retired after many years of organising and looking after the girls who formed the Service Team. The County Show staff recognised her efforts by asking her to lead the Grand Parade with the show organiser, and they presented her with a large bouquet.

In 2004 Brownies celebrated their ninetieth birthday with parties, outings and fun events. Chris Tozer, with the help of Devon Guiders and Junior Council members, organised the Region celebration at Foxlease, Fundaze, for over 5,000 Brownies from the south-west.

For Rainbows, a revised programme was introduced in September, with a new uniform and the possibility of overnight adventures, and a clearer framework for Guiders.

Guides enjoyed a large range of exciting activities as usual. Kate Harding reported:

Lynn Dixon masterminded another successful activity day at Barton Hall when 400 girls had the opportunity to try out many and varied outdoor pursuits; there was the Hurdlestone Challenge weekend run by Teignbridge Scouts and Guides, a SPLASH 'Go For It!' day of water-based activities and camps and holidays too numerous to mention. The increasing numbers applying for Baden-Powell adventure weekends show that girls are rising to the exciting challenges of Guiding – and that Guiders are prepared to uphold the Five Essentials and give girls the chance to choose their own varied programme. No wonder there are waiting lists.

Heather Pigott reported from Axminster Division that one unit enjoyed the County SPLASH! at Exeter so much they gained the confidence to enter a raft race on the River Axe. Janet Parsons reported from Erme Valley Division that Senior Section girls paddled down the River Dart in a twelve-man canoe for SPLASH! Sue Pinn reported from Exeter Division that most districts supported the WAGGGS Walk for the World. She said that many units had benefited from having a student from Exeter University to help them.

Grace Essex from Honiton Division wrote that their Good Friday Hike had become an annual event, with Brownies, Guides and Rangers being joined by parents and grandparents, uncles and aunts.

Afterwards breakfast is mostly cooked by the dads outside and we all enjoy being together eating so early in the morning.

She also reported that the Rangers were lucky enough to be invited to meet the Royal Navy in September, when they spent the night on HMS *Excellent* on Whale Island and the next day were shown around the base, a submarine and HMS *Victory*.

Sue Piercy reported from North Devon Division that Guides and Rangers from Combe Martin and Braunton spent a weekend at Pax Lodge in London, and Jane Simons reported from Okehampton Division that North Tawton and Okehampton Guides 'had a wonderful camp at Castervaria, Dorset, with an overnight stay on Brownsea Island'. Holsworthy Guides enjoyed a narrowboat holiday on the canals around Birmingham.

Sue Bullock reported from Torbay Division that the Brownies' ninetieth birthday party was the highlight of the year.

We took the Circus as our theme and over 200 Brownies turned up dressed as clowns, tightrope walkers and even lions and tigers. We hired two professional entertainers who provided circus equipment and kept everyone entertained with the usual slapstick good humour. We invited the Mayor of Torbay . . . who soon got into the swing of things by having her face painted as a clown!

Ruth Hall wrote from Totnes Division that South Brent Brownies had had good publicity when they helped create a Remembrance Garden in the village in memory of Miss Naomi Cranch, who had been a Brown Owl involved in Guiding for over fifty years.

David Hood, a Scout Assistant County Commissioner, had been organising Guides as well as Scouts through the Duke of Edinburgh Award Scheme. For several years he had run a joint Scout and Guide Duke of Edinburgh weekend at Taw Bottom, enabling young people from all over the country to get together in groups to do their Gold Expedition on Dartmoor. He reported in 2004 on Student Scouting and Guiding in Devon:

> The Scout and Guide Club continues to flourish at Exeter University with a large Duke of Edinburgh's Award participation. The Club is known as SAGE and are members of the Student Scout and Guide Association – SSAGO. During the last year they had one team who fully completed their Gold Expedition section requirements in the Brecon Beacons on foot. Another team were very adventurous and undertook a four-day Gold practice Expedition on horseback in Radnor Forest. . . . Members of the club helped with various Guide and Scout units in the Exeter area and have recently commenced a programme of social activities. At the moment we do not have clubs at any of the University of Plymouth sites. A number of students at Marjon are interested in forming a club.

In November Devon hosted the Region Development Day in Tiverton. It was for all teams of advisers and was very helpful.

South West Region was saddened by the death of its Patron, Betty Clay, the youngest daughter of Lord and Lady Baden-Powell. She and her husband, Gervais, had lived in Somerset for many years and both took a keen interest in Scouting and Guiding. A service of thanksgiving was held in Wells Cathedral in July, the music for which was arranged and led by Sally Molligoda, who received many compliments for the quality of the music and singing.

A former chairman of Devon Trefoil Guild, Audrey Downward, also died this year. She had retired to Sidmouth from Anglia Region, where she had been Chief Commissioner. She was devoted to Guiding and was an energetic and enthusiastic member of the Trefoil Guild.

In 2005 South West Region held a Celebration of Guiding and service of thanksgiving in Salisbury Cathedral on St George's Day. 'This was a splendid occasion with a most impressive display of County and Division standards, including of course a number from Devon,' reported Kate.

The disasters of the tsunami and the Himalayan earthquake galvanised the girls into a huge amount of fundraising in many different ways, for Shelterbox and other charities. The county charity (from September 2004 to March 2006) was the Children's Hospice South West.

The highlight of the year was probably the Super September Snooozzzover. Over 2,700 people of all ages took part, and people snoozed in some amazing places, such as a zoo, a museum and a Lord Mayor's Parlour. Honiton Division snoozed at the local Donkey Sanctuary: 'Spending the night with 500 donkeys is interesting, and noisy,' wrote Grace Essex. North Devon Division used the occasion to dedicate their new Division Standard and to show it to as many of the divisions as possible. Erme Valley Guides got up early and walked on Dartmoor to see the sunrise. Trefoil Guild members camped.

Plymouth East Division held a very successful cookery competition. The districts held their own knockouts, and the Guide section finals were held in the catering kitchen of the College of Further Education. Various firms sponsored them and supplied ingredients and trophies, and they were given a signed photo of Jamie Oliver!

Buckfastleigh Brownies and Guides put on 1930s uniforms, thanks to Ann Pestell and her excellent archives, to take part in a feature film at the old railway station at Buckfastleigh.

Zero 5, the Region's annual activities camp for the Senior Section at Foxlease, was greatly enjoyed as usual. Canoeing, belly dancing, self-defence and crafts through the ages were among the activities; and Devon Junior Council enjoyed wine tasting and a medieval banquet, when they dressed up as jesters, ladies, wenches, priests and minstrels, with the food coming from medieval recipes.

There were two royal occasions. At the County Show Hannah Williams, an Elburton Guide who was on the Messenger Team, presented a posy to the Duchess of Cornwall, and while at Foxlease for a Baden-Powell Challenge Adventure, Guides from Torbay were presented to the president of Girlguiding, the Countess of Wessex, who was there to open the new Princess Margaret Lodge.

Diana Norman, Division Commissioner for Exmouth, reported:

> The most nerve-wracking thing we've completed this year, on behalf of the Division, was the purchase of a garage, which was then converted into an excellent storage unit for all our camping equipment. Sincere thanks go to Gill Brown (Raleigh District Commissioner) who raised an amazing £5,000 from supporting charities, and to the team of Guiders and husbands who moved all the camping equipment not once, but twice! A Thanks Badge was presented to Helen Ellis's husband Phil who had given up so much of his time and energy reconstructing and making new storage shelving for us. The result is splendid.

Val Faulkner reported from Plym Division:

> One challenge Plym must face in the next few years will come with the huge expansion of housing within the Division boundaries. We expect a steady increase in youth residency once the building schemes start and we must anticipate their needs within Girlguiding. The Division currently is very fortunate to have such a willing group of adult leaders and supportive families who strive to provide activities, which are varied, exciting, fun and safe for our members while they also lead very busy lives.

The Commissioners' Conference, now an annual event for all Commissioners in Devon, was held at Escot House. They heard about a new recruitment initiative, Project 50K, and they were updated on the CRB process.

At Bowerman's Cottage, Chris Tozer took over from Hilary Howard as chairman of the Management Committee, and set up the Friends of Bowerman's, to help spread the load of fundraising and volunteering for the cottage.

The Trefoil Guild nationally had been consulting and debating the question of membership. Anneliese Barrell, who was retiring as County Chairman, reported:

> The outcome was welcomed and members expressed their joy and relief that the Trefoil Guild is at last to become part of Guiding UK. The way is open to develop our image, explore our potential and to encourage new members.

International Adviser Joyce Blackwell reported, as always, on the various opportunities abroad that Devon girls had experienced. She also wrote:

> A number of Guiders attended our first GAINING training. This is the in-house County training for Guiders wishing to take groups abroad as all Guiders need to attend either a County or Region training before leading a group. Module 12 (International Endorsement attached to your Camp or Holiday licence) is being worked on by a number of people, with the help of the Outdoor Team.

In 2006 the theme for the Commissioners' Conference was 'Let's Communicate', and as Kate Harding reported:

> It included an insight into listening skills from a professional management consultant, discussions and workshops on communication such as meetings, dealing with parents and making the most of the media. National initiatives included Project 50K which was concerned with the need to recruit more leaders, and Project Perception, which included live radio broadcasts and the making of a TV news item. This was to "raise the profile of Guiding, promoting it to employers and the general public as a modern, relevant and worthwhile organisation." Project Streamline would promote internet access, "Challenging us all to improve our personal communication skills."

Kate continued:

> Heather Pigott and her team of recently appointed local Mentor
> Coordinators will be working to maintain standards in training our
> new leaders, while Joyce Blackwell, our ever diligent Registration
> Secretary, continues to encompass revised data systems, keeping
> all records up-to-date and so oiling the wheels of communication
> throughout our large county.

Kate also warmly thanked Frances Franklin, who was retiring
from the job she had done for many years of stuffing envelopes
and distributing the monthly newsletter *Devon Star*.

In addition to the usual trainings for Guiders, the county held its
first residential training, at the Belgrave Hotel, Torquay,

> which was a resounding success. Gill Hardy and her team of Devon
> Trainers provided many varied and enjoyable sessions . . . and
> the good food and comfortable surroundings made everyone feel
> valued. For the more outdoor activity-minded, Ann Werry, Eve
> Townson and the Outdoor Team ran an action-packed weekend at
> Broadleas, with a wide range of activities for Guiders to try.

Lady Clinton, Patron of Girlguiding Devon, this year kindly gave
a new shield, which it was decided would be awarded to groups
undertaking local Community Action projects. "A vital part of
Guiding has always been helping other people and through this
challenge we hope to further raise awareness of the good things
our young people do for others," said Kate.

Rangers celebrated their ninetieth birthday in 2007 with a party
for all the Senior Section at Crealy Park, and many of them went to
the Pink Party, one of the activities at Zero 6, the Region weekend
for the Senior Section at Foxlease. Senior Section Adviser, Janet
Parsons, reported:

> The evening included a barbecue, party games (organised by
> Devon Senior Section Team) and the unforgettable band 'Stoyic'
> – it was a hard job protecting them from the girls!

The Queen's eightieth birthday was celebrated with local parties, and thanks to a generous donation from Sheila Wooldridge a DVD of Guiding activities in Devon was made and sent to the Queen, and another to the Countess of Wessex. Grace Essex did an excellent job of supervising the production and the distribution of the DVD. Some Exeter Brownies took part in recruitment challenges and were filmed by ITV's *Westcountry News*. The Region Chief Commissioner, Gill Slocombe, said: "The Brownies behaved professionally and naturally for the cameras."

Lorraine Richards, Queen's Guide Adviser, reported that there were now seventeen girls (Senior Section and young Guiders) working for the Queen's Guide Award. Amy Page, from Torbay Division, had completed her award this year; she had taken part in an Outward Bound Course and expedition to Borneo, and took part in a Japanese Exchange.

Eve Townson, who had been a Guider and Commissioner in Honiton Division for many years, and had taken over as Outdoor Team Coordinator, reported:

> I experienced an interesting opportunity to watch Gorge Walking (to assess the safety aspects for Girlguiding Devon) at Okehampton YHA for a Unit camping at Taw Bottom. I watched as a non-Guide group donned wetsuits, waterproofs, life jackets and helmets and waded upstream and in some places into jump pools. . . . The Guides who took part thought it was great and I can't wait to take my own girls there.

She also reported that in 2006 twenty-two girls from ten units achieved their Camp Permits, as well as three Senior Section Permits, and four Guide and one Senior Section Camp Licence.

Much enjoyed by many girls was the Big Gig in Wembley Arena. Girlguiding UK launched the 'Guiding Star' competition, the eventual winners of which would be asked to perform at the Big Gig in October 2007. Auditions would take place in divisions for the County Final in February 2007. In the Guide programme there were several new ideas launched to tempt both Guides and Guiders – Go for It! Be a Sport, Go for It!, Space, and Go for It! Camp Out.

All girls and leaders were asked to make suggestions for

celebrating the centenary in 2010, and the answers were being collated.

Axminster Division had an excitement in 2007. Commissioner Julie Graham reported:

> The year started with our part of the county being thrust into the media spotlight with the beaching of the MSC Napoli offshore at Branscombe. Chaos ensued and our beaches were closed to everyone. However, 1st Seaton Guides decided that they had to do something to help with the clear-up operation. Birds were coming ashore covered in oil, so they collected old towels from all over Seaton and took several car loads to the RSPB Rescue Centre where the birds were being washed and nursed back to health.

This was one of the community projects entered for the Clinton Shield Challenge, along with others such as planting flower beds; the winning entry was the establishment of a fair trade ethos within the town and Community College of Ivybridge. Erme Valley Senior Section were congratulated on their computer-generated report, and were presented with the shield by Lady Clinton at a county reception in June (which took the place of the annual meeting that year).

The county was raising money for Shelterbox in 2007, and Babbacombe Rangers in Torbay Division raised £1,510 for the charity by holding discos, having purchased their own disco equipment with the help of a grant of £1,200 from TOFFY (Torbay Funding for Youth).

A tragic event in March saddened the whole county: Mavis Budden, County President since 2001 and a previous County Commissioner, died following a road accident when she was driving home from a Guide function (a car on the wrong side of the road hit her car). A service of thanksgiving for her life in Guiding was held in St Andrew's Minster Church in Plymouth in October. In recognition of her years of service at many levels both to Guiding and the Trefoil Guild, people attended from all over the country as well as Devon to pay tribute to her life. It was a very moving occasion.

Mary Jones became the new president in September. A previous

Division Commissioner for Axminster, Mary had been one of Beryl Hitchcock's Assistant County Commissioners.

Four honorary life members also died this year: Betty Hinchliff, a former Division Commissioner for Teignbridge and warden of Taw Bottom, and Margaret Roberts, a former Division Commissioner for Plymouth East and then their president; also Vivien Chanter, a former Division Commissioner for Tiverton and an Assistant County Commissioner, and Muriel Foden, a former Division Commissioner for Tiverton. 'Their dedication to Guiding in Devon will be sadly missed,' wrote Kate Harding.

In the summer of 2007 the competition Guiding Star reached its climax. Kate Harding reported:

> Girls aged 10 to 25 were invited to become popstars, either as individuals or groups, and the prize was to play live on stage at the national Big Gig pop concert alongside some famous popstars. Each Division held heats and Devon organised a county finals day in March. After workshops on make-up, performance skills, use of microphones, etc, the evening concert was very lively and was followed by a disco for all performers and the audience. Our winners in the different age groups, Flik Hore from Plymouth East and Natasha Quick from Okehampton, gave two good and very different style performances and went forward to represent Devon at Region level. They also sang as part of the Region Annual Event in Plymouth in May.

The South West Region Annual Event was held this year in Plymouth. The afternoon review was held in the Guildhall, where the pillars had been decorated by all the divisions, and the evening gala dinner for 200 guests was held at the Holiday Inn. Kate wrote:

> Masterminding things for us was Jan Pritchard, Plymouth East Division Commissioner, who worked tirelessly liaising with Region and coordinating teams of workers to cover every aspect of domestic arrangements, the afternoon review and the evening dinner. . . . Altogether the Region Event was judged a great success and a definite highlight. My thanks to all members who helped to show SW England what Girlguiding Devon can do.

Rainbows celebrated their twentieth birthday with all sorts of parties, including a fun day at Paignton Zoo, 'Rumble in the Jungle', organised by Rainbow Adviser Fran Mewse and her team, for Rainbows from all over Devon. A popular resource for Rainbows was 'Right Now', which suggested lots of interesting things for the girls to learn and discover.

Fran, in her report for the year, commented on how happy the Rainbows that she met were, and wrote:

> I believe that it is important that we spread this feeling of enjoyment and happiness to the young girls that are in our care. . . . As we head for 2008, let's LOOK for new challenges, LEARN about how to make a difference, LAUGH at disappointments along the way and LOVE everybody.

Devon Junior Council had a busy year helping at events round the county. For 'Rumble in the Jungle' they decorated a room for the Rainbows with balloons and banners, animal signs and a birthday cake. For Guiding Star finals at Teign School they organised the lighting, music and staging and worked with each girl, showing them how to improve. Chairman Zoe Viggers, reporting on their year, added, 'It was a fantastic day.' She also described their work as Service Team for the Hurdlestone Challenge, and 'the trek of a lifetime' to Everest Base Camp with the hot-air balloon. (See page 184).

In 2008 the annual report changed. Instead of a fifty-page A4 glossy magazine it became Our *Snapshot* of Devon 2008 – still glossy, still A4, but with only six folded pages. Sue Bullock, the new County Commissioner, wrote in her 'Introduction': 'Welcome to our new look Annual Report. I do hope you like the new format.' It had various straplines, such as 'We promise equality and diversity!' 'We give our girls and young women a voice!' 'We provide a unique girl only space!' and 'We're relevant to today's girls!'

> What is Girlguiding Devon? It is a game with a purpose. It provides opportunities for girls and young women to be challenged by new adventures and take pride in achievement.

And Girlguiding Devon's Statement of Purpose was given:

> Girlguiding UK enables girls and young women to develop their
> potential and to make a difference to the world.

There were no individual reports as before from the divisions and
from the advisers. The main activities of the year have been edited
as 'Devon Highlights 2008' on one page, with lots of captioned
photos on all pages, a half-page of 'Travellers' Tales' and a slot for
the Trefoil Guild. There is a list of vice-presidents, etc., and brief
statistics, but no accounts.

'Highlights' include the farewell party for Kate Harding on her
retirement as County Commissioner. In memory of Mavis Budden,
two sundials had been placed at Bowerman's Cottage and at Taw
Bottom. £12,808 had been presented to Shelterbox following
eighteen months of fundraising. Two hundred Guides and older
Brownies had a fun action-packed day of activities at Barton Hall,
Torquay, provided by PGL instructors.

In May, as in other years, forty-eight Guides and Senior Section
girls and six leaders 'provided a well appreciated messenger
service' for the Devon County Show. Four lucky Guides met HRH
the Duchess of Cornwall when she visited the show.

The South West Region Macmillan Coffee Morning challenge
was supported by many units, including forty Brownies and
Leaders, who held a coffee morning at Plymouth Ski Centre. Eight
young women from Devon took part in the highest ever coffee
morning on Everest. (See page 185.)

Cynthia Saunders, Trefoil Guild Chairman, mentions Trefoil
Trails as being one of the highlights of their year:

> The four cross-country meetings took place in glorious sunshine,
> with oodles of enthusiasm, fun and excellent food!

Unfortunately there wasn't room for her to explain what the trails
were! She also wrote:

> The Katie Lee legacy enabled Guilds to have outings throughout
> the summer, and also trips to the theatre and gang shows.

The Guilds raised £6,663.64 for Devon Air Ambulance as a result of sponsorship for the trails.

In her introduction to the 2009 *"Snapshot"*, the County Commissioner, Sue Bullock, wrote:

> 2009 has been another highly successful year for Girlguiding Devon. . . . Our members have had a great time challenging themselves, learning new skills and having lots of fun. We still hold the unique position of being not just girl only but more importantly girl led. Our young people are able to decide for themselves what they want from Guiding and as leaders we have the knowledge and skills to enable this to happen.
>
> This year also saw the introduction of Project Streamline which enables us to record details on the new Girlguiding database. This excellent facility will greatly reduce the time we all spend on the administrative side of our roles.

Sue also reported:

> Our website is now fully operational and we are both delighted and impressed by the number of "hits" we receive from within Devon and around the rest of the country.

A secure 'Members Only' area was launched at the end of the year.

As a build-up to the centenary, Girlguiding UK launched a challenge, 'Change the World'. Units could choose from eighteen partner charities, who sent out information and activities to raise awareness, take action and raise money. Many Devon units took part and raised £20,000. The different projects were judged for the Clinton Shield competition, which was awarded to the 5th St Budeaux Rainbows in Plymouth. They chose the Woodland Trust as their charity partner and planted trees in a local park to raise awareness of both the Woodland Trust and Guiding.

The fifty Guides who were providing the messenger service at the Devon County Show were privileged to meet the Countess of Wessex, who is the president of Girlguiding UK. She was presented with an engraved vase from the centenary catalogue to remind her of her visit to Devon.

Every year there were girls who gained prestigious awards

through their Guiding. In 2009, seventy Guides received their Baden-Powell Challenge Award, five Senior Section girls received the Chief Guide Challenge Award and three girls received the Commonwealth Award; fourteen girls also gained Duke of Edinburgh Awards, and eight adult leaders were presented with the Devon County Standard Award.

Instead of the annual meeting this year, there was an evening 'June Jolly' for invited guests, vice-presidents and selected Guiding personnel held in a hotel in Tiverton. Sue Bullock reported:

> We were greatly entertained by a superb fashion parade of Guiding uniforms from the past 100 years with a fascinating commentary from Ann Pestell, our Archivist. Chris Tozer provided us with a quiz on all things Guiding with questions that were both historical and from the present day. This was followed by an enjoyable buffet and time to look at the displays and the new Centenary merchandise.

Centenary celebrations started in September 2009, with launch parties all over Devon.

'2010 was the year we celebrated our Centenary – a chance to show the rest of Devon that Girlguiding is still as relevant today as it was 100 years ago and we have 8,500 members to support that,' wrote Sue Bullock, the County Commissioner, in her Introduction to the 2010 *Our "Snapshot" of Devon*. She continued:

> There have been many changes over the last 100 years . . . BUT we remain focussed on providing today's girls and young women with an up to date and exciting programme which is girl-led in a safe girl-only space. This is something that our young people continually tell us is what they want and what they enjoy as members of the world-wide organisation with 10 million members.
>
> This exciting programme of weekly meetings, residential events, community action projects and overseas visits is provided by a very special group of Adult Leaders and supporters in Devon. We rely on the dedication and commitment of these leaders to enable our girls to become confident women of tomorrow with the life skills to make decisions for themselves and for their future.

Celebrations took place all over the county and there were special ones too. Rainbows went to Paignton Zoo in September for the Rainbows Go Wild event, as well as having their own Princess Parties. Brownies celebrated with the Gorgeous and Golden resource and a weekend at PGL Barton Hall for the Big Brownie Takeover. The highlight for the Guides was the centenary camp at Woodlands, near Dartmouth, when over 800 girls and 200 adults came together for an action-packed fun weekend. Participants and visitors were encouraged to put pieces into a large mosaic depicting Devon Guiding, which is now displayed at Woodlands as a permanent memento of the centenary.

There was a Centenary Ball for adults – a great success, with excellent food, stories from leaders of their international experiences, and a disco.

During the year units worked on the Devon Centenary Activity challenge, a resource full of great ideas compiled by Devon leaders; 4,000 badges were awarded for this, across all sections.

The 1st Crownhill Guides from Plymouth won a national competition and were chosen to create and build a balcony display at Hampton Court Flower Show, where they were thrilled to be photographed with the Countess of Wessex.

A new initiative this year was the launch of Devon Senior Council – a group of sixty-plus ladies who wished to continue supporting Guiding with their knowledge and skills. They became a very effective Guiding Support Team to help at events.

Special Reports for 2002

FROM GUIDING IN DEVON TO BGIFC IN KUWAIT

From the Senior Section to Rainbows!

There could be no greater contrast from the green, moist hills of Devon that we left in August 2001, to the sandy, scorching, flat deserts of Kuwait, now our new working home, and yet those familiar words rang out shortly after our arrival, "I hear you were involved in Guiding in the UK. How about Rainbows? The leader is giving up and they might have to close . . ." Newly married (just before our departure), Mike, now known as 'Rainbow Mike' (one of my Unit Helpers), has had a rapid introduction into our Guiding family and all that it entails!

British Guides in Foreign Countries offers girls and women overseas, in 41 countries, the opportunity to participate fully in the Guiding programme. Normally, at least 50% of our membership are British girls and our Leaders are either trained UK Guiders living abroad or Guiders who complete the Leadership Scheme in their BGIFC country. Each country runs as a District, with a District Commissioner, a BGIFC team of Advisers and a BGIFC Commissioner. Liaison takes place almost exclusively via email, due to distance and poor mail systems. Orders from Trading, for example, can be very interesting and the postage extremely costly! We are kept up to date with Girlguiding UK through regular contact with our BGIFC office at CHQ, London and termly newsletters. "Guiding" is sent to us, but we might be dealing with 'pumpkin ideas' in December!

The nature of BGIFC is 'change' – Guiders and girls may settle into Units on arrival in Kuwait only to find that their families are being transferred to another country within the year. Transfers are numerous, the summer 'panic' for Leaders is a regular occurrence, but thankfully so too is the arrival of new women in September of each year, as recruitment begins.

BGIFC Kuwait is a relatively small, but thriving District. Our four Units – 1st Salmiya Rainbows, 1st Salmiya Brownies, 7th Kuwait Brownies and 14th Dromedary Guides – are all bursting with healthy waiting lists. Our weekly meetings take a very similar format to those in the UK and Devon – with some essential adaptations! All four Units, for example, undertook the GA Adventure Out Challenge; for most of it, however, we 'ventured in' to complete our Challenges due to the heat of Kuwait. For much of the year our Units meet in temperatures averaging 40 degrees! In respect of the local customs and faith, our Units will not meet during the month of Ramadan, though we are able to hold special meetings or District events after dark when the daily fast has been broken. At present we are looking forward to planning our World Thinking Day event, joining forces with the USA Girl Scouts, the Kuwait Girl Guide Association and the Armenian Guides – a truly international affair in a country with such a diverse mix of cultures. This tremendous diversity is refreshing – my Rainbows have no difficulty in chats about other cultures, nationalities, family in other parts of the world, though religious discussions are avoided and saying, 'Thank you for your good in our world' becomes our focus. As Guiders we do 'censor' certain GA materials that we feel may be of a sensitive nature – remembering always that we are guests in another country.

Our Units are looking forward to a Rainbow 'sleepover' (three hours only!), a Brownie Kuwaiti evening, a special ceremonial and presentation evening with our active Friends of Guiding group, a Guider and Family social evening (when it gets cooler), a District campfire on a beach (one event that is more challenging here in Kuwait), a training for all Unit Guiders in Middle East Districts to be held in Dubai in January 2003 and the BGIFC Camp and Training at Foxlease in July 2003. As we look forward to these events and many more, Guiding in Devon seems very distant and BGIFC Kuwait all-consuming – yet on hearing girls at meetings, making the same Promise, in the same uniform (short sleeved!), singing the same songs and Guiding with the same excitement and anticipation, it is quite easy to forget where you actually are!

Whilst geography, climate, culture and religion may divide us, more so now than ever in this part of the world, how reassuring it is that Guiding continues to break down barriers, respect differences and celebrate diversity.

AMANDA WELDON
Rainbow 'Sunflower'
District Commissioner – BGIFC Kuwait
(Previously Erme Valley Division Commissioner, Devon County Senior Section Adviser etc!).

In 2011 at a special ceremony in the grounds of the British Embassy, attended by Ruth Sara – the BGIFC Commissioner – and local dignitaries, Amanda was presented with the Laurel Award for exceptional services to Girlguiding. Together with her husband, Mike, and their two adopted Ethiopian children, she returned to Devon in 2013, since when she has been Outdoor Activities Adviser for British Guides Overseas (formerly BGIFC) and a Guider and trainer in Devon.

Two Devon Guiders were the leaders of a CHQ trip in June 2002. The girls came from as far afield as Ulster and Guides Cymru.

CAMP 5RO2 – SINGAPORE

After months of planning, fund-raising and a briefing weekend we all met at Heathrow wearing our Singapore polo shirts and zip-up tops. Imagine our surprise when we were asked if we could be filmed for BBC's Airport programme; what a start to our trip. Twelve hours later we arrived at Changi Airport, exhausted but very excited. The first thing that we noticed was the incredible heat as we left the airport but it was also very pretty with lots of trees and flowers planted by the sides of roads.

When we arrived at the camp, colourful banners greeted us about the environment and protecting it. The 5Rs were the theme of the camp: recycle, reduce, reuse, remember, and refuse. The camp was also celebrating 85 years of Guiding in Singapore.

There were Guides and Brownies from India, Brunei, Taiwan, New Zealand, Australia, Philippines and Bangladesh as well as the Guides from Singapore. They were really welcoming towards us and always wanted autographs, addresses or to swap badges. We took part in lots of activities, some about the culture and traditions, but we were also given the chance to do canoeing and other adventurous pursuits. It's very difficult to take part in activities like raft-building when everyone speaks a different language!

Guiding in Singapore differs from Guiding in the UK. Singapore girls in school have to do an extra-curricular activity such as Guiding. All of their Guiders are teachers who have to take an extra-curricular activity and are not volunteers as UK Guiders are and, because Guiding is part of their job, they do not do the extra training that we do.

After arriving back at HQ we were greeted by our home-stay families. Everyone was really nice and friendly. Most lived in apartments, some in large houses, and nearly all had maids to help with the housework.

We then had the opportunity to explore more of Singapore on our own. Highlights included a visit to the zoo, a night safari, a trip to Clark Quays and the Singapore River, Chinatown and Little India, Sentosa Island and the Dolphin Lagoon. It was here that we had the opportunity to touch some very rare pink dolphins. On the last day we went to Raffles Hotel for afternoon tea. Raffles is all painted white and is absolutely gorgeous. Tea was served on a three-tier cakeplate. The top layer had savoury pastry, the second layer had sandwiches and crackers with pâté, the bottom layer had two small cakes with fruit on top, two scones with clotted cream and jam, and three chocolate cases with fruit in them. This was our bit of luxury!

We now have memories and friendships that will last forever . . .

HILARY HUGHES AND SUE BULLOCK

Special Reports for 2003

DELTA – A COUNTY CAMP HELD OUT OF COUNTY

A fine day in the summer, Sunday 24th August saw the invasion of Foxlease by Girlguiding Devon – yes – DELTA camp had arrived, after months of preparation. Six hundred of our members participated, all age groups from 7 to 97 plus . . . even including at least two young babies!

Brownies filled the holiday houses and other Brownies camped, Guides camped, with Young Leaders assisting, our brilliant (in more senses than one – DJC (Devon Junior Council) rushed about doing everything asked of them – and more, and the Trefoil Guild resided in the House, some camped and some did a mixture of the two.

The programme was different from previous County camps in that the daytime activities were entirely the responsibility of the individual camp leaders . . . no millions of activities tickets! So, if a quiet, leisurely camp was required, that was what was held; if a wild and adventurous one, so be it! The activities WERE many and varied, good use being made of Foxlease activities, the surrounding beauty of the New Forest and the close proximity to Brownsea Island.

There were a few daytime "county" activities e.g. Drum Crazy workshops. Drum Crazy being a Totnes firm, specialising in African drumming and use of boomwhackers etc. . . . a fantastic experience for ALL ages.

The Opening Ceremony will stay in the memories of many I think. The fire was just embers, quiet singing started the ceremony, recollections of Friendship Camp shared, then . . . WOW . . . dancing, twirling, rainbow umbrellas with torches behind in the dark, the camp flag was hoisted, the fire rekindled very dramatically and joyful singing ensued. DELTA had begun.

Other evening activities went with just as much of a swing.

Monday – a Disco, thanks to Steve Ennis from Axminster. Tuesday a brilliant Village Fayre, each sub-camp running at least two stalls and we raised a lot of money for Taw Bottom Showers with these two events. Wednesday evening, everyone said the idea was brilliant (pardon the pun) . . . a campfire floating on Foxlease' Lake. The drawback was we were not allowed as much of the field as we had been led to believe, so the shape of the singing group, well, shall we say, "left a lot to be desired". However, after the main event any adults who could do so, remained and had a superb time singing by the lake and campfire.

Thursday evening, It's a Knockout Finals. DJC had been running the sub-camp heats all week. Brownies had their finals in the afternoon, Guides in the evening, by which time it was raining. Nothing daunts DJC . . . the Finals went ahead – just a change of venue from the grass to the court in front of the Barn. This in fact proved to be a better venue anyway as lighting could be more easily rigged up! Another great evening.

Then . . . Friday . . . Our Closing Ceremony. We started with all 600 "Drum-Crazing" in front of the House – amazing! The self-discipline the leaders had instilled during the workshops was truly brilliant. Following this, everyone went to the rear of the house for a campfire. They were all given snap-lights and all told to snap them to light at one go. It all looked so pretty as they waved the lights. Then, movement again, to the side of the House for a superb Fireworks display to end our Closing Ceremony before the flag was lowered and everyone returned to their sites for their own final ceremonies.

Judging from the vast postbag of "Thank Yous" we all received afterwards, it was a good camp, a different camp and a camp to remember. My thanks to EVERYONE who made it so.

Chris Tozer

Travellers' Tales for 2008

In July, 40 of us of mixed abilities from all over UK gathered ready for a voyage of a life-time. Our adventure started with a crew parade in Liverpool and with "Open Ship" i.e. showing people around. Once out at sea we headed for Northern Ireland and the start of the race. Nellie (our ship "Lord Nelson") amazed everyone by being fourth over the start line. All that lay ahead now was unexplored ocean and Norway! During the voyage we experienced weathers from Arctic to Mediterranean! We even saw dolphins and whales.

Life onboard ship was hard work but fantastic fun. Spirits were high throughout and we never failed to have a sing-song. We came 17th in our class out of 19. We may not have won, but we didn't give up and we proved we could do it! The memories will be with us for life.

FIONA RAVENSCROFT

In July 2008, five of us set off on our Gold Expedition in beautiful Teesdale. We spent four hot days navigating our way over 80km of moorland with knee-high heather, along the Pennine Way and through bogs, carrying tents, kit and food for the entire journey.

We all had our low points, feeling unwell, sore feet, and exhaustion, but as a team we picked each other up when feeling down and worked together. We all found out that we were capable of doing something very demanding physically and mentally. Managing to finish was a fantastic feeling, although we were shattered and it is the hardest thing I have ever done!

SARAH NORKETT
Combe Martin Guides Duke of Edinburgh Group

Laura Warne (née Maddock) one of the Devon Young Leaders involved, describes the following amazing feat. Laura is now a Brownie Guider in Tavistock.

EVEREST 100

The Everest 100 project, to get 100 Guides trekking to see Mount Everest for the Centenary, was instigated by Devon Guides and quickly became a SW Region Centenary Challenge.

It started in September 2007 with Devon Guiders, Young Leaders and a support team taking a jointly branded Girlguiding UK/Wrigleys hot air balloon on expedition to Nepal. The team had commercial ballooning skills and wide travel and mountain experience – in addition to years growing up around Dartmoor.

Despite atrocious conditions which blocked land and air routes, the combined team made it high into the Everest area and achieved a world-first hot air balloon tether above Syangboche, with the towering peaks of Everest, Ama Dablam, Lhotse and Nuptse as the backdrop. The Everest07 tether, at just under 13,000 feet set an unofficial world-highest record. An attempt to continue to Everest Base Camp was thwarted by a washed-away ravine bridge at Phunki Tenga. The team from Devon included Zoe Viggers, Cathy Warne, Bethan Shillabeer, Kate Faithorn, Alice Inman, Abi Jerome and myself. Unfortunately, I had a pneumothorax at the last minute and was stood down, but returned to lead two treks in 2008. Rachel Myers and Jenny Smith, from neighbouring Counties, made up the Young Leader team. After completing the trek, the balloon was inflated at the Nepal Scouts HQ in Kathmandu for a national parade. The expedition won praise from the international ballooning and mountaineering communities.

The Everest 100 moved on with The World's Highest Coffee Morning, a charity trek in partnership with Macmillan and Somerfield. Devon was well represented by Zoe Viggers, Jenny Dart, Emma Hogg, Penny Challans, Lauren Calley, Emma Greenacre, Jo Smith and myself. From neighbouring counties came Kerry Blewitt, Lizzy Johns, Sophie Herrmann and Gail Snook. Again facing weather and fitness obstacles, the full team carried all the equipment to complete and broadcast World Record Altitude Coffee Mornings at the 13,000′ EVH and Dingboche at 16,000′ on the Khumbu Glacier. An advance team went onwards through icy conditions to enjoy a Coffee Morning at the old Gorekshep Everest Base Camp and on top of Kalapattur at 18,000′. Supporters of the trek raised a considerable sum and unique publicity for Macmillan.

Both pioneering treks involved highly capable Guides and a skilled expedition team under tight media itineraries, permit restrictions and challenging conditions. To extend an accessible 'Mountaintop Moment' opportunity to as many Members as possible, SW Region then enabled four regular-itinerary Everest encounter treks into 2009 with a specialist adventure travel operator. This saw some of the Everest 2007/8 Devon Young Leaders assisting with the treks – and many more Guiders from the Region able to experience the awesome wonder of trekking high up in the Himalayas surrounded by some of the world's "highest mountains".

Chapter 10: SEA RANGERS

When Guiding was in its infancy, many girls wanted to be involved with boating, both inland, on rivers and canals, and on the sea. So in 1920 the Executive Committee decided to set up a scheme for Sea Guides. The thought was that Britain being a maritime nation, many girls, as well as boys, felt 'the call of the sea'; and whether they lived by the sea or near water inland, they wanted to do something along seafaring lines. It was also thought that the extra training and activities offered to Sea Guides would help to hold older girls and attract those who were not interested in joining Guides. The scheme would also offer special Guide activities to girls in the Royal Naval Girls' Schools. The training would make girls useful for the WRNS, and would enable ex-WRNS to continue serving the nation by becoming Guiders in the Sea Guide Branch.

Activities included boat handling, signalling, knowledge of tides, sea fishing, sail and flag making, engineering, swimming and lifesaving, rowing, hornpipe dancing, etc. It was for girls of sixteen and over; each girl had to pass the ordinary 'Tenderfoot' test, then be enrolled, and then pass the Senior Guide test. She then went on to take a Trade badge 'so that, in case of emergency, she may be able to offer her services as a trained clerk, motor driver, cook or domestic worker . . . telephonist, electrician, engineer . . .' One trade only was allowed, 'the object being not to make the Guide a "Jack of all trades" but a master of one.' (*GG Gazette*, August

1920.) There was also a Sea Service badge equivalent to the King's Scout in the Sea Scouts.

The Head of Sea Guides was Dame Katherine Furse, GBE, who realised that there were many girls who were not drawn to ordinary Guiding but who had 'the romance of the sea in their blood and were delighted to find an outlet for it'. She suggested that every county should have at least one company of Sea Guides, and she hoped one day to start Sea Guides under sixteen and Sea Urchins under eleven. She also stressed that 'boating is a luxury, not a necessity', and Sea Guides could find plenty to do nautically in an inland town:

> They learn the theory of sea subjects and they dance hornpipes and sing sea shanties and . . . get a really nautical atmosphere into their evening.

There were in fact Sea Guide crews all over the country, inland as well as on the coast. (*GG Gazette*, June 1923.) Dame Katherine Furse (by now Assistant Chief Commissioner) came to Devon in November 1925 to speak at an All Day Conference for Commissioners, Guiders and secretaries in Newton Abbot, chaired by Lady Clinton.

Rose Kerr wrote:

> The Sea Guides form but a small part, numerically, of the Guide Movement, but they have a spirit of their own, and have created a tradition of service which is special to them, and which has been a definite contribution to the Guide Movement as a whole.

Sea Guides became Sea Rangers in 1927, when the three branches of older girls (Cadets, Rangers and Sea Guides) amalgamated.

The companies of Sea Guides and Sea Rangers were known as 'crews' and were named after well-known ships, either from the past – for example *Victory* – or a current Royal Navy ship, when there was often friendly communication between the crews. The earliest crews of Sea Guides in Devon were SGS

Valiant in Sidmouth (1925), SGS *Dunraven* in Cockington (1926), SGS *Farnborough* in Torquay (1926), SGS *Revenge* in Plymouth (1927) and *Centaur* and *Venture* in Teignmouth (1927). There were Sea Ranger crews in Plymouth, Salcombe, Dartmouth, Totnes, Torquay, Paignton, Brixham, Topsham, Exeter, Exmouth, Sidmouth, Seaton, Bovey Tracey, Bideford and Ilfracombe, and two Lone crews.

The following is a list of later Devon boats (with possible omissions):

Bideford or Barnstaple	SRS *Dynamo*
" "	SRS *Lundy Gannet*
Bovey Tracey	SRS *King Alfred*
Brixham	SRS *Churchill*
Dartmouth	SRS *Research*
Exeter	SRS *Tenacity*
changed to	SRS *Bigbury Bay*
Exmouth	SRS *Phoebe*
Ilfracombe	SRS *Eclipse*
Paignton	SRS *Daring*
Plymouth	SRS *Revenge*
	SRS *Devonshire*
	SRS *Musketeer* (YMCA)
	SRS *Pegasus*
	SRS *Salpa* (Devonport)
	SGS *Revenge*
Salcombe	SRS *Ringleader*
Seaton	SRS *Ambush*
	SRS *Sea Devil*
Sidmouth	SGS *Valiant*
	SRS *Scorcher*
Teignmouth	SGS *Centaur*
	SGS *Venture*
	SRS *Widgeon*
	SRS *Bold Pathfinder*
Topsham	SRS *Orpheus*
	SRS *Vengeance*

Torquay	SGS *Dunraven* (Cockington)
	SGS *Farnborough*
	SRS *Farnborough*
	SRS *Eagle*
	SRS *Delight*
Lones	SRS *Druid*
	SRS *Hydra*

Much fundraising took place to acquire a boat – usually a rowing gig, sometimes a sailing dinghy. Local people, especially any with naval connections, were very helpful and generous in enabling the girls to obtain a boat and keep it afloat.

Admiralty recognition was a target that many crews aimed for. Before being inspected for this recognition, individual crews had to have:

1. A high all-round standard.
2. Been registered for at least one year.
3. A minimum membership of twenty Sea Rangers, exclusive of Guiders.
4. An attendance record of at least sixty per cent, winter and summer.
5. A minimum of two warranted Guiders.
6. Acquired a boat, or be doing its best to acquire one.

Permission to apply had to be given by the District Commissioner, who must be satisfied that the crew had cooperated in the district and done some general Ranger training. The forms also had to be signed by the Division Commissioner and County Commissioner before going to Imperial Headquarters. The inspection was carried out by WRNS officers, who checked on the nautical side of Sea Ranger training. Once recognised, the crew could fly a special pendant and members could wear a special arm badge. They then had to have an annual inspection.

In 1946 the Girl Guides Association (GGA) acquired an ex-WW2 motor torpedo boat known as MTB *630*, laid up in Dartmouth, for use as a Sea Ranger Training Ship. She had been one of the flotilla commanded during the war by Lieutenant Commander Sir Peter Scott, RNVR, the famous naturalist. After restoration she was commissioned in Brixham with a service of dedication attended by the Imperial Chief Commissioner for Sea Rangers, Lady Finola Somers, Miss Sylvia Clarke of Torquay, who was the Sea Ranger Commissioner for England, the County Commissioner, Mrs Ledger, and local VIPs. Sylvia Clarke was the first skipper of the training ship.

There was sleeping room on board for thirty-two, and the engine room, with the machinery removed, would be used for lectures. Training would be in all aspects of seamanship, including the manning of boats ten-to-twenty feet long and the handling of motor launches and small sailing boats. An extract from Sylvia Clarke's logbook for 1946 reads:

> First training on board for 20 county coxswains. This was to be an experimental week, no fixed programme or ideas. They hoped with discussions they would come up with a formula for future trainings. Ha! Ha! It was chaos, everyone had their own idea but over the weeks they found a general routine that suited everyone.

She was moored in Dartmouth and was used for Guiders' trainings until 1952, when she became a centre for Sea Rangers. Sylvia Clarke wrote:

> Many hundreds have now spent a week or more on board, and know and love the little ship with the long history.

In 1956 Sea Rangers from all over the UK, South Africa, Australia, the USA, Belgium, Holland, Denmark and India took part in trainings, and some were lucky enough to be on board during the week of the tall ships' visit to Dartmouth.

Soon after MTB *630* was commissioned an exciting event occurred. The skipper of SRS *Duke of York*, which was based on the Thames, took her crew for a week's training on MTB *630*, and to everyone's delight the Princesses Elizabeth and Margaret, who were members of the crew, were allowed to go with them. They all came by train to Kingswear Station and were taken to the ship by naval launches.

> The Princesses slept in the starboard after cabin [wrote Miss Clarke], and joined in all the usual ship's chores. Three hectic days followed – on Tuesday the whole crew went to sea in a MTB, Princess Elizabeth's personal standard flying at the masthead, both Princesses on the bridge, and the Sea Rangers manning ship with the sailors, down the river, where the ferry was stopped in mid-stream, and all the naval ships were manned and piped as they went by.

The next day they all went to Plymouth to visit their namesake, SRS *Duke of York*, and the third day they went to Torbay to watch the international dinghy races, the Princesses on board Sir Philip Hunloke's yacht, the *Windstar*. Miss Clarke also recorded 'the Princesses' gaiety and happiness and wholehearted enjoyment of the holiday'.

Again, in 1949, Princess Elizabeth came on board MTB *630* when she and Prince Philip visited the Royal Naval College. In April 1951 Princess Margaret, who was now Commodore of the Sea Ranger Section, paid an informal visit to MTB *630* in Dartmouth and inspected the Sea Ranger crews from Torquay, Paignton, Brixham and Dartmouth. Tea, served in the engine room, included an iced cake with a model of the MTB on top.

By 1960 MTB *630* was showing her age, and a new training ship, another old naval MTB, was acquired. The Sea Ranger Adviser at CHQ, D. Dakin, accompanied by Sylvia Clarke and Vice Admiral Peile, visited Devonport Dockyard to see the new MTB being refitted. Rescued in a dilapidated state from a river, she was now in a cradle out of the water, stripped of old gear and cleaned, ready for the Sea Rangers to paint her. A huge amount of fundraising was going on to help pay for her. She was commissioned by Princess Margaret, who was now Chief Ranger of the British Commonwealth and Empire, and named *Golden Hinde* on 28 July 1960.

Golden Hinde was used for trainings for the next few years, but in 1968 she failed her annual survey by Britannia Royal Naval

College, who reported that the ship was in 'a dangerous and positively unhealthy condition'. The Executive Committee of the GGA decided that it would cost too much to repair her, and she should be handed back to the Navy. They also decided they could not consider taking on another ship. 'The cost of conversion is high and the season is short.' It was hoped that trainings could take place at other facilities round the country.

Teignmouth had a Sea Guide company as early as 1927 – the SGS *Centaur*. These Guides took on the job of looking after the war memorial, and had the idea of helping with the mending at the local hospital. There was also another crew about the same time – SGS *Venture*. In 1942 Teignmouth Sea Rangers launched SRS *Widgeon*, and at their first anniversary party, to which Dawlish Rangers were invited, they were presented by Captain Pellowe, RN (retired), with a plaque with the ship's crest and motto from the officers and ship's company of HMS *Widgeon*. Sea Rangers restarted in Teignmouth in 1953 with the launching of SRS *Bold Pathfinder*, named after a MTB stationed in Gosport; a photo of eight Sea Rangers and their skipper at the carnival in 1958 appeared in the local paper. In 1955 it was reported that they were rowing or sailing every week from June to October, instructed by a Mr Whitear, who lent them his boat.

One of the Torquay crews, SRS *Delight* (named after one of Sir Humphrey Gilbert's ships), was started in 1940 by Miss Sylvia Clarke. Sylvia had been captain of the 4th Torquay Guide Company since 1921 and later captain of the 4th Torquay Rangers. She had been District Captain, District Commissioner, Division Commissioner, County Camp Adviser, and during the war she worked with the WRVS in emergency feeding after the Exeter and Plymouth blitzes. She was appointed Assistant Commissioner for Rangers (Sea Rangers) for England, and in 1942 she was given a new award – the Ranger and Sea Ranger Diploma.

SRS *Delight* gained Admiralty recognition; when they reapplied in 1956 one of the crew described the inspection by a WRNS chief officer, reporting that among other things they did semaphore to music, danced a hornpipe and sang sea shanties.

A crew was formed in Paignton in 1941 and took the name *Daring*. (Sadly HMS *Daring* was sunk in 1942.) Activities were limited in wartime, but they worked on Morse and signalling, first aid, mapping and hornpipe dancing, and they were joined by Torquay and Brixham crews for a talk on the WRNS. Another crew was SRS *Churchill* in Brixham, formed in 1941 by Miss Anne Hopkins, who was still skipper when they celebrated their silver jubilee in 1966. The crew's numbers were always above thirty, and they gained Admiralty recognition for sixteen consecutive years and won the Princess Elizabeth Cup many times. They also camped, took part in Ten Tors Expeditions and travelled abroad. In 1991 there was a reunion to celebrate sixty years, the crew by now being part of the Sea Ranger Association and not the GGA (see page 200).

All crews kept logbooks, a few of which have survived. In the 1948 logbook of SRS *Devonshire* (Plymouth) is a list of the crew and the 'capacity in which serving'; this included 'Keeper of Colours, Ship's Writer, Purser, Shantyman, Cupboard Keeper, Chief Pew Polisher . . .' The logbook for SRS *Ambush* (Seaton) for 1949 listed the crew as the skipper, numbers one and two, the boatswains and coxswains of the port and starboard watches, 'special positions': two ship's writers, 'shantyman', librarian, two stewards and a sickbay steward, and twelve members in the starboard watch and eleven in the port watch – 'A very flourishing crew!' SRS *Ambush* was commissioned in 1947 and the Seaton District Commissioner, Mrs Rossiter, gave the crew a real ship's bell. On 15 January 1948 SRS *Ambush* in Seaton received a telegram from HM Submarine *Ambush*, 3rd Submarine Flotilla, Rothesay, Bute, saying, 'Every good wish to you all'.

In July 1948 Rangers from all over Devon attended Empire Ranger Week. Based at the YWCA in Exmouth, they took part in the local swimming gala; the outdoor campfire and the tennis tournament were rained off! On the Sunday they all assembled at Exeter Central Station, where the RSM from the Royal Marines Infantry Training Centre took charge, and headed by the band of the Devonshire Regiment the Rangers marched past the Guildhall, where the mayor and County Commissioner took the salute. Then at a special Empire Day service being used throughout the world and 'most beautifully conducted' in the cathedral by Canon Hall, the lessons were read by Miss Sylvia Clarke, a Cadet, a Ranger, a Sea Ranger and an Air Ranger. Tea in the Civic Hall followed.

SRS *Ambush* featured in an unusual inter-county event in July 1950. A Scroll of Friendship from the Girl Guides in South West England was carried from Land's End via ancient tracks to Oxford, where it was handed to delegates from Egypt at the World Conference. When it reached East Devon, it was carried to the Iron Age fort of Blackbury Castle in Axminster Division, where it was received by the Division Commissioner, Mrs Rossiter, and was then carried in relays via Colyton and Seaton to the mouth of the River Axe. A crowd had gathered there to watch the crew of HMS *Ambush* receive it and row it upriver to Axmouth, where it was piped ashore, and kept safe overnight by the Division President, Lady Pridham. (See page 37.)

In 1952 Miss Muriel (Molly) Pearson was warranted as skipper of the newly formed SRS *Research* in Dartmouth. Under her leadership the crew worked hard and successfully, winning the Princess Elizabeth Cup in the 1960 regatta with their senior crew, and the junior crew came second. The following day ten crew members took part in a parade and chapel service and formed the colour party at Britannia Royal Naval College. An interesting story concerns the Royal Navy Research Ship *Research*: she was built in Dartmouth between 1938 and 1952 of teak and non-ferrous metals in order to research the earth's magnetism – the only non-magnetic ship in the world and the navy's only brigantine-rigged sailing ship. But the development of the gyrocompass made her redundant before she was finished, and her first and last voyage was to a breaker's yard in Plymouth. Fortunately SRS *Research* had a happier life!

In 1957, when the centenary of the birth of Lord Baden-

Powell was celebrated, there was a World Camp at Windsor, and before and after it over ninety international and Commonwealth guests were entertained by Guide families in Devon. One of the highlights was tea on the Sea Ranger Training Ship on the Dart. A Sea Ranger from SRS *Delight* was one of a group representing England at the Danish camp. In the late 1950s a very successful weekend for Devon Sea Rangers and Rovers was held aboard MTB *630* at Dartmouth and it was hoped to repeat it. Combined activities between Rangers and Rovers resulted in the formation of a County Rover/Ranger Committee in the 1960s.

Support and encouragement had always been provided by Britannia Royal Naval College in Dartmouth, and in 1958 they hosted the South West Area Regatta, at which Devon Sea Rangers, drawn from six different crews, tied for first place with Hampshire. The Devon girls were congratulated on their smartness. In 1959 there was a Devon Sea Ranger weekend at the college. The four local crews (Dartmouth, Brixham, Paignton and Torquay) attended and took part in the parade and divisions and the Dartmouth crew provided the colour party.

In 1958 twelve Sea Rangers from SRS *Delight*, Torquay, spent ten days in Belgium and visited the Brussels Exhibition. From SRS *Bigbury Bay* (Exeter), nine Sea Rangers went to Holland and met Dutch Sea Rangers and Scouts.

In 1959 SRS *Delight* visited HMS *Delight* at Devonport by invitation of the Captain, and formed a guard of honour for the unveiling of a memorial to Sir Humphrey Gilbert at Compton Castle.

SRS *Daring* (Paignton) acquired a shed at the harbour as a Headquarters in 1959 and bought a sailing dinghy. Among other awards, they gained two Coast and River Bars for a survey of the River Dart from source to mouth, and a survey of the Torbay coastline. This crew celebrated its silver jubilee in 1967. A new twenty-two-foot-long gig, the *Cyleen*, which they had watched being built in a local boatyard, was launched by the Guide County President, the Hon. Mrs Mildmay-White, JP.

Plymouth West's crew, SRS *Musketeer*, celebrated their

fifteenth birthday in 1959; by then they owned four boats, the latest being a fourteen-foot dinghy which the crew had built themselves. They visited the Plymouth Breakwater Lighthouse, taking fresh food, books, etc., to the keepers.

Pat Pilditch, Division Commissioner for North Devon, reported in 1959:

> The Bideford Land Rangers have become "Combined-Ops" with the formation of SRS "Lundy Gannet", and in the near future hope to register an Air Section, as the RAF station at Chivenor are helping them get off to a "flying start".

The *Lundy Gannet* was named after a trawler that had been built in Lossiemouth in 1949 and worked from Bideford until the early 1970s carrying cargo and stores to Lundy.

In 1962 SRS *Churchill* of Brixham had a 'splendid' new headquarters, opened in October by the County Commissioner, Mrs Shelagh Eastley, and in 1963 used it to entertain members of South West Area Trefoil Guild, who were having a conference in Torquay. The crews of SRS *Churchill* (Brixham) and *Daring* (Paignton) entertained a number of foreign visitors and took them boating. A Brixham Sea Ranger was selected to attend the Jubilee Camp in Trinidad in 1964.

Plymouth Sea Rangers from SRS *Musketeer* helped staff a camp for disabled Guides from Dame Hannah Rogers School in Ivybridge in 1963; the crew adopted this Guide company and had periodic reunions, and helped three children at the RN swimming baths each week. In 1970 the *Musketeer* crew repaired and redecorated a casement on Drake's Island to use as a base for boating.

Ten Sea Rangers from Plymouth West helped at the Scout jamboree in 1964, and twelve attended the Rover/Ranger South West Devon weekend at Maker, near Torpoint. Also that year a Sea Ranger crew restarted in Topsham and attended a county Sea Scout weekend at Lympstone. During the 1960s and '70s Topsham's crew SRS *Orpheus* were greatly helped by the Royal Marines at Lympstone with sailing instruction, camping at the Turf Hotel on the Exe, and in the winter use of their gym and swimming pool. This crew, skippered by Laurie McClintock from 1963 to 1982, acquired over the years two sailing dinghies, two prams, a four-oared gig and six or seven canoes. They had some contact with their namesake, a submarine, HMS *Orpheus*.

SRS *Churchill* (Brixham) celebrated twenty-five years in 1966. With a crew often over forty in number, they were started in 1941 by Miss Anne Hopkins who was still the skipper twenty-five years later. She was awarded the Beaver for outstanding service to the Guide Movement, and had written the original 'Sea Ranger Handbook', *Sea Sense*. Miss Armitage was another excellent skipper to this crew, who took part in many activities other than boating – for example, camping and trips abroad.

This report was in *Guiding in Devon*, 1967:

> In 1967 three members of the Paignton crew, SRS Daring, went to Gosport with other Devon Sea Rangers to participate in the County Championship for the South and South-West. Full of pride they returned after an exhilarating weekend aboard the Training Ship FOUDROYANT, having tied for first place with Hampshire in the regatta, in which seven counties took part.

The 1970 and 1971 County Regattas were held on a Sunday at Britannia Royal Naval College and started with a service in the chapel. Eight crews (a record number) took part in the races, in what turned out to be the last occasion of its kind.

There was one Lone Sea Ranger crew in England in 1958, and that was based in Devon. When it became too big it split into two – one crew in Yorkshire and the other in the south. There were then two Devon Lone Sea Ranger crews – SRS *Druid* (1954–62) and SRS *Hydra* (1963–5); these became 'active' crews in 1960, but numbers dwindled and in 1962 Angela Graham (County Ranger Adviser) agreed to skipper an amalgamated crew – Lone SRS *Hydra* – by writing letters every month with all sorts of challenges, and each of the eight or nine Sea Rangers in the south-west passed it on to the next. HMS *Hydra* had been a warship commanded by a Graham relative and had been used to chase out slave ships.

There was always much friendly rivalry between the Devon

crews and every year regattas were held, usually in Torbay, Totnes or Dartmouth, with rowing races, the crews competing for various prestigious awards, including the Princess Elizabeth Cup and the Angela Graham Cup.

The skipper of SRS *Delight*, Sylvia Clarke, had a great sense of humour, and wrote this wonderful piece in Devon dialect for *The Ranger* magazine for October 1957:

SRS Delight goes Cruising (with apologies to Jan Stewer)

We was at Sea Rangers one turr'ble wet cold evenin last winter when Rosemarie zuddenly zed 'Let's go and see this y'er Thames river us y'ears so much about – I bet tiddn a patch on the Dart'. Zo Skipper, 'er sez, 'All right, let's,' and sure 'nuff, come Easter Tuesday, eight of us ups and ketches train to a plaace up-country, called Thames Ditton. Skip had hired a boat, Maid Madeleine her was called, and us diddn 'arf get a shock when we zaw 'er – she were an outsize Maid, sure 'nuff – luked 'bout the size of the Queen Mary to us. She were a luvley boat wi' a big saloon, two cabins, a bridge, and a nice lil galley wi' Calor gas and 'lectric lights everywhere – proper job it were; up top there were a sun-deck wi' arm-cheers an' all.

Skip and No. 1 and some of us had to stand on a box thing to steer cos us waddn' tall enough to luke out the winder and see where us was gwine, wi'out un.

Well, chap from boatyard tuke us out on river, and showed us how to drive, and steer, and how injin worked, and then us went dru one of these y'ere locks what they has on the Thames. Us haddn' never zeen a lock afore, and Skip and No. 1 zed arterwards they vair shook at the knees the furst one or two we went dru. Bimeby, us went off on our own, and us diddn' go very far first night cos twas dimpsey by then, and we tied up alongside of Hampton Court, where Chief Guide do live. Us Rangers went and explored the maze, and none of us diddn' get lost neither. Next day, us went up to Old Windsor, and zaw lots of interesting plaaces, Runnymede and Magna Carta Island, and the RAF Memorial; and we zaw herons and moorhens, and two kingfishers, and best of all, the liddle baby wild duck like li'l balls of fluff following their mothers. Thames were much purtier than us'd thought, and now we knew why tis called the 'said Noble River'.

Skip had put us into two Watches, four in each. One was 'Below Decks' and did the cooking and washing up and shopping;

and t'other Watch steered and read the map of t'river, and were bow and stern-sheetmen. Skip and No. 1 took boat into and out of locks, 'cos they've got their Power Boat certificates, but we steered the rest of the time.

At first, Skip kept pressin' the Klaxon button by mistake for the starter button, and zuddenly there'd be a great skritch when us waddn' expecting it, and us'd jump out of our skins.

Thursday us moored at Windsor and went to zee Castle an' everything. That evenin' Skip tried to go into a lock broadside on, but twouldn't work. Us sorted things out in the end, and lock-keeper were nice, and zed it were a proper nasty wind. But lock-keeper's dog were watchin' too, and I zaw un give us a proper snooty look. Us tied up for the night by zum willow trees by bank, and by time we'd 'ad our zupper, twere dark. Friday us went up river some more, dru Maidenhead, and as far as Boulton's Lock, but then us turned round, cos we haddn' a lot of petrol for injin, and diddn' want to run out afore us got back.

We spent one night moored up to Magna Carta Island, and then went down zo far as Kingston. Zeeing as 'twas Zatterday 'twas a fiddling job steering and trying to avoid the sailing races and rowing eights and canoes and volk in rowin' boats, all auver river, but the Maid dodged them all. Our last mornin' us runned out of water, zo us called in on the Sea Cadets at Raven's Ait. The officers were ever zo nice to us, and zeemed quite interested when they 'eared us come from Devonshire, and wanted to y'ear all about our trip. Then, twas nearly over, and us took Maid Madeleine back home, and the boatyard people thanked us for bringin' 'er back so punctual and zo clean and tidy.

We Dempshire Dumplings won't never forget our trip on Thames river – 'tis a proper job, and I can't zay no more than that. S.G.C.

Sylvia Clarke had many interests and skills; she excelled at skiing and golf as well as sailing, and she was very generous – she was reputed to have paid for the purchase of a lifeboat. She died just before her 100th birthday, having expressed a wish not to reach 100!

In 1973 a decision was made at CHQ that the Sea, Air and Land Rangers should be amalgamated and called Ranger Guides, wearing the same (Land Ranger) uniform; thus the Sea Ranger Branch would no longer exist. The County Commissioner, Angela

Graham, who was a keen sailor herself and as Ranger Adviser for Devon from 1962 to 1966 had taken a great interest in the Sea Rangers, went to London to plead with the Chief Commissioner, Mrs Ann Parker Bowles (later DCVO, CBE) to retain the Sea Ranger Branch. Angela wrote in the annual report:

> For many of us 1973 will hold some bad memories. This report would not be complete without some mention of the painful struggle on behalf of the Sea Rangers to retain their name and uniform. Many of our Devon "Seas" travelled to London at their own expense, to plead their cause together with some thousand others, but to no avail. As a result two good crews from Brixham and Topsham felt obliged to sever their ties with Guiding; a sad outcome of a sorry and one would have thought unnecessary business. Those crews who decided to remain members of the Girl Guides Association had a hard time deciding, and it is good to know that they are still part of Devon's Guide family.

The result of this debacle was that the majority of Sea Ranger crews round the country broke away from the GGA and formed their own body, the Sea Ranger Association (SRA). Supported and part-funded by the Royal Navy, it carried on where the original Sea Rangers left off. Some crews tried to belong to both organisations out of loyalty to the GGA – the crew in Plymouth East was one such, under Monica White – but gradually the influence of the SRA took over, especially with regard to their very popular uniform. Of the Devon crews, Torquay belonged to the GGA and the SRA for two years, then left the SRA and became Torquay Central Rangers – 'Rangers with a sea bias' – under the leadership of Valerie Stephens. SRS *Daring* of Paignton amalgamated with the Britannia Sea Scouts who were only too happy to take over their boats, which really belonged to the GGA. "It was a 'right how to do' trying to sort out the ownership of the boats," Valerie remembered. Paignton amalgamated with the Sea Scouts, who took the Sea Rangers' boats and became the 6th Paignton Britannia Unit and are still going. Brixham Sea Rangers, who owned a cabin on the quay, joined the SRA and probably gave them the cabin.

The Salcombe skipper (and one-time District Commissioner)

Daphne Foster, who was an eccentric Guider, but very popular with the girls, was so incensed with the new ruling that she turned up at the county annual meeting wearing her Sea Ranger uniform!

By the mid 1980s the GGA had second thoughts, and the Devon County Commissioner, Rosemary Howell, was asked to sound out officers in the SRA to see if they might be willing to come back into the Guide Movement. The answer was a resounding NO, as they were perfectly happy with their status quo, having the backing of the Navy.

Sea Ranger Taps:

- Pipe down.
- All is well.
- And our light shining bright through the night.
- Hands below.
- Watch on deck.
- Pipe down.

Chapter 11: BOWERMAN'S COTTAGE

Bowerman's is situated at Lower Barracott, up a narrow lane under Easdon Tor, on Dartmoor, in the parish of Manaton. It belongs to Girlguiding Devon and is used by groups of all ages for holidays, meetings, trainings, social occasions, or just days out.

Originally a stone barn with a slate roof, it stood in a corner of a field which was part of Tor Hill Farm, belonging to farmer Shilston and family. When Mr and Mrs Shilston senior retired, they converted the barn into a two-up, two-down cottage with kitchen and bathroom added. Then in 1964 the Shilston family sold it and the two Misses Bindloss bought it as a holiday cottage.

One of the sisters, Betty Bindloss, was Devon's County Commissioner, and she allowed small Guiding groups to use the cottage. The first Guide group to stay there was the 1st Cockington group in 1965 with Hope Rattey, and the first Brownie group was the 1st Kingsteignton group in 1966 with Barbara James. It was equipped for eight and had two bedrooms, a cosy sitting room, a kitchen with a Rayburn and electric cooker, fridge and immersion heater, a bathroom, a scullery and a grass garden. Two adults and six children were the limit, and they paid eight shillings per night for four or less and two shillings per head per night for up to eight people.

By 1969 Betty had retired from Newton Abbot to Manaton, so did not need Bowerman's, and the sisters decided to sell. The cottage was offered to Devon Girl Guides; Betty gave her half, and the county bought her sister's share for £2,840. (In 2009 the cottage was valued for insurance at £230,000.)

To enable more people to stay and enjoy the moor, plans were submitted and passed to enlarge the cottage, and fundraising took place. By spring 1970 the work was done – a third bedroom, day room, toilets, washbasins and shower had been added, and the cottage was re-roofed.

During the early years it was mainly used from spring to autumn, although a few hardy folk would venture there in the winter, sometimes having to use water from the stream for toilets and washing, and fetching drinking water from Betty in the village when the cottage supply froze. "It was great fun!" Betty acted as warden, and one of the chores she did was to bring the mattresses downstairs to keep them aired and take them back up for the next group, as the only storage heaters were downstairs.

During the 1970s and '80s many improvements were made, often by visiting families and Trefoil Guild members and husbands, and new items given and much gardening done. Numbers of users rose – nearly 700 in 1977. That year the original soakaway packed in, and Mr Shilston allowed a new, much larger, soakaway to be dug in his field. In 1984 the stream overflowed and flooded the sitting room with mud and silt, and again the farmer helped by erecting a concrete tunnel so it shouldn't happen again.

In 1986 and '87 there were burst pipes and floods in the kitchen at the start of the year, and extra stopcocks were installed. 1986 saw the installation of an external fire escape, and all doors were made fireproof. Purchases included a wall-to-wall carpet in the day room, a new electric cooker and a water tank.

Betty Bindloss retired as warden in 1988, and Doreen Smith took over until 1999. A Management Committee was set up in 1992, the first chairman being Frances Franklin. This year a new fire escape and safety rail were installed, and night storage heaters put in.

In 1993 a picnic table was bought in memory of former County Treasurer Bill Wyatt. A new roof on the day room, a new porch in the kitchen and a gifted fridge-freezer were among other improvements. Fees were now £2 per person per night, plus electricity.

Fundraising cream teas had taken place before 1992, first at

Manaton and later at Widecombe; in 1995 they raised £527.

In 1997 the outside of the cottage was repainted, the garden fence renewed, and a much needed new shed built.

In 1999 Jean Busby became chairman of the Management Committee. There was now no 'resident' warden, so the checking of cleanliness was done by the Management Committee in rotation.

From 2000 to 2003 much refurbishment was done, using legacies left by Hope Rattey, Betty Bindloss, Kit Harper, Doris Twelvetrees and Frank Rowlands. This included double glazing throughout, work on the kitchen, Guiders' sitting room and bathroom, the addition of a 'night toilet' upstairs, and the conversion of the Rayburn to oil; and a UV water filter was installed. Using part of Hope Rattey's legacy, a car park was created with space for six cars, and the gateway widened.

In 2004 Hilary Howard succeeded Jean Busby as chairman of the Management Committee, and she was succeeded in 2005 by Chris Tozer, who set up Friends of Bowerman's.

In 2006 a business plan was created with a rolling programme of repairs and improvements. That year oil-fired central heating was installed, using part of a generous legacy from Frank Rowlands, and this resulted in the vinyl flooring being replaced with quarry tiles.

New fire regulations in 2006 meant major expenditure to make the ceilings fire-retardant, replacing most mattresses with fire-retardant ones, and rehanging the fire doors, etc. Also, when the spring supplying all the water to the cottage nearly dried up, a borehole had to be sunk. With the help of a water diviner, this was done in 2007 and a pressure vessel set up in the shed.

A professional team of gardeners working as volunteers kept the garden in good shape, and a new team of housekeepers was set up. A silver-birch tree had been planted in 2002 in memory of Valerie Dampney, and in 2010 a sundial was placed in the garden in memory of former County Commissioner and County President Mavis Budden.

By 2010 plans had been made as to how to spend the legacy of £45,000 left by Florence Slade for the sole use and benefit of Bowerman's Cottage. Major refurbishments included decorating and re-carpeting or re-flooring the entire cottage, new curtains or blinds for all windows, emergency lighting in all rooms, renewal of the flat roof, complete refurbishment of the kitchen with semi-industrial units, creation of a utility room, improvements in the bedrooms and washroom, and the extension of the paved area in the garden. After a three-month break, the cottage was reopened over the weekend of 4–6 March 2011, when the Babbacombe Rangers celebrated with a banquet.

Members' fees in 2011 were £6 per head per night, which was as usual only a small annual increase.

Author's Note: This information has come from the booklet *Bowerman's Cottage: Celebrating 40+ Years*, written by Chris Tozer.

Chris writes in her introduction to the booklet:

The Trustees of Girlguiding Devon are very supportive of the work done to ensure that, whilst moving forward to accommodate 21st century members, the very special character and atmosphere of Bowerman's are not lost.

Betty Bindloss made it clear that Bowerman's was to be a "halfway house" between the comforts of home and the "strange basics" of camping. Today's Management Committee believes this IS still the case, bearing in mind most campsites now have showers and other mod cons. At Bowerman's girls learn to respect and treat with care property belonging to others; they learn to work together, play together and, in its special surroundings, they learn to live with and love nature.

Chapter 12: TAW BOTTOM

By the 1960s several counties had their own permanent campsites and Devon was lagging behind. The trigger that started a search for a site in earnest was the 1980 Scout and Guide Jamboree at Crediton. The organising committee for the jamboree had to decide well beforehand on the charge they would make to participants, and it was difficult to assess what contingencies might arise. A big event will make a profit or loss, and it was agreed that this would be borne one-third by the Guides and two-thirds by the Scouts. This seemed a fair division as the Scouts, having experience of large jamborees, did more of the organising.

The jamboree resulted in a profit, and Devon Girl Guides received one-third of this – viz. £6,000, which the County Executive decided to put towards the purchase of land for a county campsite. Much fundraising would also be needed. The search began for land, and Exeter-based land agents Stratton and Holborow were asked to help. Two or three pieces of land that were on the market were looked at, but for various reasons were not suitable. Tim Key of Stratton and Holborow, who was a great help in negotiations, then suggested advertising, specifying what was wanted, and this worked. Lawrence Jones, a farmer at South Tawton, had some surplus land by the River Taw that had previously been part of the Wood Estate owned by the late Colonel Lethbridge. The fifteen acres were overgrown fields with boggy areas where the land drains were choked up, and trees, particularly birch, were spreading fast. The steep hillside at the back of the site consisted of old oak woodland and gorse and scrub in the middle. Access was via a gate and path on the east side of the river at Sticklepath – this path was not a public right of way, but Colonel Lethbridge had allowed local people to use it for dog walking, etc.

When members of the County Executive – the County Commissioner, Outdoor Activities Adviser and the two County Camp Advisers – went to look at it they had to slash their way through brambles and bracken. But the site had potential. In its favour were the facts that it was in the middle of Devon and close to Dartmoor; the busy A30 main road, which ran through the village of Sticklepath and had to be crossed to reach the moor, was about to be re-routed to the north of the site; mains water which supplied the farmer's fields was close by, and the main sewage pipe for Sticklepath ran close to the river and could be tapped into; there was potential for several camping areas, plenty of wood for fires, the woods and river for activities; and it was a very beautiful site. Lawrence Jones offered vehicle access via a lane from South Tawton that ran between his fields that led to, and was maintained by, the council sewage works downstream of the site. Advice was sought from land managers and foresters known to the County Commissioner, and it was agreed to 'go for it'. A price was agreed and the fundraising began in earnest.

A key player in the establishing and running of this site was a dedicated Guider, originally from Plymouth but now living at Whitchurch near Tavistock – Barbara Lillicrap. At this time – 1980 – she was Division Commissioner and Camp Adviser for Tavistock and Okehampton Division. She was thrilled that the site was on her patch, and set about fundraising in a big way. A decision had to be made as to what to call the site; the local name was Taw Bottoms. Barbara suggested that Taw Bottom (without the s) was more dignified, and so it was named.

Angela Graham, former County Commissioner and now County President, wrote an appeal letter to vice-presidents and others in October 1981, telling them about this exciting project, describing the fifteen-acre site and pointing out

The advantages of having our own place, always accessible, with permanent equipment and shelter available . . . are indisputable. It will also facilitate training and thus make camping possible for more people.

Bowermans became ours through the generosity of Miss Betty and the late Miss Dorothy Bindloss. This time we may have no such benefactors and the decision to go ahead represents a considerable act of faith. The purchase of the land alone is £17,000. We shall need to put up solid shelter, equipment stores, facilities for disabled Guides, as well as a building to provide indoor training facilities. We hope for a substantial grant from the Education Authority but we cannot rely on this. Meanwhile we have to dip into our reserves, and borrow. . . . I have been asked to organise the raising of funds and I am sure you would agree that we must try not to involve the Guiders too much as they have enough to do without it. I badly need help of every kind. . . . We are hoping to raise £55,000. It is a daunting prospect but let us remember that we have never yet failed to reach our target in raising money for other causes. Now that we need something for the future of Devon Guides, surely we must not be ungenerous nor fainthearted?

This resulted in donations of £1,500 and four interest-free loans of £100 from vice-presidents. Other donations included £50 in 1982 from Devon County Agricultural Society following the Guides' help at the County Show; £9,860 in 1983 from Devon County Education Committee towards the building of the main wet-weather shelter with kitchen, toilets and washing facilities; £500 from Soroptimists International, Torquay, and £500 from the CLA (Country Landowners' Association) Charitable Trust towards a toilet for the disabled. Over the years Trefoil Guilds also made generous donations.

One of the most successful of the county fundraising enterprises was the sponsored Knit for the Needy, organised by Barbara Lillicrap for the week of 15–20 November 1982. Units held two-hour sessions of knitting, which meant that many Guides and Brownies had to learn to knit! They knitted six-inch squares, which were then made up into blankets and presented to Oxfam and Save the Children. This raised over £8,000. Sales of special badges, tee shirts, tea towels, notelets, key rings, etc., also raised funds.

From the beginning there was great support from the local community. The chairman of South Zeal Parish Council, Bill Cann, who later became chairman of Dartmoor National Park Authority, was enthusiastic and helpful, as was the local MP, Sir Peter Mills, and the vicar of South Tawton, the Reverend John Ellis.

The site was not viable until a road from the sewage-works lane had been put in. Lawrence Jones kindly gave access over the wooded area between the sewage-works lane and the beginning of the Taw Bottom land. The road was constructed most expertly by Bill Penberthy, a contractor from Monkokehampton, who over the years was a tower of strength, finding and clearing old field drains, bringing in water and taking out sewage, and dealing with problems that arose from time to time. Another local man who over the years has been worth his weight in gold is Ian Woods, a builder and plumber. From the beginning he has not only worked on the site, putting up buildings and repairing damage, but has looked after the site with great diligence and devotion. He also cuts the grass on the camping sites and keeps it all spick and span.

The purchase of the fifteen-acre site was completed in June 1982, and the official opening and first camp were in May 1983. Unfortunately it was a very wet weekend, and several intrepid Guiders camped in the mud on what became Oak site. At the opening the County Commissioner, Rosemary Howell, welcomed the guests and spoke briefly about the search for and acquisition of the site. Bill Cann officially opened the site by breaking the Guide world flag, the vicar (whose cassock was spattered with mud!) blessed the site, and Sir Peter Mills, Mr Thorpe (of Devon County Education Committee) and Lawrence Jones all spoke. The County President, Angela Graham, then presented Rosemary Howell with the Laurel Award for her vision and perseverance in bringing the search for a Devon Guide campsite to fruition. Trees were then planted to mark the occasion, and tea was served by the Guiders who were camping.

In recognition of local interest, an open day was held the

following year, and this notice went in the parish magazine:

> Devon Girl Guides invite parishioners of South Tawton, South
> Zeal and Sticklepath to an OPEN DAY at their camp site at Taw
> Bottom on Wednesday August 22nd 1984, 2–9 p.m. See a Guide
> camp in action and have a cup of tea with us. Camp fire singing
> at 8 pm.

VIPs and others were invited; Lady Morley, the recently
appointed Patron of Devon Girl Guides, was among the guests
and showed great interest in the site as she toured round.

The main building (which was later called The Longhouse)
was erected in 1984–5. At that time the site was in a loop of
land surrounded by but not in the Dartmoor National Park. This
anomaly was eventually rectified. However, planning permission
had to be granted and an architect sought. A surveyor who worked
for Devon Clinton Estates, Dick Coates, offered his services for
free. His wife, Hanniker, was a Guider in Exmouth Division.
Dick drew up the plans and acted as surveyor.

Planning permission stipulated that the building was to be a
wet-weather shelter, but was not for sleeping in. When built it
consisted of a room twenty-two by twenty-one feet, a kitchen with
sink, eight flush toilets (one for disabled Guides), and washing
facilities in two rooms. In 1987 an extension was added, making
an open-sided but covered dining area, and over the years the
kitchen has been greatly improved.

An intention from the beginning was that the site should be
used for camps for disadvantaged children, to be run by the
Guides. The first such camp was held in 1984. Called Rainbow
(and later Spectrum) Camp, it was for girls aged ten to fourteen
from deprived homes, very large families, foster and children's
homes, girls who had suffered abuse or who had a parent in
prison. There were often sets of sisters, but most did not know
anyone else when they arrived; however, they soon made friends.
It was funded by the WRVS (£10 per girl in 1984, rising to £30 in
1991). Mrs Avril Chapman, the Exeter WRVS Holiday Organiser,
arranged the selection of the sixteen girls through social services
in Devon and Cornwall, and was always a great help, organising

the transport and providing sleeping bags and kitbags for the girls. The WRVS also provided a cooked meal on Activity Day.

The camp was staffed by three or four Guiders, helped by four to eight Rangers or Young Leaders or Guides, some of whom were fulfilling the Duke of Edinburgh Award Gold Residential or Silver Service clauses. They all agreed it was very hard work, but worthwhile and rewarding. The first camps were run by Mrs Brenda Gunby, Guide Guider in Wembury (and in 1986 Division Commissioner for Plym Division); she set a very high standard of good camping, fun and learning for the participants, and loving care for those needy girls. Chris Tozer, Guide and Ranger Guider in Torquay and previously Outdoor Activities Adviser, took over in 1986 when the camp managed to survive Hurricane Charlie!

The camp was run on the Guide Patrol system, with the girls helping with various tasks. Cooking was originally done on wood fires, but although fun this was too time-consuming, so they reverted to using the kitchen with its gas cooker. Among the activities they all enjoyed was walking to South Zeal to buy postcards, etc. (the shopkeepers gave the girls special discounts), swimming and shopping in Okehampton, a farm visit, a Backwoods Day (run by Scouters and Guiders), crafts, nature trails, fun sports, a barbecue, a campfire and a visitors' afternoon. Help of various kinds was received from the Trefoil Guild, Cadover Division and Wembury Guides, Devon Girl Guides, and especially the warden of Taw Bottom, Barbara Lillicrap. This special camp continued until 1991, with the exception of 1990. It was an inspirational piece of service to the community, of which Devon Girl Guides, and in particular all those who were involved in the tremendous hard work of running it, could feel proud.

It had originally been intended to build on the site a holiday house for training Guide and Brownie Guiders in running residential holidays as opposed to camping. Brownies at that time were not allowed to camp and Pack Holidays were becoming very popular; busy Guiders also found that holidays were often easier to organise than camps. The original rough costing for this was £50,000. After much thought and discussion at the County Executive and as a result of a county referendum, the executive decided Taw Bottom was not the right place for a holiday training house. Bowerman's Cottage was popular and much used, with improvements continually being made, and it was decided that another such property to be owned by Devon Girl Guides was not needed. There were also various District Headquarters that were suitable for Brownie and Guide holidays.

The first camping sites to be developed were Oak, which to start with used The Longhouse for a wet-weather shelter (its own shelter was provided much later), and then Ash, just down from Oak. This had a purpose-built shelter. Beech site, nearer the river, was made by the clearing of trees and scrub, and in 1986 was given a much appreciated shelter by Totnes Division, which was replaced some years later by a bigger building. A fourth, smaller, site, Hawthorn, behind Beech, was in use by 1989. Its first shelter was a redundant summerhouse given by friends of Assistant County Commissioner Loveday Fergusson. Eventually it deteriorated and was replaced by a purpose-built shelter. All sites were equipped with a cooking grid for wood fires on a concrete base. For toilets and washing facilities Oak and Ash used The Longhouse, while Beech and Hawthorn shared a toilet block partly hidden among the trees between the two sites. At this time flush toilets and running water (although cold) were a great improvement on the original trench latrines and water carried from a communal tap, found on earlier campsites; but by the twenty-first century girls were demanding hot showers as provided on commercial campsites. So in 2003, at some expense, these were installed by Ian Woods. Calor gas provided the heating. As a result of this (which seemed an unnecessary luxury to older members of the movement!), camping numbers, which had been dropping, started to go up again.

A new venture at Taw Bottom was launched in 1988 – a Duke of Edinburgh Gold Award Expedition Week, organised and run for many years by David Hood, Assistant County Commissioner for Scouts, helped by Foky Bradshaw, Devon Guides' Outdoor Activities Adviser. Young people could come for the week and form groups, get some training in, say, map reading, and then go on to Dartmoor for three days to take the test. The Enterprise clause for Queen's Guide was also assessed. This initiative was hailed as 'a splendid example of Scout and Guide cooperation'.

In the 1989 annual report, the warden, Barbara Lillicrap, wrote:

> Looking at my photographs of Taw Bottom from the day in 1983 when a small group . . . ploughed through brambles and stood gazing and suggesting what might be possible, gradually the most beautiful campsite has materialized.

That year as well as the usual camps there were two large Brownie fun days, and the Trefoil Guild had a County Day there.

It was hoped from the beginning that the site would be used in term time by schools, and the large grant made by Devon County Education Committee towards the purchase of the site had been made with this in mind. Barbara Lillicrap was good at encouraging and helping schools to camp, and in 1990 Wilcombe (Exeter) Middle School camped there for the fourth consecutive year. Schools have continued to use the site over the years.

In 1990 Foky Bradshaw (previously Outdoor Activities Adviser and Ashburton Division Commissioner) started a support group, Friends of Taw Bottom. A small committee chaired by Margaret Branch (previously Exeter Division Commissioner) planned money-raising social activities and all adults, in and out of uniform, were invited to become Friends. It was proposed to build a camp store for equipment and a shelter for Ash site, and £2,000 was raised by subscriptions and donations, including a generous gift of £500 from Lady Amory.

1991 saw a record of over 3,000 'bed nights'. The fitness and nature trails on site were very popular.

A Trefoil Guild member from Sidmouth gave £500 for the creation of a 'Quiet Corner' for Guides' Own Services and relaxation and meditation. A flat area by the river had been earmarked for a quiet area and trees thinned to let in light. It has always been a good spot for wild flowers – primroses, wood anemones and bluebells among others. In due course benches in memory of Madge Greenwood of Sidmouth Trefoil Guild were put in a circle round a focal point, a pile of stones, replaced in 2010 by a special stone to commemorate the Guide centenary. A concrete ramp with handrail was put in to enable wheelchairs to access the quiet area. Fires were not permitted here – there was a dedicated campfire site, with benches, below Ash site and near the river.

1992 saw the tenth anniversary of Taw Bottom, and an open day was held in June. Guests included the vice chairman of Devon County Council, the chairman of West Devon Planning Committee, county counsellor and chairman of the parish council Bill Cann (who had performed the opening ceremony) and many local people. This day was a very good PR exercise. Laurie Pearson (Outdoor Activities Adviser) had organised a weekend camp for Guiders with their Patrols and some Brownies came for a fun day, so guests could wander round and see the site in use. Friends of Taw Bottom served tea for the visitors. The local paper ran a piece written by 'Our South Zeal Correspondent' Ursula Radford:

> Invited recently to visit the County Girl Guide camp site at Taw Bottom, I was pleasantly surprised to find an 18 acre area which has been developed by the unstinting hard work of many supporters from near and far over the past 10 years into something which is of tremendous value to girls from Devon. A delightful wooded valley has been enhanced with a fitness trail designed to propel the pulse rate of participants; a nature trail to nurture the need for observation and understanding; quiet areas; picnic grounds; a campfire circle; and a number of camp sites which are supported by the purpose-built provision of facilities sufficient to provide for any eventuality the British summer can inflict upon visitors.
>
> All of this had been discreetly provided to enhance the natural beauty of the area being enjoyed by many young visitors. In use every weekend throughout the best of the year and continually during holiday periods, the financial investment is obviously being recouped many times over, and future investment will provide even more value. To this end a 'Friends of the site' organisation has been formed, and contribution details can be obtained from Mrs. E. Weir on Chagford 43221. Beyond this, local people can do much to assist the Guides by simply walking through the area occasionally, enjoying its tranquility, and thereby discouraging vandals who have all too often been the cause of heartbreak.

In fact there was some vandalism during the summer of 1994 when local boys broke into The Longhouse. A piece in the *Okehampton Times* reported:

> Not satisfied with vandalising equipment and stealing food from store tents the tearaways have even disturbed tents at night shining torches into tents and frightening youngsters.

Elizabeth Weir, secretary of the Taw Bottom Management Committee, who lived nearby at Chagford and had always been involved in the setting-up and running of the site, commented:

> It's boys who have not got enough to do and just want to create mayhem.

The police had been informed and PC Heard officially warned the boys. Doors to The Longhouse were changed and shutters put across the kitchen window. The only other problems were a lot of litter left one summer by local teenagers using the shelters near the path from Sticklepath, and occasionally dog walkers, so notices were put up to ask walkers to respect the camping areas, and pointing out that there is no public right of way through the site.

During 1994 a new shelter was erected on Ash site, called the Welch Shelter after Joan Welch, who gave a generous donation towards it. Friends of Taw Bottom organised a Pixie Pie Lunch, which raised enough money to purchase a large Calor-gas cooker for The Longhouse. Once again Mrs Claire Fowler and her band of Scout and Guide helpers did an excellent autumn tidy-up. For many years Shaldon Trefoil Guild spent a day in May spring-cleaning The Longhouse, and their work has always been greatly appreciated.

In 1995, thanks to Friends of Taw Bottom, the new shelter was erected on Hawthorn site, and on-site cooking facilities were improved by the provision of purpose-forged fire stands. Camp equipment, which was kept in a storage shed and was enough for a camp of twenty-four Guides and their leaders, could be hired for a modest sum, and there were trolleys to take equipment to the different sites. Fees in 1995 were £1 per head per night. A caravan was kept in the car park. Originally donated by Elizabeth Bowden (formerly Division Commissioner for Taw and Torridge), it could be hired for £10 per week, and was popular for Guiders' husbands or any frail Guider or helper who could not manage in a tent.

Taw Bottom was advertised in *Guiding* magazine for the first time in 1996, and this resulted in bookings from Bristol and Dorset. Devon Scouts and Cubs as well as schools were regular users. The site was particularly valuable for training camps of all kinds.

1997 saw the retirement of three of the original team – the dedicated and hard-working warden, Barbara Lillicrap, the gracious and untiring secretary of the Management Committee, Elizabeth Weir, and the chairman, Rosemary Howell. Betty Hinchliff, Guider and Commissioner from Teignmouth, who had camped there many times with her Guides, took over as warden and treasurer, greatly helped by her husband, Bryan. Laurie Pearson became chairman and Anne Veale (Ranger Guider from Exeter who with Ann Fitzroy had camped there from the beginning and had made the original nature trail) became secretary. The Camp Adviser for Taw Bottom was Jane Simons, who with her mother, Monica, lived and Guided in North Tawton; they were always a tower of strength, and Monica became warden in 2003.

Beech site was enlarged in 1997, and the concrete path to the quiet area completed. Bush Bashing took place over a weekend in October as usual, now organised by Sue Brown; five Senior Section girls, three Guiders and two Scouts took part. Bush Bashing had been going on periodically from the early days of the site, the girls (and adults) being taught how to cut brambles and gorse by a dedicated forester, Gordon Douglas of Fountain Forestry. (Another of their foresters had erected the post-and-wire fence along the riverbank as a safety barrier.) Gordon Douglas loved the site, and he looked after the quiet area for many years, even in retirement, keeping it clear of undergrowth and fallen branches.

The highlight of 1999 was Campsite Capers, an open day in May when over 600 visitors took part in many different activities, in good weather. The newly refurbished kitchen was opened and much appreciated by its users. In the autumn South West Water started on a major pipe-laying project through the site, coming down through trees and scrub and then straight through the middle of Beech site. They promised it would be completed and the grass returfed by April 2000. In the event it wasn't finished and Beech site was unusable throughout 2000. Eventually they restored the site, planted trees and put up a screen by the river to hide the ugly pipe connections. Elizabeth Weir fought hard to get compensation from South West Water, and won!

Campers were also deterred by the fact that 2000 was an exceptionally wet year, and Taw Bottom was not helped by the unfortunate flooding of the quiet area with raw sewage in April (the main sewage pipe was blocked up at Sticklepath) and South West Water's slowness in dealing with the problem. Ian Woods, as ever looking after the Guides' interests, spotted and reported it. To help restore the site generally, in 2001 Dartmoor National Park supplied trees free under the Amenity Tree Scheme; hazel, alder, buckthorn, birch and oak were planted near Beech site.

For another reason 2001 was also a difficult year – Taw Bottom was closed from February to August because of the foot-and-mouth disease outbreak. Twenty-two camps and events had to be cancelled, but from the second week in August till the end of the season the site was fully used.

Thanks to much fundraising, 2003 saw the introduction of hot water and showers in the toilet block for Oak and Ash, the same facilities to be ready for Beech and Hawthorn by 2004. This was very popular, and bookings went up, including Guides and Scouts from as far as Sussex, and schools, youth groups and a church camp.

The twentieth anniversary of Taw Bottom in 2002 was celebrated with a day of activities, including dancing with the local morris dancers, and a cream tea. Many compliments were received on how good the site was looking – this was thanks to the hard work of many volunteers and to Ian Woods, who now kept the grass cut with a ride-on mower purchased in 2002 and paid for by Friends of Taw Bottom. Day bookings were available for Rainbows, Brownies, Guides, Senior Section and Trefoil Guilds, and activities on-site included archery, a fitness trail, nature trail and orienteering.

Barbara Lillicrap died in 2003 and many tributes were paid to her: 'She so loved it at Taw Bottom and spent many hours working and camping there.' A rowan tree was planted on Oak site in her memory. Monica Simons of North Tawton was now the warden and she, together with her daughter Jane, is still looking after the site and the campers with great energy and effectiveness.

The entrance road was repaired in 2005 and the car park surrounds cleared. Trefoil Guild members planted a willow arbour in the quiet area in memory of Katy Lee, whose large legacy was being shared and enjoyed by Devon Trefoil Guilds. 2006 saw more improvements – Oak site was terraced and extended to provide a larger, more level, camping area; part of the Beech and Hawthorn toilet block was converted for men's facilities; and a new fridge-freezer was put in The Longhouse kitchen.

Laurie Pearson retired as chairman of the Management Committee in 2006. Laurie, with her husband, Clive, had been a tower of strength during the development of the site and in influencing high standards of camping over twenty years. It was Laurie who introduced archery and taught it for many years, and Laurie and Clive planned and constructed the popular fitness trail. Ann Werry took over as chairman and has also worked tremendously hard and successfully to maintain and improve the site, greatly assisted by the indefatigable and devoted warden since 2003, Monica Simons.

The winter storms brought down some mature trees; a tree surgeon inspects the large old trees most years and work is done on them accordingly. Beech site was enlarged again, and the shelter improved. The twenty-fifth anniversary was celebrated in 2007 by the planting of twenty-five beech, hazel and rowan saplings.

In 2008 a sundial was placed at the top end of Ash site in memory of Mavis Budden, a former County Commissioner and

County President, who was tragically killed in a car accident. Previously garden seats had been placed in memory of two great Guiders, campers and County Camp Advisers, Hope Rattey and Joan Richards.

A new shelter was built on Oak site so that The Longhouse dining shelter could be used by other groups. Friends of Taw Bottom continued to hold enterprising and enjoyable fundraising events, such as the annual Trefoil Guild Fun Day and Harvest Lunch. The centenary of Girlguiding in 2010 was celebrated at Taw Bottom by the placing in the quiet area of a cube-shaped white stone with commemorative wording and the centenary logo, designed so girls can take rubbings.

Camping and day visits and trainings continue. Long may Taw Bottom prosper!

Chapter 13: INTERNATIONAL GUIDING – VISITS OVERSEAS

Rose Kerr, in *The Story of the Girl Guides* (1932) wrote:

> Perhaps the greatest achievement of the Guides, and the one which holds out the greatest possibilities for the future, is the growth of the Movement all over the world, and consequent development of friendship and sisterhood among the girls of different nations.

By 1911 units of Guides or Girl Scouts opened in Canada, New Zealand, South Africa, Denmark, Sweden, Finland and Poland, and other countries followed over the next few years.

The two world wars stopped international travel temporarily, but by 1947 it had got going again. In the Devon annual report for that year the County Commissioner, Miss Parker, wrote:

> Parties of Rangers had successful trips to France and Switzerland, making valuable contacts with young people of other countries.

In the 1957 annual report for Devon the Commonwealth and International Representative, P. Allen, wrote:

> Centenary [of the birth of Lord Baden-Powell] Year has brought the International side of Guiding very close, with the World Camps in the Philippines, Canada, Switzerland and Windsor, and on our own doorstep, over 90 International and Commonwealth guests being entertained in Devon homes before and after the Windsor Camp, under the Hospitality Scheme. Guests and hostesses enjoyed this shared experience, and to be welcomed as a member of the family in an English home was undoubtedly one of the

highlights of the trip for visiting Guides and Rangers. . . . Guides and Rangers came to Devon from . . . Canada, Nigeria, St Lucia, St Vincent, South Africa, S. Rhodesia, Kenya, Grenada, Mexico, India, U.S.A., Australia, France, Switzerland and Luxembourg. . . .

Devon has been proud to send two delegates abroad this year, Sea Ranger Bosun Leila Stockman, S.R.S. Churchill, Brixham, went to the Philippine World Camp as one of the eight delegates representing Great Britain, and Sea Ranger Morag Halliday, S.R.S. Delight, Torquay, was one of a party representing England at the Danish Camp. Very good reports have been received about these two Rangers.

County Commonwealth and International Representative (CCIR), Mrs Colwill, wrote in the report for 1961:

The many overseas visitors welcomed to Devon during the year included a Nigerian Guider, a Ranger from New Zealand, and Trainers from the Philippines [sic] and Canada, while the fact that a former Devon Guider is now running an African Guide Company in Nairobi is a further proof that Guiding knows no frontiers.

The following year she wrote:

The queries which are dealt with by the County Representative are many and varied, and are by no means restricted to the planning of holidays abroad for the many parties who now contrive to travel in this way. Introductions, information on foreign badges and mottos, interviewing candidates for overseas invitations are all part of the day's work, and recent activity among Commonwealth Knowledge candidates has prompted many enquiries too.

Sylvia Clarke (see Chapter 10) succeeded Mrs Colwill as CCIR, and in the report for 1964 wrote:

In July and August we welcomed approximately a hundred Girl Scouts from Colorado in five separate parties, staying in Torquay. These groups were entertained to tea by the Ashburton Guides, spent an evening with the Brixham Sea Rangers, and visited Guide camps on the moor. They also went to the International Scout camp at Torquay while it was in progress. It is interesting to note that they were unable to complete a far too strenuous and tiring programme of sight-seeing arranged for them by a Travel Agent, and enjoyed much more meeting our Guide folk and going on shorter and more leisurely trips. Guiders planning visits abroad might perhaps take note!

She reported that in 1965 a cadet from Elburton had an interesting and exciting time at the Italian International Gathering, staying first with an Italian family and then joining a group consisting of Danes, Swiss, Greek and Italian Rangers to study art and drama in Florence.

The following year four Sea Rangers from Brixham, Paignton and Sidmouth enjoyed a fortnight in Holland as guests of the Dutch Water Guides. They spent a week on a barge, sailing, rowing, canoeing and sightseeing, and a week staying with the Guides.

Mrs Kathleen Thomas took over as County Commonwealth and International Adviser (CCIA) in 1968, and the next year she wrote:

It is obvious from the number of enquiries received that there is a very keen interest in Overseas Guiding in Devon. Many Guides and Brownies have worked for badges and planned Patrol and Six activities which have required much research and study regarding the country of their choice. Several Companies have travelled abroad, Switzerland being the popular choice, and three Ranger Units have stayed at Our Chalet.

In 1970, Diamond Jubilee Year, Devon was allocated one place at the International Camp, Vastkeest '70, in Sweden. Deborah Hodge, a Ranger from Tavistock, was selected, and had a

fantastic time and learnt new camping ways, many of which would be frowned on in England. The Swedes are very handy with knives and axes, and they use the latter in preference to mallets!

In 1971 Kathleen Thomas started what soon became standard practice – a weekend at Bowerman's for potential candidates for international events. She elaborated:

Representatives came from most of the Divisions and from the Lone Ranger Company. The experiment proved most worthwhile as we were able to get to know each other in a way which is quite impossible at a short interview. A programme of international interest was planned. . . . The girls took part in lively discussions on many aspects of International Guiding, and for relaxation there was walking on Dartmoor, a film show, a singsong with international flavour . . . There are so many opportunities for travel. . . .

This resulted in four of the candidates who attended gaining places at an International Camp in Sweden and a Young Pioneers' Exchange visit to Romania.

In 1975 a World Conference was held in Sussex, and contrary to expectation this generated a lot of interest in World Guiding. Gifts were made for the delegates, and international evenings and camps were held. Also, as a result of 'twinning' between Devon and Common Market countries, Guides from France visited Devon. 'The visits definitely presented problems but we hope that these have now been sorted satisfactorily and in future we shall see many more of our continental friends,' wrote Kathleen Thomas.

In 1977 Devon had four delegates at international events, including Diane Bowles from Exeter, who was one of three representatives from the UK at the Juliet Low Seminar at Our Cabana, Mexico, and Barbara Marsh, District Commissioner for Axminster, who led the UK party to the International Camp in Norway. 'Once again Devon proved that not only can it produce the calibre of girl required to represent the United Kingdom but can raise a large proportion of the money to finance her,' wrote Kathleen Thomas.

1978 saw seven Devon girls selected to represent the Region or the UK, including Rosemary Rimes, who was one of the UK Rangers due to go to the Argentine International Camp, but it was cancelled because of political unrest. (She was subsequently given a place at an International Camp in Western Australia). They all received encouragement and financial backing from the county.

They come back full of enthusiasm and ready to pass on their experiences to others [wrote Kathleen]. It is interesting to note that almost every girl fortunate enough to attend an International event over the past few years is still in Guiding, either as a Guide or Brownie Leader or a member of a University Guide and Scout Club.

In 1979 ten Devon girls represented the UK at International Camps, and a young Guider from Plymouth East, Cheryl Strike, went at short notice to Our Cabana, the Guide centre in Mexico. On her return she visited many units to speak of her experiences and show her slides and a fascinating collection of craft, art and souvenirs.

1980 was a very special example [of International Guiding[with the grand Scout and Guide Jamboree at Crediton and the unforgettable Inter-Link Camp at Foxlease [wrote Kathleen Thomas]. Probably the most worthwhile results from these camps are the lasting friendships that have been made, not only with those from abroad, but with other Scouts and Guides in this country. A real spin-off from the Jamboree has been the visits to Denmark of two groups, one from Plymouth and the other from Crediton. Both Leaders cannot praise enough the hospitality they received or the way their Guides and Rangers conducted themselves throughout the time in Denmark.

Following the visit of Kathleen Thomas and Chris Tozer to Fiji (see page 356), this link was kept going, and books, charts and other items of equipment were distributed to the areas they visited, paid for by units round the country. The requests for penfriends were not so successful because of poverty in Fiji – the cost of an airmail stamp could be beyond their means. However, correspondence with the Ranger and Guide who came to Interlink Camp was kept up, and Budleigh Salterton Trefoil Guild adopted a unit from one of the country areas. Sala, the Fijian Guide, asked for photos of the royal family, and many were sent. The Lones also sent songbooks and charts. Devon's other Branch Association link, Grenada, had suffered a recent crisis and letters of concern were written.

In 1984, because of the popularity of the selection and training weekend at Bowerman's two were held instead of one, and both were rewarding. More Guiders were wanting to take their units abroad, so trainings were held to help and encourage them. A young Ranger Guider from Exeter, Nicola Durman, was one of three from the UK to go to India to help in a Service Camp for handicapped children in Sangam (see page 99).

Two Devon Rangers, Sarah Bartlett and Amanda Weldon, both from Tiverton Division, represented South West Region in 1985 in Greece and Mexico with Experiment in International Living. They spent a month living and working with the families in whose homes they were staying. Amanda fortunately returned home just before the disastrous earthquake in Mexico City, where she had been living, and she heard that the family were all safe.

Fiji was hit by a devastating hurricane in 1985 and Devon responded by sending £320 via the Fijian High Commissioner and £50 raised by two units, which went direct to Lautoka Division, which had suffered the most. The money was used to replace books and uniforms for the Guides and Brownies.

The jamboree at Mount Edgcumbe was the biggest event in the international calendar of 1986, and all who participated saw World Guiding and Scouting in action and many lasting contacts were made.

Kathleen Thomas reported that in 1987 over 120 members from Devon enjoyed camps and holidays in Europe. One group staying at Our Chalet were Guiders, some of whom had done sterling service to Guiding in Devon, but who had missed out on the chance to go abroad. The aim of this group was to encourage Guiders to take their units abroad. At a Region selection weekend in Exeter an Exeter Ranger was chosen to attend the first ever International Camp in Nepal (see page 140).

Kathleen made a valid point:

Since the proportion of members enjoying the experience of International Guiding is small, all the outward and exciting publicity created by these special events must not minimise the importance of the quiet and steady interest in World Guiding. The hundreds of other girls who are being encouraged by their Guiders

225

to appreciate the world-wide picture of Guiding by bringing it into the programme are also receiving a vital experience.

Sheila Wooldridge took over as Commonwealth and International Adviser in 1989 and reported that it was a good year for overseas invitations. Boating Adviser Ailsa Faulkner joined a sailing expedition in Swedish waters, and two Devon Guiders took a Region group on a Sailing Camp in Sweden, which was challenging as it included 'less able' boys and girls as well as able bodies from several European countries. Two girls attended a huge gathering to celebrate eighty years of Scouting in Denmark. A Young Leader went to a special centenary camp in Kenya, one joined Venture Scouts on a special mission to Ethiopia (see page 144) and another went to a jamboree in India.

> Our International Opportunities event moved to Woolacombe and we are so grateful to Mrs Rita Sandifer who enabled 20 of us to have a most memorable and happy weekend.

Pirates 1990, Devon's International Camp at the County Showground, enabled 600 Guides to experience friendship with the 232 overseas visitors who came from seventeen countries. Sheila Wooldridge commented:

> I shall never forget the effect of the unexpected arrival of ten Kenyans on a small village on Dartmoor.

Sheila also wrote about the Youth Exchange Forum, which is a national group within the Education Service to encourage exchanges of young people within Europe.

> I have been a member of the Devon Forum from the start and find that the Girl Guides Association is held in very high esteem. Our expertise in foreign travel is being used by the Forum and at a Training Day in February we are contributing market stalls and workshops.

A thirty-pence supplement on members' subscriptions each year had enabled a fund to be set up for overseas travel, and this was proving a great help financially for the girls who were selected. In return, they were expected to report back and share their experiences.

In 1993 the World Association of Girl Guides and Girl Scouts launched a Three Year Peace Initiative and in April 1994 the practical project – PEACE PACKS – was launched [wrote Sheila Wooldridge]. Working in partnership with the United Nations High Commission for Refugees (UNHCR) all 128 countries (WAGGS members) were asked to help the nineteen million people who 'have no place to call home'. More than half this number are children who have known little but fear, pain and hunger. They do not go to school and have little or no privacy. So the girls are being asked to put together school supplies and personal items in individual bags to brighten the lives of their sad refugee peers. So far 850,000 Packs have been pledged. The UK Association has pledged 97,600 Packs which will go to countries in the African continent. Many Units/Districts in Devon have been busy collecting the necessary items and packing boxes, and these will be gathered together in Exeter early in March 1995. We look forward to hearing which organisation has agreed to collect up our national contribution – carrying it to Felixstowe for final transport overseas later in the spring.

Two hundred Peace Pack boxes went to the *Express and Echo* warehouse and thence to the Exeter Body Shop as this organisation had undertaken all the UK collection and delivery to the docks. Many thousands of these boxes duly reached Africa. Many of the girls who took part in this project combined it with working for the Refugee badge.

Sheila also reported:

During the past year Guiding has enabled 70 of our members to visit 16 different countries in three of the five different WAGGGS Regions. Travellers have made their way as individuals carrying an Introduction Card, with their own Units or as members of a Devon, Region or U.K. group. Cost has been a great concern this year and so we are increasingly thankful for our County International Fund which enables us to give significant help.

In 1996 a Peace Initiative was put together by the Guide and Scout Associations of Ireland, and Lorraine Richards, the new CCIA, reported that they had produced three booklets full of wonderful ideas and a thought-provoking booklet for the Senior Section. Many girls had gained the Peace badge, which could be worn on a sash or camp blanket. Another new idea this year was the Guide International Patrol Interest Pennant.

1997 saw the start of International Sleepovers. Lorraine Richards explained:

> There was a request to take International Guiding to the girls and so we held a sleepover at Bett's Centre at Plympton to cover the Plymouth Divisions and another at the Sidmouth Guide HQ for the Axminster, Honiton and Exmouth Divisions. Two more are planned for 1998. The sleepover gives the girls a chance to find out more about International Guiding and to sample the crafts, games and food as well as look at some of the world issues. During the sleepover the girls cover enough clauses to gain their World Wide Interest badge.

Two more were held in 1998, in North Devon and Torbay.

Friendship Camp in 1998 gave the girls a chance to meet Guides from other countries and to mark off another clause from the World Guiding Interest badge. An international evening was held during the camp, when the girls from all the countries attending were asked to perform a song or dance, and this was linked to the four World Centres.

There had also been World Issues Days, when a representative from UNICEF had come and covered clauses from the World Issues Interest badge, and this had given the girls a lot to think about.

There was a Russia Awareness Day in 1998, and many units took part in activities based on a CHQ leaflet – everything from circuses to food tasting, Russian dancing and crafts.

This year Devon sent three Leaders on CHQ and Region trips to New Zealand, India and Germany, and other girls were selected to go to New Zealand, Mexico, India and Scotland.

The highlight of 1999 was the World Camp at Foxlease (see

page 136). Also this year Devon was asked to host a new pilot scheme which CHQ wanted to run in South West Region. Called ICE (International Community Experience), it was held in Mid Devon and thirty girls from around the Region (ten from Devon) spent an enjoyable weekend trying different skills and finding out more about International Guiding.

Lorraine reported that 2000 was a good year for International Guiding: 167 Leaders and girls travelled overseas; another Sleepover was held in Tavistock – part of 'Taking International to the Divisions', and another two were planned for Tiverton and Exeter.

> Devon held its HOPE DAY on 24th June and there was a large International area where Rainbows, Brownies, Guides and the Senior Section could try out many international crafts and games . . . the girls made 300 juggling balls, painted over 400 hands, made 300 Thai promise necklaces and made 400+ Mexican God's eyes and paper flowers.

Joyce Blackwell, the next CCIA, reported that in 2003 International Guiding was changing.

> This is the last year that anyone has been able to take a group abroad without their International Endorsement and many other rules to follow. We have followed a strict code of conduct in the past but now the paperwork, including the forms, are changing.

She said that they had an excellent INTOPS (International Opportunities) selection weekend, but unfortunately there were few opportunities for overseas travel, partly because of the SARS virus and fear of terrorist attacks.

By 2004 she reported that all Guiders going abroad were working for, or had completed, their International Endorsement, thanks to Pat Beevers, who was overseeing those going abroad. There was a Rainbow International Challenge that year, and over 700 Rainbows took part; those who completed the challenge were awarded an 'International Bug' and unit certificates.

Joyce reported that in 2005 Devon sent a record number of

young people abroad on international opportunities. Switzerland continued to be very popular, and many units travelled with Venture Abroad or Jeka, who were very experienced in dealing with groups and offered good value for money. Three girls went to a jamboree in Iceland, two to Thailand, two to an American jamboree and one to Denmark. One girl went to Madagascar on a GOLD project (Guiding Overseas Linked to Development).

Joyce also reported:

A number of Guiders attended our first GAINING training . . . for Guiders wishing to take groups abroad, as all Guiders need to attend either a County or a Region training before leading a group. Module 12 (International Endorsement attached to your Camp or Holiday Licence) is being worked on by a number of people, with the help of the Outdoor Team.

In 2006 two young Guiders took part in GOLD projects, one in South Africa and one in Belarus. For the first time, a county group visited Canada.

Rachel Tettersell took over as CCIA from Joyce, and reported that in 2007 one Guider took part in the Mongolian Horseback Challenge, a county group of Guiders went to Sangam and a North Devon group of Guides went to Eire. The one place abroad that Brownies could go was Disneyland, Paris, and a group of Brownies, Guides, Young Leaders and Guiders from Exmouth Division went with Venture Abroad.

We stayed at Davy Crockett Ranch for three nights where we were in cabins for four people, so the girls experienced a 'looking after each other' feeling throughout the holiday.

But the most exciting event in 2007 was the successful Everest World Record-Breaking Attempt, in which several members from Devon took part (see page 184). Rachel Tettersell wrote:

A wonderful chance to show the world just what Girlguiding can achieve, both on an individual and organisational level.

The hot-air balloon challenge developed in 2008 into the highest ever Macmillan Coffee Morning in the world, and eight young women from Devon went on it.

From 2008, the annual reports were reduced to *Snapshots* of Devon, with no detailed reports from County Advisers and rather curtailed 'Travellers' Tales'. One was of a voyage on the *Lord Nelson* (see page 183). Torrington Senior Section girls and Guides went to Adelboden, home of Our Chalet.

> Our week was filled with exciting trips and visits and by the end of the week our fitness had improved with all the walking.

In 2009 two girls from Devon went to Sangam, where they took part in community projects, including making murals for a leprosy school. One girl went to an International Camp in Iceland, where, among other things, they learnt traditional Viking crafts – "a brilliant opportunity to meet new people and make new friends". Sparkwell Guides enjoyed a wonderful visit to Austria. Lesley Masey, Guider in Sparkwell for a great many years, who led the group, said, "At least two parents said, 'My daughter seems to have grown up in twelve days,' so I will say YES, it was a success."

And that comment perhaps illustrates an important feature of International Guiding.

The World Association of Girl Guides and Girl Scouts (WAGGGS) has four World Centres: Our Chalet, in Switzerland, opened in 1932; Our Cabana, in Mexico, opened in 1957; Sangam, in India, opened in 1966; and Pax Lodge, in London, opened in 1980.

Chapter 14: THE EXTENSION BRANCH
(Guiding for the handicapped)

Not long after Guiding started, it was realised that there was great potential in the programme to help children who were physically or mentally handicapped (we now use the descriptions 'physically challenged' and 'with severe learning difficulties'). The name Extension Guiding was given in 1919 for 'companies for mentally and physically defective children [who] should be enrolled under special qualifications'. Children in hospitals as well as at home, and in orphanages and 'rescue homes' and other institutions were keen to become Guides and Scouts, and doctors, realising the improvement to the children's well-being, encouraged the spread of the idea. A little book dealing with 'Guide training for the physically, morally and intellectually defective' was distributed, resulting in new companies starting up. Alternative tests for Second and First Class and proficiency badges were introduced.

For girls in their own homes the Post Guide scheme evolved, whereby children received regular letters to take the place of company meetings. Programmes were also written in Braille, and in 1929 a monthly Braille magazine for blind Scouts and Guides was published, thanks to the National Institution for the Blind. Camps were held for 'deaf and dumb' Guides and Rangers and those with other handicaps. 'Amazing results have been obtained in Institutions for Mental Defectives . . . . Guides have successfully competed with open companies in District and even County competitions . . . these Guides are learning self-respect and self-control, and are taking a pride in themselves and their doings,' said Rose Kerr, writing in 1931. She went on:

Everywhere one is struck by the amazing courage and pluck of the 10,000 Rangers, Guides and Brownies who form the Extension Branch. They are a constant inspiration to those of us whose privilege it is to play the great game of Guiding with them.

Extension Guiding started in Devon quite early on. In the 1932 Cornwall county annual report there is a mention of the Cornish Patrol of the Devon and Cornwall Blind Post Rangers; there were six Cornish Rangers in the company and they had Patrol competitions each month in the company journal and they collected silver paper, stamps and cigarette cards for good causes.

The Rangers gave half the proceeds of the sale of handicrafts to buy a woolly coat for a Devon member of the Company, who is a great invalid.

They also camped. In 1942 the 1st Devon and Cornwall Blind Rangers had eleven members 'and have now been formed into a Trefoil Club'. In 1949 the twelve members held a combined meeting in Plymouth, 'where they had a very jolly time and proved again that Guiding for the blind can be a great success'. That year eight joined the Trefoil Guild. In 1955 the company was re-registered as the 1st Devon (Ranger Posts).

In 1943 there were three Extension companies – at Exeter and Plymouth Orthopaedic Hospitals and at Starcross Mental Hospital. By 1947 there were more, including a company for 'cripples' at St Loyes, Exeter. That year Lady Fryer, who was the Imperial Commissioner for Auxiliaries, came to Devon to visit the very successful Guide and Ranger companies at Ryalls Court School in Seaton. There was also a visit by the Commissioner for Extensions for England, Lady Alethea Eliot, to see Devon Extension companies. 'Guiding is the Youth organisation which caters for invalids and handicapped girls (in their own homes and in hospitals and institutions) as well as the physically fit, and doctors and nurses pay tribute to the very real benefit that they derive from Guiding,' wrote the County Commissioner, Miss Parker.

By 1957 a new Guide company opened at Maristow House (near Yelverton), which was a school for 'educationally sub-normal children', and a new Post Pack and company opened in Plymouth. A Brownie Pack at the Angela Home, Tipton St John, was re-registered, making twelve units in the county – two Ranger, six Guide and four Brownie. A Guide Patrol Leader, Lorraine Chambers, from the Dame Hannah Rogers company (a prestigious school in Ivybridge for children with cerebral palsy) represented Devon at the Centenary Extension Camp at Beaconsfield in 1959; the Extension Adviser for England wrote:

> We are very glad to have Lorraine Chambers here. She is so willing and keen, and so well-liked and self-dependent.

(The centenary was that of the birth of Lord Baden-Powell.)

In 1958 the 1st Devon Blind Post Ranger Company went into abeyance through lack of numbers, in spite of a county-wide search for blind recruits. Many former Rangers from this company were still in Miss Thomas's Trefoil Guild for the Blind. The Exeter Orthopaedic Company also closed, but the school for 'educationally sub-normal children' at Withycombe Raleigh now had a Guide company as well as a Brownie Pack.

1960, jubilee year, was marked by the visit of the Chief Guide, Lady Baden-Powell, to the county annual meeting and a special service in the cathedral, to which many handicapped Guides went with their companies; seven Guides from Dame Hannah Rogers School had special places and the Chief Guide spoke to them afterwards. The Extension Adviser was Miss E. K. Parker, the recently retired County Commissioner; she wrote:

> It is not always realised that handicapped Guides only take alternative tests when their handicap makes the ordinary tests impossible. These tests are not easier, but are adapted so as to be within the scope of the Guide. In this Branch they are treated as far as possible just as normal children, and are given the chance to do some service, instead of having everything done for them.

In 1961 the Extension Adviser for England, Miss Hornby, spent four days in Devon, visiting all the units in special schools, and after attending meetings spoke to the head teachers, matrons, etc.

At Maristow School (for 'educationally sub-normal children') the Guides held an outdoor meeting and enrolment and cooked supper on a campfire. In 1963 ten Guides at the Royal School for the Deaf in Exeter started working for the Duke of Edinburgh Award. An Indian trainer who visited the company remarked on the wonderful alertness of the girls. Eight gained their Bronze and two their Silver Awards.

The next year two Guides from Dame Hannah Rogers School were presented by the County Commissioner with Badges of Fortitude, and in 1965 another Guide, Janet Bentley, very handicapped and who could not speak, gained her First Class badge – the first of several to get it. Two Guides from the Ivybridge company helped Miss Ruth Reed with this severely handicapped but very keen and happy company. Ruth Reed retired in 1971 after eighteen years of sterling work, and was replaced by Janet Thorpe. Beryl Paul was Brownie Guider here (see page 359), replaced in 1969 by Ruth Howell.

Mary Peters took over from Mrs Hudson as County Extensions Adviser in 1968, and appealed for more Guiders and Rangers to help run camps for the handicapped. Withycombe School Guides had had their first camp, in the school grounds, in 1962, and it was 'of a very high standard'. Some years later Miss Bond had an experimental and very successful camp for these girls at Slapton Field Study Centre, as well as a camp for twenty-one Guides in the school grounds.

In 1970, Diamond Jubilee Year, deaf Guides and partially sighted Guides took part in the County Day at Powderham Castle, and a partially sighted girl organised a sponsored swim and raised £50 for the county project. Withycombe School Guides held a Jubilee Venture Day, and they all went to camp. Dame Hannah Rogers Guides all went to the Two Divisions Camp at Prince Hall on Dartmoor and joined in many activities, including the night walk – they were pushed in their wheelchairs by willing Rangers and Guiders. 'What a never-to-be-forgotten camp this was for those Guides, and what thought and organization and help was given by so many!' wrote Mary Peters. By 1972 two former Guides from Dame Hannah Rogers School had joined Sea Rangers – one, who later became a resident at Brixham Cheshire Home, was with the Brixham crew, and the other, who was living at home in Exeter, joined the Topsham crew.

Katherine Ingamells, who took over from Mary Peters as Extension Adviser in 1974, reported on the many units in the county who had one or two disabled Guides in their number, and the problems this could pose:

> Jane who wants to take the Rambler's Badge in her wheelchair, Pat who cannot grasp all the words in the Promise because she is so backward, but grasps fully the meaning. . . . There are no concessions for them . . . they take the same tests, but they do need occasionally testers who will test them according to the spirit and not the letter of the law! . . . I am pleased for Devon that so many units are learning to cope with disability and giving disabled girls a real chance to live.

On another occasion Katherine mentions the Guides at Dame Hannah Rogers School:

> To enrol a Guide of that Company who had no speech was the high spot of my many years of Guiding.

There was a camp for Extension Guides at Foxlease in 1977 – Camp Endeavour – attended by several girls from Devon who really enjoyed it in spite of a lot of rain. Extension Guider Janet Thorpe said afterwards:

> We would like to add a big thank you to the Rangers who helped with the Guides camping under canvas. Try pushing a loaded wheelchair back and forth across uneven ground in constant pouring rain for seven days. They were very mature in their management of unforeseen difficulties coping in quiet unassuming ways. . . . True Guides in every way.

In 1979 a partially sighted Guide, Heather Taylor, gained her Queen's Guide Award (with no concessions). For her service she worked with the deaf Guides (now known as 'hard of hearing'). These Guides and Brownies at the Royal School for the Deaf in Exeter were all led by Jean Busby, who took over as Handicapped

Adviser in 1980; Katherine Ingamells said of Jean that her 'ease of communicating with these girls is a constant wonder'.

1981 was the International Year for Disabled People, and there were a lot of local events, including a Day Camp for the Disabled organised by Sidmouth District at Knowle. There was a Region camp for handicapped Guides at Woodlarks in Hampshire, to which four physically handicapped and three severely deaf Guides went, with four Ranger/Young Leader helpers and three Guiders. It was hard work for the helpers, but in spite of dreadful weather 'a very happy week was enjoyed by all'.

Celebrations for seventy-five years of Guiding took place in 1985; two handicapped Guides went to the Albert Hall Spectacular, which was a great experience, and one went to Devon's Badger Camp. A useful new publication came out for Guiders – *Be Prepared to Welcome a Handicapped Member* – giving advice and hints on coping with the more obvious handicaps. In 1986 there was another South West Region camp at Woodlarks (see page 239) which Jean Busby described:

> Four Guides, three Rangers and two Guiders from Devon units travelled to Hampshire for a week of sun and rain, fun and hard work. The swimming pool was as popular as ever, though 'Sports' must have come a close second – wheelchairs charging up and down transferring cups of water from one bowl to another, or chasing quoits was quite a sight. The Rangers were exhausted at the end of the week, but Guides and Guiders were very grateful for their untiring efforts and cheerful faces. The camp would not happen without their help – I hope they feel it was worthwhile and gave them some insight into the problems and abilities of various handicaps.

Integrate in '88 was a South West Region challenge for all units, to help girls and Guiders to understand what it is like to be handicapped and how they can help those who are. Logbooks were kept of the various challenges undertaken and judged – the 5th Exeter Brownies, 1st Modbury Guides and Sidmouth Rangers were selected to represent Devon in the Region. In 1989 Anneliese Barrell took over from Jean Busby as Adviser for Members with Disabilities (another change of title), and reported that although there was now only one special unit left in the county (at the Royal West of England School for the Deaf), there were fifty members with a disability who were being happily integrated into normal units, and this increased to 100 by 1991.

(Anneliese writes about her time as Adviser for Members with Disabilities on pages 363–4.)

In 1994 Chris Foster, a Guider and District Commissioner who was a physiotherapist working with children in North Devon, took over from Anneliese as Adviser for Members with Disabilities. She reported that in 1995 many Guides and Brownies with a disability had been to camps, holidays and outings with their units. There were trainings on asthma following Asthma Awareness Week (the following year there were 320 members with asthma), and many units took part in the 'Church and Blindness' survey. South West Region produced a challenge, Learn to Mix in '96, which many units took part in and enjoyed; as intended, it led to more awareness and understanding of disability. Guiders were also helped by a new publication in 1997, *Including Disabilities*. Also in 1997 Anne Shadrick, a Guide Guider in Bradworthy, was awarded the MBE for services to the community; she had spent a lot of her life using a wheelchair, but it did not stop her taking part in all the activities of her unit. Sadly Anne died in 2000, and Chris Foster spoke of the pleasure she had brought to others with her musical abilities and her great sense of fun.

In 2000 Katie Rippon, a Young Leader from Barnstaple with spina bifida, took part in the Queen Mother's 100th-birthday parade, and the following year was presented with the Star of Merit Award at the North Devon Scout and Guide Gang Show, in which she had taken an active part since she became a Guide.

In 2004 the Disability Discrimination Act came into force, causing some minor adjustments to buildings, but not too many problems. The disability challenge, You & Me Together, was well received and many units enjoyed taking part. The new Adviser for Members with Disabilities, Caroline Vickery, reported in the 'Review of 2006':

It is good to report that Guiding in Devon has included so many girls and leaders with disabilities or medical conditions. It is obvious from the census papers and the number of phone calls I have received that everyone enjoyed being challenged by the programme. This does prove how adaptable Guiding can be.

Woodlarks Campsite, near Farnham , Surrey, 'Where camping is fun for disabled and able-bodied together', was started by a Colonel Strover in the 1930s. Called 'The Woodlarks Camp for Cripples', it catered for children who suffered from polio, club feet and TB of the spine and who came in wheelchairs and on crutches, and Guides volunteered to help look after them. Over the years the camp went from strength to strength (in 2012 more than 400 people, both adults and children, with disabilities camped there assisted by volunteers). It is now run by a trust, but still depends on volunteers to help run it.

Janet Thorpe, who ran the Dame Hannah Rogers School Guides for many years, took them to the Region camp at Woodlarks in 1979, where they were commended on their helpful and friendly behaviour. She wrote this ditty to describe it:

On a very wet Saturday morning,
Our equipment piled high in the hall,
The coach reversed under the awning
To pack wheelchairs and walkers and all.

The journey was very eventful
With the driver not sure of his way;
The hills seemed too much for the engine
And petrol so scarce in each bay.

The quaint town of Farnham in Surrey
We eventually reached before dark;
We unpacked our bags in a hurry –
Hurrah! We'd arrived at Woodlarks.

From Devon our little contingent
Were physically handicapped all –
Near sighted, part hearing, in wheelchairs,
All playing their part large and small.

The Guides were all highly delighted
To find others from Bristol and Hants,
In fact from the whole of the South West,
From Avon right down to Penzance.

There were two camping sites which were ideal,
Plus a dormitory near the First Aid,
With shower and baths of hot water
We felt that we really were made!

The programmes were many and varied,
With riding and archery too;
The feel of the saddle and bridle
To some was a real dream come true.

Our indoor pursuits were exciting,
Enamelling pendants so gay,
Bright candles and collages various –
We seemed to be busy all day.

We made paper kites with long tails on,
To fly them, you see, was our plan.
We strapped Guides in wheelchairs to hold them,
And full tilt down steep slopes we ran.

The swimming pool bordered by fir trees
Was really a sight to behold.
The Guides and the Rangers plus Guiders
Agreed that the water WAS cold!

The camp fires were always hilarious
With songs and activities plus,
Especially those by the Guiders
(Ballet Rambert had nothing on us!)

The Rangers from Devon were super –
So helpful in sunshine and rain;
We'd all like to thank them sincerely
And hope they will join us again.

And so it was time to start packing;
As always, the end came too fast:
The great times we all had at Woodlarks,
With friendships and memories to last.

The unit at Dame Hannah's was closed in 1982 due to a drop in numbers; there were more activities organised by the school and fewer girls seemed to need Guiding. (Because some conditions such as cerebral palsy are becoming preventable, and many handicapped children can be accommodated in normal schools, Dame Hannah Rogers School – now known as Hannah's – now caters for children with much greater handicaps.) The last few Guides were transferred to ordinary Guide units in Ivybridge, where they joined in as fully as possible. Jean Busby gave a very big thank you to Janet Thorpe 'for her tireless and inspiring work with the 2nd Ivybridge Guides'.

In the early days of Guiding there were also Auxiliary Guides. In the 1929 annual report of the GGA this was written:

> Perhaps the most difficult piece of work undertaken in the name of Guiding is that of the Auxiliary Branch, which deals with companies which have been formed in Penitentiaries and Rescue Homes. The type of girl involved is usually difficult – of a low mental and moral standard, and the outside circumstances a great handicap.

There were thirty-two companies in the UK, including one in Truro. Girls were usually transferred to open companies on leaving the homes.

Social change saw the closure of many of these institutions, and girls in approved schools could join open companies. The Auxiliary Branch was disbanded in 1959, but outreach to underprivileged girls has continued.

Chapter 15: LONE GUIDING

Early in the history of Guides there were girls who lived in the country and wanted to be Guides, but were too far from any others with whom they could join up. They could become Lone Guides, working on their own and passing tests by correspondence. They were grouped into companies, which at first included girls from all over Britain, then became more local as numbers grew. Their captain kept in touch with them with a monthly letter, which went round all the members. They met very occasionally, usually at a special camp. There were Lone Guides in boarding schools where there were no Guide companies, and when families were posted abroad girls could continue their Guiding through the post. By 1925 Lone Ranger companies were started.

In 1947 it was reported that there were two Lone Guide and two Lone Ranger companies in Devon; numbers were increasing and it was hoped to open two more companies as soon as a shortage of Guiders could be overcome. All Lone Guides had now been put in touch with the nearest Guides and active Guide company.

> This has proved very beneficial and has enabled Lones to be enrolled and to receive help with Second Class, First Class and badge work.

Lone Guiders had a helpful meeting to discuss ideas and difficulties.

In 1957 there were fifty-six Lones in Devon, including twelve Guiders. Three Rangers belonged to SRS *Druid*, which was the only Sea Ranger crew for Lones in England and had in it girls from Yorkshire, Wales, London and Kent. Most went camping with other Lones or with active companies.

At Christmas 1958 Devon Lone Guides

sent a box of beautifully filled stockings and soft toys to Exeter Orthopaedic Hospital. . . . Some of the older Guides have cycled many miles to visit the recruits, giving a feeling of responsibility to the older Guides, and of really belonging to a Company to the younger ones.

In 1959 the Devon Lone Secretary, Margaret Gill, wrote:

Though it is sometimes said that Lones have no fun and never meet other Guide people, this certainly cannot apply to our Lone Rangers. This summer they had two camps of their own and had plenty of contact with active Guiding.

Activities included riding, and bridge building over the River Dart. 'Some necessary forestry was also practised when a tree fell down.' There were eleven Lone Guides and five recruits at Stover School; they had a company letter like other Lones, but worked with it in Patrols on Saturday afternoons.

Lone Guides and Rangers had a chance to see for the first time a large gathering of Guides in June 1960 when the Chief Guide visited Exeter, and then when Princess Margaret named the *Golden Hinde* at Dartmouth.

Lone numbers continued to fluctuate like active companies, and in 1962 the Lone Sea Ranger crew, SRS *Druid*, became an active crew in Ashburton. A new Lone Ranger crew under the County Ranger Adviser, Angela Graham, was registered as Lone SRS *Hydra*, but was disbanded in 1965 when no Guider could be found. Most Lone Rangers helped with Guide and Brownie units in their own localities.

An All-England Lone Guide Camp was planned for 1968, but was cancelled for lack of support; however, the Devon Lone Guide who had applied went to a camp in Scotland and had a very good time. A girl in the 4th Devon Lone Guide Company was the first Lone to gain a Queen's Guide Award, in 1969, and the County Commissioner presented her with it at a gathering in Honiton: 'The [Lone] Guides in particular enjoyed the afternoon immensely as they are so rarely able to meet together.' Miss T. D. Lowry summed up: 'A good year and a feeling that a very real need is being met.'

Greta Gray took over as Lones Adviser in 1974 and reported that Devon Lones now included girls from Cornwall as well as Somerset. She was impressed with the number of badges the Lones managed to gain, and the fact that most of them managed to get to camp. Lone Rangers were always a great help at Guide camps. Greta started the cake stall at the county annual meeting in 1975 to raise money for Devon Lones; it made £17 the first year and it became an annual event, the money being needed for postage of the monthly letter to each Lone Guide and Ranger.

In 1977 the Lones joined Oakford Guides for a 'super' camp on Exmoor, at which they were thrilled to receive a letter from Buckingham Palace in answer to a postcard they had sent to the Queen with Silver Jubilee greetings: 'Her Majesty wishes you all a most enjoyable Jubilee Camp on Exmoor.' Greta organised a successful get-together at Bowerman's Cottage in 1978 with twelve Guides and Rangers and two Unit Leaders. Two Lone Guides, Sara Haskin and Wendy Bootherstone, gained the Queen's Guide Award in 1979, and Sara, as one of four from the UK, went to the All Australia Lone Guide Camp in Sydney. There was a similar camp in Perth in 1983, which was attended by Sara's sister Kathy Haskin, who was also a Devon Lone.

Greta Gray, who was Lones Adviser for Devon for eleven years, really put this branch of Guiding on the map; with her friend Kathleen Thomas, with whom she shared a remote cottage near Oakford in north-east Devon, she helped the girls to find camps to join, arranged activities for them and made sure they always took part in county fundraising and good turns. Unity Harley, who took over from Greta in 1984, thanked her warmly for all she had done for the Lones, and also thanked a long-serving Lones Guider, Elinor d'Albiac:

The enterprise of her Rangers . . . was greatly due to her encouragement and devotion to the detailed writing in her monthly letter.

Two Rangers from North-East England joined Devon Lones in 1985; one attended a school for the deaf and the other was a member of the National Youth Orchestra. Unity Harley reported that with their contributions and those of a Lone Ranger living in Hong Kong 'our letter makes exciting reading at times'. She added:

Miss Jean Peters, the Lones Guide Guider, joined those Rangers who could get to the Cathedral Close for a picnic Birthday Tea to celebrate together the 75th anniversary before attending the Service on June 30th. . . . We all enjoyed meeting our "pen friends" for the first time!

1986 saw an increase in numbers of Lones following county-wide publicity, and now two Guide Guiders wrote the Guide letters and two the Ranger letters. Five Rangers joined the hard-working Service Crew for the Mount Edgcumbe Jamboree and two Guides camped with the Wembury Guides. The Lones at the jamboree all met Mrs Shirley Strong, Chief Commissioner for London and South-East England, at a special ceremony at which Corrie Newell received her Guider's Warrant and two Rangers were invested. A Lones Travel Fund was initiated to help subsidise the cost of Lones travelling to meetings and camps and sail training cruises. The Trefoil Guild contributed to this as well as stalls at annual meetings.

Unity Harley became Lones Adviser for South West Region in 1989, and Beryl Paul, who succeeded her in Devon, reported on a camp training get-together and a Dartmoor Letterbox hike. Lone Rangers worked in the 1990 Pirates Camp Service Team and others camped with girls from Greece. Lone Ranger Guider Corrie Newell gained her Duke of Edinburgh Gold Award.

Beryl reported in 1991 that six of the Lone Rangers were also Young Leaders in local units. She also wrote:

It was a proud day for the unit when Sarah Smith was presented with her Queen's Guide Award. . . . She had just returned from serving [with the Army] in the Gulf, and extracts from her letters home which were circulated in the Company letter make very interesting reading. Guiding had certainly prepared Sarah well for these very challenging experiences. (See page 149.)

Corrie Newell went with two other UK delegates to a Lone Guiders Conference in Australia in 1992. Other Lones went on overseas visits and a Lone Ranger sailed on the *Lord Nelson*. In 1994 Lone Guides went to the spring meeting of Dartmoor Letterbox enthusiasts, at which they produced a Lone Letterbox stamp as a 'one day special'. This gained them £30, some of which they donated to the British Heart Foundation.

Lone Guiders have to work hard in a different way to those running active units, and Beryl Paul thanked them for

> working so hard to awaken and keep the interest of our girls, some of whom they have never met, by beautifully presented Company letters which take hours to prepare, and by their willingness to travel miles to meet and share ideas with other Lone Guiders.

Mary Timmis took over as Lones Adviser in 1995 and suggested that

> with the problem of Guide units closing down, perhaps Guiders could remind their Guides and prospective Guides in Brownie Packs that they can continue Guiding in the Lone scheme. All opportunities are available to Lones within the County, internationally and, of course, having fun out of doors.

In 2000 the girls who had been Lone Guides for the past two years moved on to be Young Leaders, so there were no Lone Guides in Devon. But there was a Lone Brownie unit which had girls from all over the county. Email and audio tapes were now used in addition to the traditional letters through the post. Mary Timmis reported that for one Lone Brownie, who suffered from ME, being a Lone was 'an ideal way for her to continue as a Brownie, doing badge work when able and not committed to a regular meeting'.

After 2003 there was no County Lones Adviser and the whole branch seems to have gone into abeyance in Devon – for the time being anyway. It had certainly fulfilled a very real need over many years, and it took hard work and dedication from the girls as well as the Guiders. As Margaret Gill, County Lone Secretary, said in 1958: "It is not easy to be a Lone Guide, but a good Lone is a very good Guide indeed."

Chapter 16: HEADQUARTERS

(Author's note: It has not been easy to track the history of local Headquarters, and there may be omissions. After Ivybridge they are in alphabetic order.)

Scout Troops have nearly always had their own Headquarters – specially built Scout huts or old buildings taken over and converted. Not so the Guides, who have tended to meet in schools or village halls or in the early days in the Guider's house. Sometimes they shared a building with the Scouts, but this was not always satisfactory.

Minutes of the IVYBRIDGE Scout and Guide Hut Management Committee meetings in the 1970s reported disgruntlement among the Guides at having to clean up at times after the Scouts, and the Scouters complained that the Guiders were not supporting the joint committee as much as they were!

This hut was a redundant Territorial Army drill hall near the parish church. It was bought by philanthropists John and Pat Trahair of Westlake in about 1945 for £500 for a youth club, rent-free. When this disbanded the Scouts took it over, joined later by the Guides. Eventually the Trahairs gave the freehold to the Scouts and Guides. It is still in use.

ASHBURTON had an unusual Guide Headquarters, opened in 1962. An old building dating from the thirteenth century, it had been a pub called The Golden Fleece, in St Lawrence Lane. The name was retained, and the Guide Association was granted a fourteen-year lease on the building. It had a large room for Guide and Brownie meetings and other rooms for Sea Rangers, Trefoil Guild, etc., as well as kitchen and cloakroom. But it was not all suitable as the main room had rather intrusive pillars in it, and at some stage it closed, possibly when the lease ran out.

BIDEFORD District's Headquarters, a large wooden hut, suffered a terrible flood in 1980, having only been redecorated the year before. Three to four feet of dirty water wrecked all the equipment of the four units that used the hut. After it was back in use it was still very damp, and for some weeks the girls had activities during which they rushed around to keep warm! By 1995 there were structural problems with the hut, and a working party was set up to consider a new building on the same site. Fundraising got under way and people were encouraged to buy 'bricks' towards the new hut. Then asbestos was discovered in the old building and the cost of its removal used up all the money so far raised. It was then decided not to rebuild, and the units have met in church halls and schools ever since.

BISHOPSTEIGNTON Scouts and Guides opened a new Headquarters in the 1970s. There are now no Guides in the village, but it is still used by the Scouts.

BUDLEIGH SALTERTON District was given a Guide hut by Lady Clinton in the early days, but they did not own the land. Eventually the hut deteriorated and was condemned, and in 1992 a new hut was opened on land bought by the Guides; ownership was shared with the Royal British Legion, who had the money for a Headquarters but no land. Called the Venture Hall, it was well equipped for Pack and Guide holidays and is still used; since the Royal British Legion pulled out, it has been shared with a youth group run by the county council.

COLYTON District launched a fund in 1996 to buy a disused chapel in the town, and by November had raised over £10,000. The building was sympathetically renovated as a Guide Headquarters and opened in 1998 by Chief Guide Bridget Towle.

CORNWOOD (near Ivybridge) had from before 1966 a hut near the village and close to open moorland, the use of which was shared by the Guides and other youth groups, courtesy of the landowner, Major Parker of Delamore. Lit by Calor gas and heated by a wood fire, it had a small kitchen and chemical toilet and was suitable for overnight hikes and weekend indoor camps. It burnt down mysteriously in October 1981, and the division decided that because of its vulnerability it should not be rebuilt. In 1983, with the insurance money, they bought Pennaton Meadow near South Brent.

CREDITON District, instigated by their Commissioner, Muriel Foden, and then her successor, Patricia Coward, built their Headquarters on the edge of the town playing fields and opened it in June 1980. Ten years later it had to be dismantled to make room for a new sports ground, but they were compensated with a new building with the same facilities both inside and outside. Unfortunately in 2012 the hut was flooded due to a burst pipe and suffered serious damage; the district was helped with the repairs by a generous grant from the Devon Lones Trefoil Guild, who meet twice a year in the Boniface Centre in Crediton and are well looked after by Crediton Trefoil Guild.

EXETER Division in the 1960s leased Budlake Hall from the National Trust for camping and outdoor activities. It was an old school near Broadclyst on the old A38 and could sleep twenty-five, with a fully equipped kitchen, washroom and flush toilets, and there was a small orchard for camping. It was much used in the 1970s and '80s. Then in 1983, thanks to the determination of the Commissioner, Margaret Branch, a Headquarters was found in the city – Belmont Park Lodge in Blackboy Road, which was leased from the council and partly funded by bottle collections all round Exeter. It was opened by the Chief Commissioner, Lady (Patience) Baden-Powell, during her visit to Devon in 1983. It was described as a superb Headquarters, with a training/conference room, a committee room, office, kitchen, cloakroom and toilets. It was used by the county as well as the division for a number of years. But a bigger, Guide-owned, building was really needed. Then in 1998 the old Assemblies of God church in Buddle Lane came on the market and was bought by the division and renovated as their Headquarters and used for county meetings. It was also let out to local organisations. Plans are now afoot for further development, possibly as Headquarters for the county as well as the division. It is now called Trefoil Lodge.

FREMINGTON, near Barnstaple, had a Guide hut from June 1967. At the opening ceremony the Guiders gave a 'mannequin parade' of clothes they had made themselves. It is not known what happened to it.

HOLSWORTHY District built a Headquarters which was opened in 1993 by Lord and Lady Morley, who lived near Yelverton. Lady Morley was Patron of Devon Girl Guides, and Lord Morley was Lord Lieutenant of Devon and had always taken a great interest in the Guides and Scouts.

NEWTON ABBOT District had a Guide hut near the road at the bottom of Combeshead School playing field. When Loveday Fergusson became District Commissioner in 1969 it was in a bad state, but with the help of prisoners from Chaddlewood Open Prison and local well-wishers, it was restored and used regularly for some years. Eventually it was dismantled when the school needed the land for a car park.

OKEHAMPTON Guides and Brownies, after much fundraising, had a hut built in the town in 1981, but with no water or electricity it was of limited use. Then the town council wanted the site back for housebuilding and gave them another site in the skateboard park. Guiders, parents and friends moved the old hut, board by board, and erected it on the new site, and it was officially reopened by the Mayor of Okehampton on Thinking Day, 1995. But after a few years it started to deteriorate and suffered from vandalism, so it was abandoned and the units moved to the church hall.

PAIGNTON owns a purpose-built camp store. In 1981 the two districts in Paignton were busy raising money for a store when feisty Guider Doreen (Do) Scattergood, who worked for the council's planning department, persuaded a local builder to donate a small plot of land that he owned to the Guides, for a camp store. Jacqui Leigh, a former trustee and treasurer, wrote:

> The idea grew, and the Local Association, as we were then known, worked tirelessly with coffee mornings, begging letters etc. L.A. members and Guiders all worked manually at weekends to clear the site, and the building was eventually built, and was opened by Assistant County Commissioner Loveday Fergusson.

Looking like a smart garage with an up-and-over door, it is beautifully fitted out to store camp equipment, and the gate on to the road has a trefoil on it.

PLYMOUTH EAST DIVISION built a large Headquarters near Mutley Plain, which was opened in 1963 by HRH the Princess Royal (Princess Mary, President of the GGA). After improvements were made, in 2003 it was named the Rosamond Stevens Hall after a well-known and well-loved Guider and Commissioner. It is used for Brownie, Guide and Ranger holidays and activity days as well as regular meetings. The division are very proud of their large Headquarters.

PLYMPTON District opened its prestigious Betts Guiding Centre in 1980; it was named after nurse Sister Betts, a stalwart Guider of the old school, who was a great influence in the lives of many girls and women in the 1950s and '60s. It is much used, including for Guide and Brownie holidays.

SALCOMBE was raising money in 1968 for a Guide hut, encouraged by Guider Daphne Foster, who kept the hut going for some years. It must have closed at some stage, because it is recorded that thanks to friends in Salcombe, including Guide parents, and a grant from the Dartington Trust, it was reopened in 1993. But eventually it was decided that it was too expensive to maintain, and it was sold to the Methodist church next door.

SIDMOUTH District built a very well-designed Headquarters called Lawn Vista at The Byes Park and opened by the County Commissioner in 1986. Like Budleigh Salterton, being in a seaside town it is very popular for residential holidays.

SOUTH MOLTON District's original Guide hut had its roof repaired in 1976, and fundraising over many years resulted in a new building opened in 1987. But by the late 1990s it was deteriorating; the district could not afford to repair it, so it was sold. The interest from the sale is paid to the division annually and used for trainings, etc.

TAVISTOCK has what is probably the most interesting building historically as a Guide Headquarters. Situated in the middle of the town, it was built as a large stone warehouse straddling the canal that was built in about 1803 to take the copper from the Duke of Bedford's mines down to the Tamar at Morwellham. Barges could sail into the warehouse for loading and unloading. Later it was used as a granary, and then after several changes of ownership it came into the ownership of Mrs Mary Gallup, a gentleman farmer's wife from Brentor. She was a JP, an active supporter of civic and charitable concerns in Tavistock, and was District and then Division Commissioner for the area. She generously gave the warehouse to the local Guide Association and it has ever since been known as 'The Guide Hall'. A framed scroll hangs in the building:

> This hall is given to the Rangers, Guides and Brownies of Tavistock District in memory of the late King George V by one who has faith in Guiding. 1936.

It is used by different units and other organisations, and much fundraising has gone on over the years for its maintenance. In the

1990s the old railway sleepers supporting the ground floor were found to be rotten, so for some time the small meeting room downstairs had no floor – just the waters of the canal underneath! Fortunately fire-precaution work was included when the floor was replaced, as vandals broke in in 1994 and started a fire in the camp store, but it did not spread. Since 1997 it has been in the hands of the Guide Association Trust Company, with a local Management Committee, and within the limitations of its listed-building status many improvements have been made. Kate Harding adds:

> Situated as it is at the entrance to the main town car park, the big blue doors remain both a symbol of the heritage of this former mining town and the strength of Guiding in the area, and . . . our wonderful, historic HQ will for ever be known to everyone as 'Tavistock Guide Hall'.

A beautiful hut for TEIGNMOUTH District in the grounds of Teignmouth Community School was opened in 1978 by the Bishop of Crediton, Wilfrid Westall; this followed years of fundraising and the help of a generous benefactor and the Job Creation Scheme. It is used now by the school as well as the Guides.

TIVERTON district from about 1961 had the use of a large wooden hut that had been a classroom at the old Heathcoat Junior School, which was now a factory shop and offices for John Heathcoat and Co. This had been arranged by Lady Amory, and the Guides and Brownies could use it for as long as they wished; they also had the use of part of the field next to it. No rent was paid, but occasionally working parties were formed to maintain the hut. By the early 1970s a change in management at the Heathcoat factory made it clear that the Guide use of the hut was not popular, so the District Commissioner, Mrs Dorothy Gardiner, a very determined lady, suggested they look for other premises and persuaded the factory to give them some help. An upstairs hall with a downstairs flat in St Peter Street, Tiverton, came on the market in 1973 and was bought and opened in 1975.

Since then improvements have included two inside toilets and a shower, a camp store and a committee room, and the kitchen has been improved. It is well used and is suitable for sleepovers and Pack Holidays.

WOODBURY, after many years of hard fundraising, opened a joint headquarters with the Scouts in 1977, and this is still in use.

There were times when the county had use of property the Guides did not own. One such was Bradley Manor, a small and unspoilt medieval manor house on the edge of Newton Abbot, now owned by the National Trust, but still a family home. Soon after the war, Mrs Woolner, who lived there, decided to let part of the house to Devon Guides. Miss E. K. Parker, the County Commissioner, wrote in the county report of 1948:

> Early in the year, I had the pleasure of opening North End, Bradley Manor, as a centre for Devon Guiding. It has proved of immense value as a centre for Guiders' Training, and Cadets, Rangers, Guiders and Lone Guides have all had weekends there, while for the whole of August it was used for Brownie Pack holidays. During the first ten months, over 300 people made use of it.

The large wooded grounds were also a great asset to those staying there. Miss Cobham, chairman of training, commented that the weekends there were 'most happy gatherings'.

Some lucky companies had their own special meeting places. Brentor Guides and Brownies met in a room above a barn in the Vicarage garden in the 1920s, but when the Vicarage was sold they had to move to the village hall. Then in 1970 the old Vicarage changed hands again, and the new owner and her daughter repaired the barn in the garden and allowed the Brownies to use it again. Brown Owl, A. Neale, had been one of the Guides who used it all those years ago!

There was a fairy-tale cottage on the beach at Wiscombe, near Kingston in South Devon, which was let to various organisations, including Guides from Plymouth and nearby areas. Described as 'gloriously isolated', it was reached by a cart track through woods to the sea. The advertisement read:

> The beach is the last unpopulated one left in South Devon and there are opportunities for bird-watching, swimming, fire lighting and all sorts of adventurous and interesting expeditions.

It had a living room, equipped kitchen, running water and flush toilet, and close by were old stables converted for sleeping up to twenty-two. There was space for two or three tents. The beach was part of the Flete Estate and the cottage had been a Victorian 'tea house' (there was one on each of the estate beaches) where Lord and Lady Mildmay and family and friends would take tea served by liveried staff. The cottage at Wiscombe was very popular and much used, but by 1967 it was abandoned as the sea took its toll; the cliff crumbled and the cottage fell into the sea. (See page 383 for the story of a camp there.)

Collecting jam jars, 1947–8.

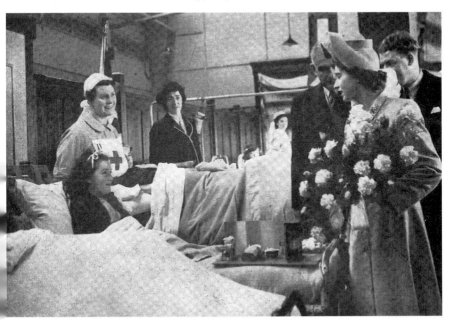

Princess Elizabeth with 39th Exeter (Princess Elizabeth Orthopaedic Hospital) Guide Company, 1947–8.

The founder.

Jennifer Evans, Pack Leader of the Plymouth Post Brownie Pack, teaching Brownie knots, 1957. Photo courtesy of the Western Independent.

The County Commissioner presents the Badge of Fortitude to Cynthia Miller of 1st Devon Post Brownie Pack, 1959.

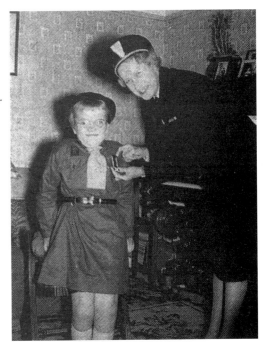

Princess Margaret, Chief Ranger of the British Commonwealth and Empire, is piped aboard the Golden Hinde, *when with her husband she attended the commissioning service and named the ship, at Dartmouth, 1960. Photo courtesy of the* Western Morning News.

Thinking Day, 1962. Photo courtesy of the Herald Express, *Torquay.*

The County Commissioner, Mrs J. E. Eastley, MBE, JP,
at the St George's Day Parade at Exeter, 1961.
Photo courtesy of the Express & Echo.

Opening of The Golden Fleece, Ashburton, 1962.
Photo courtesy of H. R. Rivers, Newton Abbot 400.

2nd St Budeaux Guides Discoverers' Challenge Hike, 1964.

St George's Day Parade in Exeter (and an envious onlooker), 1965.
Photo courtesy of the Express & Echo.

Dawlish Golden Jubilee, 1968 – Mrs Saltav cuts the cake.

Pioneering at North Devon Division Camp, 1966.

The launching ceremony for the new handbooks, Torquay, 1968.

264

The Chief Guide at the Spa Ballroom, 4 November 1967.
Photo courtesy of Torquay Times *Ltd.*

BROWNIE
SEA DAY

Brownie Sea Day, 1970.

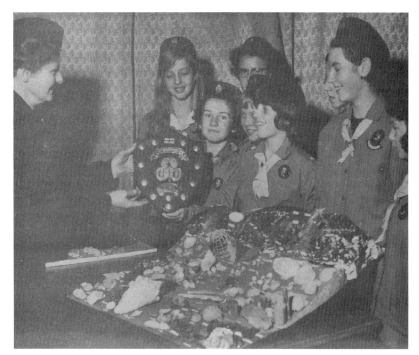

Operation Shoreline, 1968.

The Queen Mother at Brixham, 1969.
Photo courtesy of the Herald Express, *Torquay.*

The exhibition at Torre Abbey, 1969 – The Architects at Work.
Photo courtesy of the Torquay Times.

The County Commissioner, Mrs. A. T. J. Graham, 1971.

Diamond Jubilee Camp, 1970.

Royal Naval inspection of SRS Churchill, *Brixham, who gained
Admiralty recognition for the seventeenth consecutive year in 1971.
Photo courtesy of Charles Risk, Brixham.*

*The Queen at Dartmouth, 1972.
Photo courtesy of the* Herald Express, *Torquay.*

The County President, Lady Amory, 1972.

Brownies collect for land at £10 per acre, 1972.

Sidmouth Guides and Young Leaders prepare for camp with advice from
Mrs C. T. Richards, 1973.
Photo courtesy of the Sidmouth Herald.

*Brownie jubilee year, handing over the keys of the minibus at Hawkmoor,
1974. Photo courtesy of the* Herald Express, Torquay.

*Shebbear Guides and Brownies distribute loaves to the sick and elderly
during the recent shortage, 1974.*

Teams of Guides ring the parish church bells at Ottery St Mary, 1974. Photo courtesy of the Ottery News.

1st Oakford Guides – spring-cleaning the church, 1975.

The arts week at Honiton, 1976 –
a scene from the Elizabethan Sheep Shearing Festival.

Brownie Pow-wow, Exmouth Division, 1976 – 1st Exmouth Pack.

274

*At the AGM at Totnes, 1976 – Mrs Owen Walker, JP,
Chief Commissioner (on the right), with Mrs Angela Graham.*

*The Eight-Point Challenge – exploring the arts and getting to know
people. Salcombe Guides decorate their boat for the Regatta Water
Carnival, 1975. They won third prize in their class.*

Judith Turner of Crownhill District Rangers takes the wheel aboard the Malcolm Miller, 1976.

Thinking Day in Kingsbridge District, 1976, celebrating their link with India. A Salcombe Patrol Leader wearing a uniform sari given by Miss Violet Caleb, a camp trainer in India.

A tasty meal! Devon Lone Guides and Oakford Guides at Summer Camp 1977 on Exmoor.

Dawlish Guides watching the inauguration of the swimming-pool hoist at Oaklands Park School, 1978 – part of Devon Guides' Silver Jubilee Project for mentally handicapped children.
Photo courtesy of the Western Times.

"Can I see you?" 1st Whimple Brownies with their Good Turn spectacle collection, 1977.

Members of the Trefoil Guild in 1978 admiring the seat in the Cathedral Close that they gave in memory of Lady Baden-Powell. Chairman Miss Sheerman is seated (left) with President Miss Bindloss. Standing on the right is Miss Phyl Fowler, Division Commissioner of North Devon. (The seat is no longer there.) Photo courtesy of the Western Times.

Presentation of the Queen's Guide Award to Heather Taylor of the company for visually handicapped Guides at the West of England School for the Visually Handicapped, Exeter, 1979. Left to right: Mr Slade (headmaster), Mrs Ronchetti (assistant Guider), Heather Taylor, Heather's mother and sister, Miss Toogood (Guider) and Mrs Branch (Division Commissioner).

2nd Appledore Brownies pointing to the fuel crisis at Appledore Carnival, 1979.

*The Honourable Mrs Clay, daughter of the founder, with her husband
and grandson and the Scout and Guide County Commissioners, at the
Crediton Jamboree, 1980.*

Torquay Sea Rangers at the launching of Squirrel *by the County
Commissioner on 22 July 1980, made possible by a generous grant
from the Seamanship Foundation.*
Photo courtesy of the Herald and Express.

Building a Saxon hut at the Jamboree, 1980.

Sereana and Sala from Fiji and Mrs Thomas (Commonwealth and International Adviser), 1980.

Two young guides from Dublin have fun paddling the coracle made by their patrol at the Jamboree, 1980.

Mrs June Barnes, Chief Commissioner of Fiji, and her deputy, Mrs Senimili Dyer, who visited Devon in the summer of 1980.

Swallow Patrol of 1st Ivybridge Guides won the second prize, of £150,
in a 1981 national competition for designing the 'House of the Future'.
Left to right: Lisa Wood, Patrol Leader Tracey Martins,
Michel Duval, Patrol Second Jane Sarsum and Tracey Davis.
Photo courtesy of the Western Morning News.

Lynton Guides, Brownies and a Ranger working on the Adopt and
Cherish project on Hollerday Hill, 1982. They have cleared the area
and uncovered many young trees and given them a chance to grow.
They were first in the Regional final.
Photo courtesy of the North Devon Journal & Herald *Ltd.*

A World of Song, *the festival of song and dance held at Exeter Cathedral on 28 October 1982. Some of the performers after the morning rehearsal. Photo courtesy of the* Express and Echo.

The opening of the county campsite, Taw Bottom, on 7 May 1983.

Silverton District Guides clean telephone boxes in Stoke Canon for their Service flashes, 1984.
Photo courtesy of C. J. Court, Poltimore.

Joy Zaple, assistant Ranger Guider, Plympton, with girls at the Rainbow Fun Camp, 1984.
Photo courtesy of the Western Morning News.

1st Topsham Brownies serving tea to Devon's Chief Fire Officer, 1985. Photo courtesy of the Express and Echo.

The County Commissioner receives the light from the Region Chief Commissioner, 1985. Photo courtesy of Bob Merrifield.

1st Ottery St Mary Guides in the greenhouse they won,
by decorating a pumpkin, 1985.
Photo courtesy of the Sidmouth Herald.

4th Tavistock Guides knitted 100 jumpers for Oxfam, 1985.
Photo courtesy of the Tavistock Gazette.

*Amanda Weldon receiving a Queen's Guide brooch from
Princess Margaret, watched by the Chief Commissioner, 1986.
Photo courtesy of CHQ.*

*2nd Littleham (Exmouth) Brownies, Region winners of SCF Tea Making
Competition, on their way to meet Princess Anne, 1986.
Photo courtesy of the* Exmouth Journal.

*Joyce Lady Amory watching the planting of one of her
birthday trees, 1986.
Photo by courtesy of E. Greensmith.*

Torquay Rangers on the sloop Seacrest, *1986, kindly given to Devon
Girl Guides by Mr Ian Holden, far right.
Photo courtesy of the* Herald Express, *Torquay.*

Robin Patrol, 2nd Cockington Guides, county winners of National Meat Cooking Competition, 1986.
Photo courtesy of Bob Merrifield.

Thorveton Guides 'Adopt a Footpath' under a Devon County Council scheme, 1987.

Maypole dancers at Woolacombe District Brownie Revels, 1987.

*34th Exeter Guides singing fifty songs for muscular dystrophy research
in their jubilee year, 1987.*
Photo courtesy of the Express and Echo.

One of Devon's new Rainbow units, 1988.
Photo courtesy of Dan Dalziel.

Torbay welcomes the Queen, 1989.
Photo courtesy of the Herald Express, *Torquay.*

*Plymstock West District Rangers' investiture at the top of the
Smeaton Tower, 1989.*
Photo courtesy of the Dan Dalziel.

*1st Wembury Guides demonstrating outdoor cooking at the Devon
County Show, 1990.*

Teignmouth Rangers proudly display their flag, designed and made by themselves, 1990.
Photo courtesy of the Teignmouth Post.

Rafting — one of the boating activities at Pirates, 1990.

Kingsbridge Guides after caving at their camp at Holne, 1990.

Scouts and Guides from North Devon sampling the brand-new county canoes at Bicton College, 1991.

1st Uffculme Brownies making snowmen for their Craft badge, 1991.

Presenting the county cheque to St David's House in 1991.
The final amount was over £6,000.
Photo courtesy of the Express and Echo.

Guides from Tavistock Division lend a hand with senior citizens'
Christmas shopping, 1992.
Photo courtesy of James Bird, Tavistock Times Gazette.

'Maeve the Rave' together with members of the Junior Council, 1992.

Dartmouth Guides visiting Our Chalet, 1992.

Learning a new skill at Cadover Division Camp, 1993.

Messenger Guides at the County Show meet Princess Margaret, 1994.
Photo courtesy of Herald Express *Publications Ltd. Torquay.*

1st Brixham St Mary's Ranger, Alice Hodges, at Berry Head, 1994.

3rd and 32nd Plymouth Brownies trying new skills at Pack Holiday, 1995.

Colyton Brownies with eighty marigolds at their eightieth birthday party, 1995.

'On the Chalet Steps' –
Devon Senior Section Group
visit Our Chalet, 1996.

Canoeing at Bicton, 1996.

Dartington Guides experience being wheelchair-bound or on crutches for Learn to Mix in '96.

1st Marldon Guides returning from Buckfastleigh Caves, 1997.

*1st Bradworthy Brownies disguised as sunflowers –
by Vincent Van Who? – 1997.*

*An Action Plus group from 3rd Ilfracombe setting off on what proved to
be a successful Bronze Duke of Edinburgh Expedition, 1998.*

Members of Devon Senior Section and Polish Guides canoeing beneath the Tamar Bridge, 1998.

A 4th Barnstaple Guide, Katie Rippon, mixing the chocolate pudding at Foxlease Camp, 1998.

304

Devon County Commissioners in 1999, from the twentieth and into the twenty-first century. From left to right: Miss Betty Bindloss, Mrs Angela Graham, Mrs Rosemary Howell, Mrs Mavis Budden, Mrs Beryl Hitchcock, Miss Chris Tozer.

Devon Home for Children in Mozambique built with money raised by Devon Guides, 1999.

1st Tiverton and 1st Bampton Brownies enjoy pond dipping in the Wembworthy Conservation Area, 1999.

Babbacombe Rangers making music with junk, 1999.

*"How long can we float before we get wet?" 1st Paignton Brownies at
Campsite Capers, 1999.*

*Guides each year provide invaluable messenger services at the
County Show.*

Part of the team of Kingsteignton Guides getting their bearings at the Map and Compass base at the Hurdlestone Challenge, 2000.

Bradworthy and Torrington Rainbows at the Taw and Torridge Division Thinking Day Celebrations, 2000.

2nd Braunton Rangers and Guides white-water rafting on the River Inn in Austria, 2000.

North Devon Division being awarded the Hope Rattey Trophy as winners of the It's a Knockout competition at Hope 2000.

Devon Junior Council Members at
Zero-One South West England Weekend, 2001.
"How fast can they run with only eight legs?"

2nd Braunton Guides visit the Devon Air Ambulance, 2001.

4th Brixham Brownies rock pooling at Goodrington with the Torbay Marine Ranger, 2002.

Tracey Arscott and friend relaxing on the Lord Nelson, *2002.*

Devon Junior Council showing off their pink tee shirts, by which they were so well known as Service Crew at DELTA 2003.

Taw Bottom, the county campsite, is always in need of voluntary work. Devon Junior Council were among those who gave this service to help maintain the quality of the site. Before the strimmer was used, instruction in health and safety was given.

Guides taking part in the county Baden-Powell Adventure at Grenville House, Brixham, 2005 – seen here rafting.

Okehampton Brownies celebrating ninety years at the carnival, 2004.

Exeter Division's ninetieth birthday party held at Crealy Park, 2004.
Photo courtesy of the Express and Echo.

Ailsa Walsh, Babbacombe Guider, at the Queen's Guide Reception, 2004.
Seen here with Girlguiding UK President, the Countess of Wessex.

Disneyland, Paris, January 2004. A group led by Laurie Pearson started at Totnes Station and travelled via train, coach and ferry to the Davey Crocket Ranch, Disneyland, where they were met by Venture Abroad reps. The reps proved to be very helpful and the information was first class. In keeping with the ranch theme the accommodation was in log cabins which were well appointed, clean and warm.

1st Wrafton and 1st Woolacombe Guides, here seen with Ainslie Harriet in 2004 after being in the audience for Ready, Steady, Cook.

*Combe Martin Brownies
during their annual tree
survey in 2005. This mazzard
tree was planted by the
Brownies and Guides in 2000.*

*8th Plympton Guides caving at Buckfastleigh, where two made their
promise underground, 2005.*

A group of Guiders enjoying (hopefully!) the experience of making and walking along a rope bridge, during a residential training weekend at Broadleas in 2006.

Guides from 1st Buckfastleigh while being assessed for their Guide camp permit at Taw Bottom in 2006.

In 2007 1st Hatherleigh Brownies had a day at camp, during which they tried limbo dancing.

Raleigh District Guides undertaking their Outdoor Cook badge in 2007. Not only did they cook and eat . . . they had to clear up also!

318

The Everest Expedition. In 2007 a team of young Guiders and balloonists, based in Tavistock, led a Girlguiding UK expedition to Everest, aiming to break the altitude record for a tethered hot-air balloon.

Devon Junior Council Chair, Zoe Viggers, chatting with Chief Commissioner Gill Slocombe during the County Reception in June 2007.

*During 2007 John Green (Shelterbox) was speechless when
presented with a cheque for £1,510 raised by
Babbacombe Rangers in only four months.*

*In 2009 12th Devonport Rainbows' 'Change the World'
Project was for the National Deaf Children's Society.*

*Combe Martin Guides
Duke of Edinburgh
Group, 2008.*

*2008 Devon County
Show, meeting with
the Duchess of
Cornwall.*

*"We had a wonderful time
gorge-scrambling near Okehampton.
Wearing wetsuits, buoyancy aids
and helmets we waded up-stream,
stopping often to jump off rocks into
the water and bury our heads
under waterfalls — but only
when allowed to do so!"*
Sarah, Babbacombe Rangers, 2008.

321

In 2010 1st North Tawton Rangers fundraised by taking part in the Starlight Moorwalk (a six-mile night walk on Dartmoor) and raised over £250 for breast-cancer research.

Coming together, cooperation and healthy competition at the County Centenary Camp at Woodlands, 2010.

In 2010, on the 100th day of our Centenary Year, Girlguiding Erme Valley put on a show for parents; created on the day, through workshops, and presented that night.

1st Woolfardisworthy Rainbows held a sponsored cycle ride and tabletop sale in 2010 as suggested by the girls after seeing Haiti on the news and raised £917 for Shelterbox – a great effort.

In 2010 Emma Bullock was fortunate to be given the opportunity to be an adult involved in taking a group of ten girls to Our Cabana in Mexico for a Girl Friendship session.

Launch Parties

Axminster Division

5th Sept 2009

Erme Valley Division

Exeter Division

Exmouth Division

Honiton Division

4 Plymouth Divisions

North Devon Division

Okehampton Division

4 Plymouth Divisions

4 Plymouth Divisions

4 Plymouth Divisions

Tavy Division

Taw & Torridge Division

Launch Parties
5th Sept 2009

Teignbridge Division

Tiverton Division

Torbay Division

Totnes Division

"VISION"

20th October 2010 – at 20:10
Promises were renewed across the UK...

Plym Division

Erme Valley Division

Honiton Division

...in a fun finale to our centenary year...

Exeter Division

Taw & Torridge Division

Exmouth Division

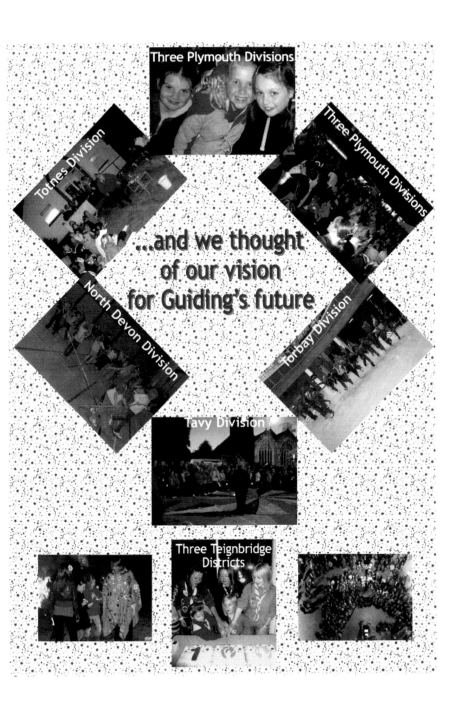

Three Plymouth Divisions

Totnes Division

Three Plymouth Divisions

...and we thought
of our vision
for Guiding's future

North Devon Division

Torbay Division

Tavy Division

Three Teignbridge
Districts

327

Amanda Weldon, Guider and Commissioner in Tiverton Division, with her husband, adopted children and mother, Jillian, a former District Commissioner. Amanda was given the Laurel award for her work for BGIFC in Kuwait, 2011.

Rosamund Stevens as a young Guide in Plymouth, about 1920.

SRS Daring.

Sea Rangers training ship Golden Hinde *on the River Dart.*

Princess Elizabeth.

*'To our District Commissioner with the best of Guide wishes from
Tavistock 3rd Coy. G.G.', 2 August 1919.*

SRS Delight, *Torquay, Skipper Miss S. G. Clarke with their Admiralty recognition pennant, 1951(?).*

Laira Sea Rangers, 1952.

Sea Rangers of SRS Delight *building their own dinghy, 1954–5.*

Lady Clinton, left, accompanying the Princess Royal, 1928.

Camp on Ash site, Taw Bottom, 1995.

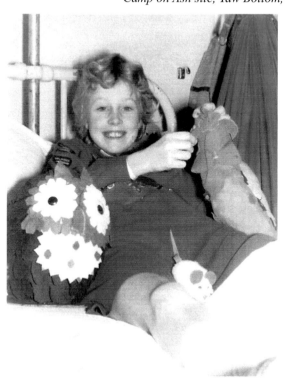

Elburton Brownie Sally Fear in Mount Gould Hospital doing her Toymaker badge, 1977.

Brownies at Campsite Capers, Taw Bottom, 22 May 1999.

The centenary stone at Taw Bottom, 2010.

Lady Clinton, Patron of Devon Girlguiding (in the middle) visiting Taw Bottom, 1999.

Centenary camp at Woodlands Theme Park, near Dartmouth, where nearly 900 girls had a weekend of fun and adventure, 2010.

The Princess Royal (Princess Mary) leading a parade in Plymouth in 1928. The Devon standard given to Lady Clinton, carried behind the Princess's standard, was dedicated that day.

Bush Bashing at Taw Bottom. From left to right: Unity Harley, Kathleen Thomas, Sheila Bromridge and Chris Tozer with helpers, 1983.

336

The first photo taken of the 1st Torquay Guides, 1913.

Foky Bradshaw, Ashburton Division Commissioner, with the new division standard, 1985.

King George VI and Queen Elizabeth in 1937, their coronation year.

Activities of R.S. Ringleader, Salcombe. 1983-84.
Eight Point Programme.

Fitness. Gig Leprechaun.

Enjoying the Outdoors
County Pony Trek Weekend.

Arts Creative Ability. Caddihoe Moot.

Relationship
Anglo-German Exchange

Homecraft. Bazaar Sweet Stall.

Giving Service
Cliff House Wood.

Mind.
Meteorology (Yacht master's course)

Character. Law. Promise
District Thinking Day Service

339

Chesterfield House,
LONDON.

July 24th 1928.

Dear Lady Clinton,

I feel I must write and congratulate you on the great success
of Saturday's Rally. It was a great pleasure to me to be
able to attend it and to see so many Guides on parade. I was
particularly struck by the way in which both the Devon and
Cornwall Guides joined in the Rally and as far as I could see
everything went off without a hitch.

I much appreciate the gift of the kite to my eldest son. I
know he will be delighted with it.

I was much impressed by the march past of the Colours, I had
never seen it done in that way before. The whole of the
march past I thought excellent. I only hope none of the
Guiders, Guides and Brownies were any the worse for the
very hot day.

I trust you were not very tired and that the presentation of
your standard went off well - I had not realised when you said
good-bye that you were not returning to Mount Edgcumbe so felt
I must write you a line.

I trust Lord Clinton will have a successful visit to Australia
and a good journey.

Yours sincerely,

Mary.

Letter from HRH Princess Mary, the Princess Royal, to Lady Clinton, 1928.

DEVON GUIDE
ASSOCIATION

1910 - 2000

CELEBRATING **90** YEARS AND
THE NEW MILLENNIUM

THE DEVON COUNTY STANDARD

In 1928, Devon's County Standard was presented to Lady Clinton (Devon's first County Commissioner, 1914 - 1943, one of the first two to be registered at CHQ), thus making it one of the oldest in the country

The emblems represent the Guide Trefoil; the Guide county badge (which was taken from the badge of the Devonshire Regiment) ; Lady Clinton's coat of arms (Antrim arms impaled upon those of Clinton); the Clinton motto "Loyalty is without shame"; sea gulls for the Sea Guides (later Sea Rangers); an owl for Brownies; and the Silver Fish, awarded to Lady Clinton for all her services to the Guide Movement.

Our Standard is very rare in that **nearly all** Guide County Standards bear the Guide motto - "Be Prepared" - ours does not.

MESSAGE FROM THE COUNTY PRESIDENT

This year we look back on 90 years of Guiding, with gratitude for the influence for the good that it has been and, as we start a new century, we can look forward to providing new opportunities to further the aims of Guiding in the years ahead.

Let us, with God's grace, rededicate ourselves to bring the joys of Guiding to the girls and young women of today and tomorrow and may we all enjoy the adventure of Guiding together.

My thanks for all you do and my good wishes go with you all.

Rosemary Howell

MESSAGE FROM THE COUNTY COMMISSIONER

With this brochure comes Thinking Day Greetings, together with my thanks for all you do for Guiding in Devon.

I have tried to give you a brief glimpse into Devon's History, highlighting a small number of the many events that have happened. I hope you will enjoy reading this and treasure it for many years as a souvenir of what has been, whilst eagerly anticipating what is to come.

In 1985, the date of the previous such brochure, Rosemary Howell, as County Commissioner, asked us all "to carry forward with God's blessing into the next century and beyond." Now that we have entered that new century, I reiterate those thoughts.

Please be proud to Guide in Devon and again, "Thank You".

Chris Tozer

COUNTY COMMISSIONERS 1914 - 1999

1914-1943	Lady Clinton
1943-1946	Mrs. Dorothy Ledger
1946-1956	Miss Katherine Parker
1956-1962	Mrs. Shelagh Eastley M.B.E.
1962-1970	Miss Betty Bindloss J.P.
1970-1978	Mrs. Angela Graham
1978-1987	Mrs. Rosemary Howell
1987-1992	Mrs. Mavis Budden
1992-1997	Mrs. Beryl Hitchcock
1997-	Miss Chris Tozer

Guiding in Devon
1910-1999

Lady Clinton	1910 -	The first Guide Company, 1st Exmouth
	1911 -	The first Guide Companies in Devon were Registered.
	1914 -	Lady Clinton was one of the first two County Commissioners to be registered at CHQ.
	1928 -	Visit of H.R.H. Princess Mary to the Devon & Cornwall Rally 21st July. Special rates of 5/6d, Exeter to Keyham, were negotiated.
Mrs. Dorothy Ledger	1946 -	Mrs. Ledger was prepared to write to employers asking for extra holiday for Guiders running camps!
	1946 -	Visit of Chief Scout to Exeter
Miss Katherine Parker	1947 -	County Quota was 1/- per head but it was strictly voluntary!
	1948 -	Trefoil Guild in Devon was formed.
Mrs. Shelagh Eastley	1957 -	A Guide & Ranger Rally was held at Oldway Mansion, Paignton, with the County Commissioner taking the salute.
Miss Betty Bindloss	1964 -	Devon was hostess to 110 American Girl Scouts.
	1969 -	Visit of Queen Mother to Plymouth & Torbay Rangers in May.
	1970 -	Bowerman's Cottage was given by Betty & Dorothy Bindloss, for a small fee, to Devon Guides.
Mrs. Angela Graham		Introduction of Sail Training Grants for Devon members aged 16+ years
	1973 -	There was ill-feeling over the abolition of Sea Rangers. Angela Graham gave a cup for Sea Rangers to row for at Dartmouth Regatta
	1977 -	"Devon Durbar", a pageant at the County Showground, (3000 participants), celebrated Queen Elizabeth II's Silver Jubilee
Mrs. Rosemary Howell	1978 -	The start of a Guide messenger service at County Shows.
	1980 -	A Guiding link with Fiji was forged.
	1982 -	Purchase of Taw Bottom, our County Campsite.
	1983 -	3 day visit to Devon by Lady Olave Baden-Powell.
	1985 -	Badger Camp to celebrate 75 years of Guiding.
		"Rainbow Camps" (which later became "Spectrum") held for "socially deprived" girls ... including one during Hurricane Charlie!
Mrs. Mavis Budden		The word "Management" was introduced into Guiding!
	1988 -	Integrate in '88, a S.W. England Challenge was well-supported.
	1989 -	"We Follow a Star", a celebration of music in Exeter Cathedral. The proceeds bought 2 medallions for the head choristers
	1990 -	Pirates, an international camp held at the new Westpoint Arena. Part of it was televised.
Mrs. Beryl Hitchcock	1993 -	Service in Exeter Cathedral
	1994 -	Saw the new style, A4 glossy, County Report "Guiding in Devon"
	1994 -	Romanian Girls Choir visited Devon and we gave hospitality
	1997 -	Many parties for Rainbows 10th Birthday.
	1997 -	Friendship Camp ... one of the wettest ever! ! Held at Powderham
Miss Chris Tozer	1998 -	Major refurbishment of, Taw Bottom kitchen.
	1999 -	Review of Division/District boundaries.
	1999 -	"Live Wire" began as a means of direct communication, to all uniformed adults, together with direct-mailing of "Devon Star".
	1999 -	Major refurbishment of County Standard.

BOWERMAN'S COTTAGE

This is a cottage, near to Manaton on Dartmoor. It was given to Devon Guides by the Misses Dorothy and Betty Bindloss. It is used for holidays, trainings and meetings for members and friends of Guiding. Its beautiful surroundings encourage everyone to learn about, understand and love the peace of the countryside.

1969

1999

TAW BOTTOM

Devon Guides are proud to own this beautiful site at South Tawton in the centre of Devon and within walking distance of Dartmoor. It has the River Taw along one boundary and contains a great variety of broadleaved trees, wild flowers, birds and butterflies, as well as wild life for the quiet observer. We hope all who visit will explore and enjoy the site and will benefit from the tranquillity of the peaceful surroundings.

Oak Site 1983

Oak site 1999

Chapter 17: THE CALL OF THE SEA

Cruises for young people on replicas of the old sailing ships that traded round the world became possible after the war. The Sail Training Association (now called the Tall Ships Youth Trust) was founded in 1956 and was dedicated to the personal development of young people aged sixteen to twenty-five through the crewing of ocean-going yachts.

The Sail Training Association's first ship was a three-masted topsail schooner named the *Sir Winston Churchill*. Built to take part in the international Tall Ships Race, it was launched in 1966, followed in 1967 by a similar yacht, the *Malcolm Miller*. Both were used by the STA until 2000, when the *Malcolm Miller* was replaced by the *Stavros S. Niarchos*, and later there was the *Prince William*.

Devon Girl Guides sent selected girls on these ships with the help of bursaries from various charities. In the annual report for 1972, the County Commissioner, Angela Graham, wrote:

> The County News Sheet contained a very good account from Rosalyn Stoneman of her cruise in the schooner Malcolm Miller, which I sent to the Devon Northcott Trust who sponsor our girls for these S.T.A. berths. What may not have been generally realised is that Rosalyn is deaf, and in spite of this she had a very good report from the ship. It is heartening to know that these girls are able to overcome their various degrees of disability, and that we, through Guiding, can provide opportunities for them to join in such activities.

Through the 1970s and '80s, Rangers (and later Young Leaders) won bursaries each year from the Northcott Trust, having been selected by a small county committee, and in 1975 two runners-up gained berths on the Ocean Youth Club's ketch, the *Falmouth Packet*. This was a smaller yacht with less expensive cruises, mostly in the West Country, thus giving more girls the opportunity to sail.

From 1978 bursaries were given by the Matthews Wrightson Charitable Trust and the Sidbury Trust and for several years the county sent a girl on both the *Winston Churchill* and the *Malcolm Miller* and three on the *Falmouth Packet*.

During the 1980s Devon Guides helped to raise money for the building of a yacht equipped so that disabled people could sail her together with an able-bodied crew. Tracks were put in for wheelchairs, and people in wheelchairs could be hauled up the mast; they could take the wheel and steer the ship as well as helping to man the sails. Called the *Lord Nelson*, she was launched in 1985, and that year an Exeter Ranger, Helen Lavers, was selected for the maiden voyage. The idea was that each able-bodied member of the crew would accompany someone with a disability, and Helen accompanied a partially-sighted Ranger. Helen wrote this account for the 1985 annual report:

OCEAN CRUISE ON THE LORD NELSON

Nobody is disabled. Ten days on board the Lord Nelson proved it.

The Lord Nelson is a masted sailing ship, equipped for handicapped people, enabling handicapped and able-bodied to work together as a team. High spirits are essential to cope with the mental and physical challenges the sea offers you. One day you could be doing mess duty, cleaning, a graveyard watch (midnight–4 a.m.), scrubbing the decks and middle watch (8 p.m.–midnight).

Our voyage was the maiden one so our route was previously planned, so we could not avoid the weather. However, besides the sea sickness, we had parties and television coverage.

Working with the handicapped is very satisfying especially

on board the Lord Nelson because you're not working for them but with them. By the end of the ten days I'd almost forgotten they were handicapped.

I think the most important thing I learned was that everybody has some sort of handicap. For example some able-bodied crew were scared of climbing the riggings, whereas the handicapped crew were not. Most of the able-bodied crew suffered from sea sickness so that the handicapped people were left to run the ship.

Gradually you get very close to each other, and it is very sad to leave everybody at the end, but the memories will stay with us permanently.

HELEN LAVERS
Ranger Guide, Exeter

When Mavis Budden took over as County Commissioner in 1987, she gave the county a Mirror dinghy, which was kept at Torquay. In the annual report for 1998 she wrote:

Our county's coastline creates a demand for boating and the Shaldon weekends for Guides, mainly spent in the county canoes, have proved very popular. The county's sloop and Mirror dinghy, based at Torquay, have given the girls the opportunity to sail and a few units have boats of their own. Seven Rangers/Young Leaders went on sail training cruises in 1988 and, despite the sometimes inclement weather, all agreed enthusiastically that it was a marvellous experience: two girls are already working and saving for another cruise.

One of the Devon girls who sailed on the Lord Nelson that year and was paired with a disabled girl called Michelle was Rachael Battye. This is her report:

TRIP ON THE STS *LORD NELSON*

I was lucky to have the opportunity to spend one week in June on Britain's most famous flag ship STS *Lord Nelson*. I did not know any other member of the crew but I met Michelle at Southampton on the Quay. The ship looked very nice with all the sails up and we took some photos of her before going on board. On board we met the Medical Purser whose name was Claire and who showed us our bunks. We made up our beds then had to go up to the main mess deck, so that the professional crew could tell us a bit about the ship. We sailed on the Monday and I was on the 5.00 to midnight watch, partnered by Michelle. Halfway through I had a go at the helm. At midnight we went to bed and the 12 to 4.00 watch came on the look-out.

In the morning after we had had breakfast we had what they called 'Happy Hour' which was cleaning the ship. Two watches cleaned the outside and two cleaned the inside of the ship. The crew is divided into four watches, Forward Port, Aft Port, Forward Starboard and Aft Starboard. I was on the Aft Port watch with eight of our able-bodied and handicapped crew. That day we were on the 12 to 4.00 watch. By this time we had arrived in Plymouth and after we had tea we went ashore together for the evening. While we were anchored in Plymouth Sound, I climbed the rigging. Some of the crew found it rather difficult, but Kieran, one of the men in charge, went up with me and I really enjoyed it. I was very pleased afterwards that I had been up so high and Michelle took a photo of me when I was at the top.

We then went to the Scilly Isles, but as we went past Land's End it was extremely rough going and we were all sea sick. However, it did not last long and it soon became calm again. On Wednesday morning we arrived in the Scilly Isles and after 'Happy Hour' went ashore to explore. All too soon it started to rain, so we found a cave where we ate our lunch. Then Claire, the Medical Purser found us and told us we had to get back to the ship quickly. Apparently there was a dock strike at Swansea, our destination and we had to get there as quickly as possible. On the Thursday evening we anchored outside Combe Martin and enjoyed a sing-song on deck. On Friday we arrived at Swansea to find the dock strike was over, so there was no problem. We went together to the Flying Angel where there was a lot of food and drink set out on the tables and people there were singing songs.

We then went back on board. I enjoyed the week very much; it was quite hard work as we were either on watch, having 'Happy Hour' or helping in the galley, but I made a lot of friends, considering I did not know any of the crew at the beginning of the week.

I should like to thank all the Guiders who made it possible for me to go.

Rachel Battye 1988

In the annual report for 1993, Sue Brown, Senior Section Adviser, wrote:

> Five Rangers accepted the challenge of the sea – all reporting exciting sailing adventures and when seeing photographs of them at the top of the masts of these tall ships, we realise what an achievement it really was.

One of these was Helen Crane who sailed on the STS *Sir Winston Churchill*. She wrote in her log:

> On our afternoon of arrival, on-board training began. We had to climb up to the crow's nest, learn about ropes, sheets, sails and the general working of the ship as well as being introduced to our Watch Officer and the rest of the permanent crew. Watches began at 9pm. . . . Today I was a galley rat and it was hard work. We had to peel thousands of potatoes, wash up, clean, set tables and so on, and I was glad to take a quick shower before my well-earned full night's sleep. . . . During our Watch from 12 midnight to 4am the sky was brilliantly clear and we could see myriads of stars – I even saw a shooting star. . . .
>
> When we arrived at the Danish port of Aalborg we were allowed some shore leave and I took the opportunity to phone home. We left again early the following morning and in the evening the weather deteriorated rapidly. It was "All Hands on Deck" to reef sails as a Force 7 gale blew up and huge waves crashed over the bow and on to the decks. The boat was keeling over from side to side. It was quite a frightening experience! However, it subsided and the following day we anchored in a sheltered bay on the south coast of Norway. We were ferried ashore in the lifeboat for a barbecue on the beach after we had swum in the beautiful clear water. . . . We finally sailed into the Humber and went ice-skating in the evening before scrubbing the decks and leaving for home the next day.

From the annual report for 1994:

> "Remember this is not a holiday" we were warned before embarking on a ten day sail training course on the Malcolm Miller. Even so, we had a wonderful time and gained some really worthwhile experience.

Organised into our three watches for eating, sleeping and working, we left Portsmouth and before losing sight of land, practised our "man overboard" and "close tacking' drills until our arms ached from hauling in the ropes. Despite it being calm, the fishes had my lunch!

As we entered the French port of Fecamp we had to "man the yard" which involves climbing up the rigging and positioning ourselves in formation along the yards – the locals love to see it. We entertained the crowd with our favourite rugby songs and just managed to avoid hitting the harbour wall. Although beautiful, Fecamp was not the most exciting place for tourists but we did visit the museum and palace where Benedictine liquor is produced and felt it would have been impolite to have refused the proffered drinks.

The wind backed up considerably and we were delayed for twelve hours. Eventually we sailed towards Dover in a Force 8 gale and my watch had to take down the fore stay sail. Waves were lashing over the fore-deck, making it slippery, we were heeling over and the wind was forcing us over to the windward side where there was nothing on which to clip our safety harnesses. I was terrified!

We made the Belgian port of Zeebrugge from where we went up the canal to Brugge with its narrow streets and canals, delicious cakes and vast selection of beers. Returning down the canal, despite having a pilot, we went aground and eventually we had to summon a tug to pull us off! So we were late leaving Zeebrugge, the tide was against us and another strong wind carried us across to Harwich from where we motored up river to Ipswich.

I would like to thank the Sidbury Trust, the Guide Association and the Sail Training Association South West Region for their generous sponsorship without which I would not have gained this valuable, enjoyable and challenging experience. Nobody leaves a sail training vessel without learning something, not only about sailing, but about themselves as well.

LAURA CRESSWELL

In her report for 1996, Sue Brown wrote:

Two young women took up the challenge of the sea and undertook sail training during the year. This is a wonderful adventure with a generous grant from the County. It is sad to say that in 1997 all places have not been taken up – it is available to anyone over the age of 16 years.

Sailing is not for everyone, and there were many other exciting activities for the girls. But there were always a few girls who went on these cruises each year.

In 2001 Sue Brown reported:

ADVENTURE ACTIVITY OPPORTUNITIES

This year Emma James, Emily White and Hannah Gunn-Johnson gave service at Cathedral Camps and Elizabeth Reed, Lucie Prothero and Angela Biden took up the challenge of the Tall Ships. The following are 'extracts' compiled from their reports.

Elizabeth Reed aboard The Lord Nelson – "An experience I will never forget. My first sighting – huge masts poking towards the blue sky; it looked magnificent. I had another chance to take the Helm, with the sails up, the ship moved off course far more easily. A wonderful sight aloft looking over the French coastline. We hoisted wheelchairs up to the crow's-nest, all heaved at the ropes: David had been waiting for this moment all week! A wonderful learning experience!"

Angela Biden aboard The Prince William – "It was a very clear evening, the stars were just fantastic; never seen them so clearly. I decided if I was going to the very top of the mast now was the only chance; it was amazing; such a sense of achievement and wonder as I looked out across Portsmouth Naval dockyard, it was one that I never want to forget. I learnt a lot about myself: I built up my ability to work in a team, to listen to others, to overcome fear and sickness. The best experience of my life!"

Lucie Prothero aboard Stavros S Niarchos – "My first glimpse – a magnificent ship. 3.30am – watched the sunrise over the horizon; one good reason for being up at this hour in the morning! Climbed the rigging in fairly windy weather, very scary, difficult to tie tricky knots aloft with one hand! But I did it; so pleased with myself; consider this to be one of the biggest challenges for me of the voyage. I took over the Helm to sail the ship out of the North Sea Canal. Truly was the voyage of a lifetime!"

Emma James at Truro Cathedral – "An extremely worthwhile experience. I was apprehensive but excited; up a 20 foot scaffold with a harness, hard hat, dust mask and vacuum cleaner! To clean the huge stone arches above the quire; not as easy as it sounds; to mask tape around the edge of huge stained glass windows and woodwork, so St Mary's aisle could be painted; to dust the intricately carved wood. It was fascinating to see the detail that close and a great sense of achievement. I felt I had achieved a great deal for the cathedral and for myself; built new friendships; fabulous experience!"

In 2002 three young women undertook a sail training voyage.

MORE ADVENTURE ACTIVITY OPPORTUNITIES

Claire Porter aboard the Lord Nelson – "I have just returned from my trip on the Lord Nelson, I really enjoyed it and two people helped me to climb the rigging, but not to the top. I had a bit of seasickness but soon overcame it. I also visited St Malo, this was my first time in France. Many thanks for helping me go on this trip."

Tracey Arscot aboard the Lord Nelson – "We travelled down Southampton Water under motor. After breakfast we set off with the tide to St Malo. All at our allotted muster stations we manoeuvred into the lock, through the port to where we were berthing and secured the ship. It was then time to go and explore!! I was at the main mast helping to pull those who were in wheelchairs up to the platform.

It was our last night on board. I was really sad to be leaving. We set off after breakfast for Plymouth – time to go aloft for the last time to stow the sails – a little more scary on the yards today, the wind was blowing and already heavy sails back onto us making it increasingly difficult to fold the sails for stowing. I was asked to stay for the next trip as Jo (the medical purser) was sick, unfortunately I couldn't stay. Work tomorrow!! An excellent experience, one that I would have hated to miss, I have met many new friends, a few of which I will never forget."

Jenny Gordon aboard the Stavros S Niarchos – "I flew from Gatwick and arrived in Athens; the ship stood in Piraeus harbour. Each bunk was a pipe cot – a canvas hammock supported by two pipes. Approaching lots of islands we had to keep a careful lookout for other vessels, especially fishing vessels; in the dark it was hard to see what was around us. Our sea legs did not suit land at all; walking came with a swaying sensation that made us feel very queasy.

Job done, I descended the mast very pleased with myself despite having shaken the whole time. I took the helm between 3am and 4am – another of the wonderful moments being on ship, the peacefulness and the gentle 'shoosh' of the waves whilst the sun went down. A naval submarine took us by surprise as it was nearly fully submerged; certainly one of the most thrilling moments on the bridge. The voyage challenged me: I learnt more tolerance, developed more patience, the whole experience unlike anything else I have ever undertaken. It is sure to change my outlook on life."

MY TRIP ON TALL SHIP, TENACIOUS

As a Young Leader, about 12 years ago, I was given the opportunity to sail on the *Lord Nelson*, after which I had the bug and wanted to repeat my experience. Last year Devon County offered a place to an adult in the 25–65 year age group, I applied and was successful.

After considering the cost of trips and work commitments, dates that were convenient to me were all fully booked on the Lord Nelson. However, since my last trip a second purpose built Tall Ship, Tenacious has been built by the Jubilee Sailing Trust. Built in their Jubilee Yard in Southampton by shipwrights and volunteers of mixed ability it brought the JST ethos of integration ashore. When I sailed on Tenacious it was just two and half years old with all the advantages of modern technology and all the charm and excitement of an 'old' ship.

On registering I was told I was to buddy a lady named Louise, who had had polio and walks with the aid of crutches, or uses a wheelchair. We left West India Dock and had a lovely run down the Thames where I went aloft for the first time. The following day our destination was Zeebrugge, after which we entered the canal in order to proceed to Brugge. We tied up in time for lunch and then had the rest of the day free to explore the beautiful city with its cobbled streets, mediaeval buildings and canals (not good for the wheelchair users).

The following morning we made our way back to Zeebrugge then headed towards Terhausen, a pretty Dutch town. From Holland we started the surprisingly long run back towards London.

Before going on board this time, I made a personal challenge, when going aloft I wanted to get at least to the first platform unaided, I had not managed this as a Young Leader on the Lord Nelson. I achieved this going down the Thames, and in Ternhausen a group of eight of us climbed to the second platform, then one at a time we were able to climb to the top of the mast, 38.05m high. On entering the Thames estuary I worked on the sails, this time I got to the end of the yard working on the curlings, and then realised I was only being held on by my harness – No Hands – I had pushed all my challenges to the limit.

I was approached to become a relief medical purser and have spent a weekend looking into this when the ship was in Falmouth in July. I have also spent a weekend in Southampton on a Watchleaders course.

Thank you Devon for giving me this fantastic opportunity.

CAROLINE VICKERY

Following the demise of Sea Rangers in the 1970s, local boating carried on, and in 1980 Chris Tozer (Outdoor Activities Adviser) appointed Valerie Stephens as Boating Adviser. During the 1980s Ashburton Division Commissioner Foky Bradshaw, who lived in Shaldon and was very keen on all water activities, started county boating weekends based in Shaldon, which included rowing, canoeing (kayaking) and sailing. The county gradually obtained several canoes, and this activity became very popular.

By the 1990s Plympton Guider Joy (Zaple) and her husband, Clive Ashford, were running canoeing weekends and trainings, and in 1996 Clive was appointed Assistant Boating Adviser (Canoeing) and in 1999 Boating Adviser.

In 2000, canoeing days were reported at Exeter, Ilfracombe

and Plymouth, and several units and districts had canoeing days or evenings. In 2002 canoeing days were held at Tiverton and Exeter. Boating Adviser Clive Ashford was thanked for his enthusiasm and commitment.

Many units have included canoeing as part of their unit programme, using the facilities at Haven Banks, Exeter.

Chapter 18: GUIDING MEMORIES: SOME GUIDING LIVES

FIJI, 16 July – 11 August 1981

Chris Tozer, who was County Outdoor Activities Adviser from 1973 to 1985, described her visit to Fiji with Kathleen Thomas:

In 1980, SW England held an international camp, Interlink 80, and Devon raised money to enable Fijian Guiding to be represented. We raised so much it was decided to send two adult members of Devon Guide Association over to Fiji in 1981, to train, pass on ideas, help in any way they could and to continue to forge the link made. I was one of the two very fortunate people to go, with Mrs Kathleen Thomas (Tommy), who was the County Commonwealth and International Adviser. In addition to trainings of all sections and age-groups we also trained Commissioners, despite neither of us being a trainer.

Our time was incredibly full of meetings, receptions, discussions, speeches, socialising and eating far too much and far too often! For example, day one, after 37 hours of travelling we arrived, had a cup of tea, breakfast, <u>then</u> went to bed for a couple of hours before attending a reception at 11.30 am, another at 1.00 pm, had a meeting with Sereana, one of the two who had gone to the Interlink 80, visited our first school with Guides and had a great deal of food at each place.

This proved to be the pattern throughout our two weeks' stay. We had a truly marvellous time but certainly learnt how <u>not</u> to be a hostess. No time allowed even to breathe.

During our first week we were hostessed by Muslim families. As it was Ramadam, daily there was a strong smell

356

of curry from before dawn. In the 19th century Queen Victoria had sent many Indians to Fiji to do the work as the indigenous population were not renowned for hard work. This did cause some problems as the Indians were not allowed to own land. The second week we lived with indigenous Fijians. Everything was more relaxed, food included suckling pig cooked in a Lovo oven (under the sand and wrapped in leaves and mutton yes . . . mutton, not lamb) BBQ. (very large chops!!).

We visited over 30 schools, meeting some 600 Brownies, Guides and Rangers. All Guiding is within schools, run by teachers. All are incredibly enthusiastic, willing to learn and wear their uniforms with pride. Wherever we went we were treated like royalty, everyone being delighted to meet us and even, many times, asking us why we were not in London for the Royal Wedding! One day we received Yagona – the welcoming ceremony usually reserved e.g. for the Queen.

Places we visited:

The hydro-electric power station for the whole island, a Chief's Buru (home) a gold mine where we had our photograph taken holding a gold nugget worth £12,000, a leprosy hospital and saw where (and how) shoes are made for the terribly deformed feet, a museum to hear of their history and heritage, Fiji Broadcasting Corporation to make a broadcast and a satellite transmission centre where Guides link to others abroad.

What did we learn whilst there?

No need to panic about wet weather alternatives for events!

When describing e.g. how to play ladders, be explicit. Girls run between the legs not <u>on</u> them!! Luckily everything was played barefoot, though not so good when doing barefoot orienteering in a mangrove swamp with toads.

Garlands made with real flowers also had many real ants which ran around our necks! These, when no longer needed, are thrown into a river, not a dustbin.

Fijian-time prevailed! If the time for the next event hasn't actually arrived, we're not late!

Tea made with condensed milk and a great deal of sugar doesn't resemble tea at all.

The indigenous Fijians are, like the Welsh, wonderful singers. These Guides also camp but the Indian Guides do not. We learnt Fijian plaiting.

What did we impart? I would like to think they gained as much from us as we did from them. We 'put our all' into our many trainings and activity sessions but this list is not as long as the one above.

Despite Fiji, at the time, being a developing nation they certainly taught us a great deal about humanity, loyalty, having a faith, but not how' to hostess people. Many days Tommy and I were absolutely shattered by about 9.30 . . . in the morning! As we spent little time in the capital Suva but most time in little villages we certainly learnt how the bulk of the population live and work together in harmony.

It was a truly marvellous experience; one of the best of my Guiding career, for which I thank Devon County Executive of the time. On my return I started a Guide Unit in Babbacombe (Torquay), using Fijian Patrol badges – Anthurium, Bougainvillea, Hibiscus and later these were added to with Orchids and red and white Roses as the unit grew. 1st Babbacombe Guides still is a thriving unit.

Chris Tozer has done a huge amount of Guiding in Devon and South West England. She has run Ranger, Sea Ranger and Guide units, has been County Ranger Adviser, Outdoor Activities Adviser for the county and Region, Programme and Training Adviser, trainer, mentor, chair of Bowerman's Management Committee, County Editor and has held various posts at Foxlease and Guide Headquarters. She was County Commissioner from 1997 to 2003 and wrote about some of her best moments in this post:

Probably one of these was purely the meeting and chatting with the vast number of friends I have made through my Guiding. It has never ceased to amaze me how, despite at times having to make difficult decisions, the friendships made then remain to this day.

Achievements, truly within the spirit of Guiding, were the local meetings held, especially in the Division of Tavistock and Okehampton, during the review of boundaries within Devon which resulted in the Division being split in two; Tavy and Okehampton Divisions. The two towns are so far apart across Dartmoor they had little in common with each other for joint events, apart from the vast distances to travel.

Other successes which gave me great satisfaction during my time as CC were the revival of DJC [Devon Junior Council] and the creation of our own Singing Circle, both of which survived and flourished for many years though both have now folded [2017].

An event which gave me great pleasure (and I hope to those attending) was Hope 2000 – a day of activities at the newly-created Westpoint on Midsummer's Day in the year 2000. Approximately 5,000 of our young members took part and even the weather was kind to us.

. . . and some of my other treasured memories include being presented to the Queen in St James' Palace; and the totally unexpected privilege of being asked to be County OAA at the tender age of 26!

Chris can surely boast that twenty-nine of her former Rangers, Sea Rangers and Guides have become Guiders – a wonderful endorsement of her Guiding skills. She was appointed County President in 2014.

BERYL PAUL

I first came to live in Devon in 1956, and very soon I was contacted by the District Commissioner, Mrs Mabey, and asked if I would take on the 1st Teignmouth Guides. Their Guider had left and a mother with no Guiding background was trying to run the unit. She welcomed me with open arms and became my lieutenant. It was quite a challenge as it was a large, lively unit. When I asked them if they went for hikes, etc., they said that they never went out from the Guide hut as there was nowhere to go! As I had been Guiding in Birmingham and took my Guides out a lot, I was astonished, and we soon started going on Saturday hikes and cooking on the banks of the Teign.

Mollie Brice was the Guider of 2nd Teignmouth – the grammar-school company – and she took me under her wing, took me to Dartmoor and drove me to trainings, etc. In 1957 Betty Bindloss, the Division Commissioner, organised a division camp at Buckland in the Moor, where five or six units camped separately but close together, with some organised activities. One was a paperchase on Buckland Beacon in the evening, and some of my Guides got lost. Betty drove me round in her car under the moor looking for them, and when they were found (it was then dark) she put me to bed with a hot drink because I had been so upset! Rosalie Hacon was in the camp next to us with a boarding-school company, and she asked me to get my girls to talk in whispers as her girls were not used to noise!

We had other company camps, and when 2nd Teignmouth camped at the World Camp in Windsor Great Park in 1957 I took a coachload of Guides to visit for the day. An abiding memory was when Lady Baden-Powell came on to the platform and everyone threw their berets in the air.

I left Teignmouth in 1959, and my Teignmouth Guides came up to Stratford-upon-Avon to camp together with my new unit the following summer.

I returned to Devon in 1966 to take up a teaching post at Dame Hannah Rogers School in Ivybridge. Ruth Reed, a physiotherapist at the school and also a County Camp Adviser, roped me in to helping with the Guide unit at the school, of which she was a captain. All the girls were Brownies, Guides or Rangers, and they all enjoyed their Guiding very much as it was completely different from school. In those days about half the children were mobile, and with the mobile girls pushing the chairs of the immobile we were out of doors as much as possible. We went on nature trails, treasure hunts and even did some outdoor cooking. Badge work was adapted so that even Cook and Laundress badges were possible from a wheelchair. I remember Sally, who had no speech and was chair-bound, with only movement in her big toe, lighting a fire with two matches and cooking on it for her Second Class!

A highlight from this time was an indoor camp, held at Dewerstone Scout Hut on Dartmoor. All the Guides and Rangers went, with some local Rangers coming to lend a hand – very good for them and for our girls to mix. We even did some outdoor cooking and there was a lovely outdoor campfire.

I became Brown Owl to the seven Brownies at Dame Hannah's and persuaded Ruth Howell to come and help. She brought her Brownie-age daughter, who later went in for children's nursing, and says that it was her time with DHRS Brownies that made her decide on her career.

The new Guide programme was launched in 1968. I was District Commissioner and also a Trainer, and we had been training Guiders towards the Eight-Point Programme for some time (which was not always welcomed by the Guiders!) and we had been asked to have a big ceremony with the press, etc., in each district when the handbooks arrived. We had decided that the whole of Ivybridge District should come to Dame Hannah's, where a pony and trap would bring the books to be distributed. But something went wrong and the books were not ready on the expected day, so the launch had to be put off at very short notice. Eventually, though, the books were ready and there was a good gathering to receive them.

In 1969 Beryl Paul went to Kenya and then Rhodesia as a full-time Guider Trainer. Later she ran the Guide Club in London and then, back teaching in Devon, she was in turn Kingsbridge District Commissioner, Totnes Division Commissioner and Devon Lones Adviser, and she edited Devon Star *for ten years – and joined the Trefoil Guild.*

VALERIE STEPHENS

I joined the 1st Marychurch (Torquay) Guides in 1947 as a result of going to a hobbies exhibition in the town hall. The Guides had a display showing a camping scene, and there and then I decided to be a Guide. We followed the Guide programme of the time, and I became Patrol Leader of the Chaffinches and then the Kingfishers. The highlight of the year was going to camp. This was always at Miss Needham's farm at Manaton, which seemed a world away from home, both in distance and way of life.

A number of my friends already belonged to the Sea Rangers, and when I heard that it was planned for them to have a Crew Holiday, staying in Woking and going to London for the coronation, I decided to join them, and the following year, 1953, we saw the coronation procession from the Mall – quite an experience!

My Sea Ranger days were happy ones, and I particularly liked the boating aspect of it, whether in and around Torquay Harbour or participating in local regattas – Dartmouth being a favourite because of all the activities going on, especially the fair. Being a Ranger gave me many opportunities I would not otherwise have had, like sailing to France and the Channel Islands. Visiting Belgium for Expo 9 and holidaying in Austria gave me a taste for travelling abroad.

Before college I helped with the Brownie Pack and then a Guide company, but I ended up staying with the Rangers as their leader from 1959 to 1985. In 1979 I became District Commissioner for Torquay North District, but my Rangers were in Torquay Central District, which caused problems and extra work at times. Then I was asked to be Division Commissioner, a position I held for eight years and thoroughly enjoyed as I got to know units and Leaders from all three Torbay towns.

With the pressure of my teaching work increasing, I decided I had to give up something – I was also County Boating Adviser at the time and treasurer for Torquay Districts – so I gave up as Ranger Leader, and remained as an Assistant Leader because I had the boating qualifications needed for the summer programme. I finally finished in 1993. A gap of five years and I was back again as Division Commissioner for a further six years, until it was dictated that I came out of uniform.

Having retired, I became a member of the Trefoil Guild, so I have been a member of the Guide movement for sixty-one years. I have gained a lot by being a member of such a worthwhile association – fun, friendship and knowledge – and am very grateful for everything and everyone who has contributed to my Guiding life.

ANNELIESE BARRELL

Anneliese Barrell, Guider, trainer and hard-working Trefoil Guild member, writes about her role as the County Adviser for Members with Disabilities.

It was in 1989 that I was asked to take on this role. I was a paediatric physiotherapist and was also working with young adults with a learning disability, which gave me an insight into the problems that can be experienced by young people and their families when having to cope with what is often unknown and very frightening. I was also a licensed trainer and tutor, which meant that I was often asked to train other Guide Leaders about disability and to enable them to meet disability without fear of the unknown and of being helpless in an emergency.

At that time there were two special units for Guides and Brownies with disabilities – one in Exeter at a school specifically for children with a hearing impairment and the other at the Dame Hannah Rogers School for children with cerebral palsy in Ivybridge. Our then County Patron, Lady Morley, who had a hearing disability, wanted to visit the Exeter unit with me. I remember her sitting with the girls, showing them a craft and expecting quite a high standard of performance. She took a great interest in what they and I were doing.

Integration was not as it is now. There were these 'special schools'. But girls with a disability which could cause issues with other girls and their Leaders (for example, those with a learning disability, behaviour or communication problems) were not usually welcomed into mainstream units. Thankfully this has all changed, and disability is becoming more widely accepted as being part of the 'norm' and girls are integrated where possible.

My role was very rewarding and enjoyable; it was not without its difficult times, but the joy of seeing someone who was disabled become fully integrated into a Guide or Brownie unit was wonderful. Often I would be asked to visit a unit to assess what was happening when a girl was causing anxieties because of her disability. The solution was usually so simple and the issue was resolved, having initially been caused by fear of the unknown.

I remember a very enlightening experience when asked to visit a Brownie Pack where there was a very disruptive Brownie causing all sorts of problems and behaviours among the other girls. I started by observing what was happening: she was trying to get involved in the activities, but I could see that she was having communication difficulties, not being heard and being ignored, so her behaviour became increasingly difficult. I tried signing to her using the Makaton sign language and she responded immediately and calmed down. I talked to her Brownies and the Brown Owl, explaining that she was only difficult because she was unable to get people to understand her. The six then had to do a competitive activity and the sixer, realising that the girl was trying to join in, let her and she helped them produce the winning result. The change was noticeable, the other girls realising that they had a part to play in helping her to understand. Just a small intervention could bring about big changes. But it was not always like that – I did have to recommend to some parents that for the sake of others in a unit their daughter had to be excluded. These occasions were rare and occurred when outbursts of violent behaviour caused health and safety issues.

I was also involved in Riding for the Disabled and acted as physio for several groups. The Guides in my Guide unit also helped with the local RDA group, and that introduced them to girls less able than themselves and gave them an insight into what it was like – one girl with cerebral palsy described it to me as "being shut in a telephone box shouting for attention and not being heard by those outside".

I really enjoyed the training part of the role, which I undertook for the South West Region, as I met and trained other advisers and also learned from them. I think that being the Adviser for Members with Disabilities was one of the most fulfilling roles that I have had in Guiding. I became very aware of how much we ask of and depend on our leaders, and also on the parents and the girls in order to work, play and have a good time together. To change perceptions and encourage happy and meaningful integration was always my aim and I hope that I achieved it most of the time.

SHEILA WOOLDRIDGE

Sheila Wooldridge and her husband, Alan, came to live at Lapford in Devon when Alan retired from the army. She soon became involved in Guiding – she was Division Commissioner for Tiverton from 1984 to 1987, and then when this large division was divided she became Commissioner for the new division of Mid Devon from 1987 to 1993. She was County Commonwealth and International Adviser from 1989 to 1994.

Sheila writes about her time Guiding in Germany with BGIG (British Guides in Germany), 1973–9.

I spent a busy and interesting two and a half years as Commissioner for Guiding in Berlin. There was a very international aspect as the city was controlled by French, American and British forces. It was also a time of liaison with the German Youth Organisations, who were very involved with rehabilitation work. The time came for this group to be readmitted to the Scouts. Because the groups were both boys and girls I was part of the organisation for preparing for this special event, and we spent many happy occasions sharing events with British Scouts in Berlin.

When Alan moved to Rheindahlen – the headquarters of British forces – I was approached by the retiring Commissioner for British Guides in Germany to take over her role. It was agreed by the military that I could have transport to enable me to visit all parts of this very large area, including Berlin. I was very fortunate to find a secretary and good friend – an RAF wife. I had responsibility for several thousand girls and their Leaders, most of whom would frequently be on the move in and out.

I had excellent communications and support from London with memorable visits from Vivienne Vaughan-Cox, who was responsible for all British Guides overseas and was such FUN! I've never known anyone better at Brownie games. Sheila Walker, the then Chief Commissioner, who was a very special lady, spent a whole week with me, travelling far and wide. Stella Cunliffe, a highly respected Guider from South-East England came to help and support our outdoor work. She determined that I would go to camp (not allowed in Birmingham in wartime when I was a Guide) – she succeeded and we had a delightful few days in North Germany, helped as always by the military, and I have fond memories of sleeping serenaded by nightingales. Our Camp Adviser was a teacher in one of the army schools so was with us for several years and later became Guider-in-Charge at Waddow.

I was invited to join in the UK County Commissioners' Conferences, which were always a learning experience for me, as in BGIG we always had flexible rules to suit our often unusual situations and differing communities. A memorable invitation was to Westminster Abbey for the Lady Baden-Powell Memorial Service.

Liaison with British Scouts was always good and much valued. I was invited to speak at one AGM to explain the Guide Association's position on remaining a single-sex organisation – a somewhat intimidating afternoon!

1977 was the Queen's silver jubilee. She was to visit British forces for a special parade to take the salute. I organised a competition for all units to write a letter of congratulations to the Queen. The best were sent to London, and along with the acknowledgement came an invitation for the winning girls and their leaders to meet the Queen . . . DURING THE PARADE! What a day!

Just before I left, Vivienne arrived to join in my final Leaders' gathering, and I was surprised and very honoured to be presented with the Beaver Award. It is one of my proudest possessions, and because this award no longer exists it is often a talking point when worn on special occasions.

I continued to speak up for BGIG at council meetings for a short while after returning to Devon, where I spent an interesting and involved thirty years within Guiding and later the Trefoil Guild.

Colonel A. G. Wooldridge, OBE, Sheila's husband, Alan, was honorary treasurer to Devon Guides from 1991 to 1998 and looked after the county's finances extremely well.

BERYL HITCHCOCK

In June 1946 I made my promise as a Guide with the 1st Pinhoe Guide Company at the age of twelve years. This was of course just after the war ended and I had only just moved to Pinhoe with my parents.

During the war I was an evacuee, having been sent from London, with many other children, on the train, with my gas mask and little case at the age of six. I spent a short unhappy time in Heathfield, Sussex, but came back to London after a family tragedy.

After a short while back in London I came to Devon as an evacuee for five quite traumatic years.

Eventually I was reunited with my parents, but had meanwhile become a very insecure teenager with not much confidence in myself.

Joining the Girl Guides changed all this, as fortunately my captain was a person who encouraged us all to face challenges and to achieve success in whatever we attempted to do. The Guide Promise and Laws became a way of life for me and were always at the heart of all I did in Guiding and otherwise. My favourite Guiding activities were camping, all outdoor activities and international events.

I became a Patrol Leader, a Company Leader and a cadet and eventually became captain of the 1st Pinhoe Guides and Brown Owl to the 1st Pinhoe Brownies. I married and had twin girls and another daughter, who all became keen members of the Guide movement.

Guiding had given me back my self-esteem and confidence, and all through bringing up my family and helping my husband to run a business I never gave up. After running a district and division I felt very privileged to have been asked to become County Commissioner for Devon Guides. During this time I obviously travelled around the county and met some amazing Leaders, who were all encouraging young people to become secure and confident adults through Guiding.

I am now a keen Trefoil Guild member with many Guiding

friends throughout the world; and although I experienced Guiding in other countries and overseas, I will always be thankful that I became a Girl Guide in this wonderful county of Devon.

LAURIE PEARSON

There are so many special things that have happened in my Guiding life over the last fifty years, but apart from the time spent with the girls, it has to be the out of doors. Boating was the activity that brought me back into Guiding when I moved to Devon. The local Sea Ranger crew, SRS *Research*, desperately needed someone to help with the boating and that was all I was going to do, I said at the time – that lasted just six months! I soon became a Leader, not only with the Rangers but also with the 1st Dartmouth Guide Unit.

My love of the outdoors soon led to taking the unit to camp. A few years later, much to my surprise, I was asked to be the Division Camp Adviser. This meant that I got to visit camps held in the division and being part of the County Outdoor Team, which included helping at camp training weekends. How I enjoyed these times! Then I got another surprise: I was asked to be the South West Devon County Camp Adviser. What experiences I enjoyed over the next five years, making new friends, working with a great team of advisers, learning so much and having fun at the same time!

Then came the ultimate honour: at a Region Outdoor Activities Weekend, Mavis Budden, who was then County Commissioner, asked me to be the County Outdoor Activities Adviser. This was the icing on the cake. 'Could I really do this?' With lots of support and encouragement I said yes please, and how glad I am that I did! Over the next seven years I worked with a wonderful group of advisers in the county, then in the Region, helping to organise both county and Region camps and Activities Weekends. We had so much fun working with the Guides at Patrol Leaders/ Seconds Activities Days, organising trainings for camping and the Walking Safely Scheme (this enabled me to enjoy walking in the Peak District to gain my own qualifications). After enjoying archery at Activities Weekends, I took up the challenge to be an instructor; this gave me great times working with units both locally and at our beautiful county campsite. Canoeing became popular in the county, so canoes were purchased for the county – more great fun organising County Canoe Camps. It also gave me the privilege of meeting Prince Edward at a Youth Day at Bicton Park. He thought our canoes looked like bananas – they were yellow with black fenders at each end!

When the time came for me to finish as Outdoor Activities Adviser at our county camp, aptly named 'Friendship', I felt sad, but looking back I had enjoyed so many wonderful times, visiting parts of the county and Region that I would never have discovered had it not been for Guiding and, most of all, the many great friends that I have made over the last fifty years – thank you, Devon, for treasured memories.

Laurie's Scouter husband, Clive, was always a great help to her and to Devon Guiding, especially with manual work at Taw Bottom.

KATE HARDING

After poor experiences as a child in South Yorkshire at two failing Brownie Packs and a Guide company that sometimes had as few as six members and never went to camp, I had, by my mid teens, determined that Guiding could be great if tackled properly. So, at sixteen I was running a Brownie Pack and, being keen to prove myself, was frustrated to be denied access to trainings and made to wait to take the written test for a warrant until I was eighteen. Little did I know this was just the start of an amazing journey through Guiding, which eventually took me to becoming a County Commissioner.

University in London followed, where I joined the Scout and Guide Club, only to find that most members just wanted a good time rather than getting involved with units. There were some fun events, however, and a camping trip to the Norwegian mountains was definitely a highlight. Throughout the three years I also ran a Brownie Pack in a very rough and disadvantaged area of St John's Wood (there certainly was a seedy side to that part of London in those days), where I felt the children needed something to belong to even if the parents gave no support.

In Nottingham for a year doing my teacher training, I contacted the Brownies at the local church, and helped there with the Guide unit too. This was an exciting time in Guiding, with a new programme being introduced.

My first teaching post was in Twickenham and I soon found myself a Brownie Pack at a church near Kew Gardens, where the friendly and enthusiastic vicar, who had daughters in the group, was very supportive. I first came across the concept of the district meeting, and I developed a style of record keeping that stayed with me all my Guiding life; I now have a wonderful archive to dip into and recall faces from the past.

With my husband, John, I moved to Devon in 1971, and as a qualified Brownie Guider was soon approached by the local District Commissioner in Tavistock – who asked me to take over a Guide unit! Then within three months the attached Brownie Pack was leaderless too, so I stepped in there as well and remained running both units until 2010.

Annual Guide camps and Pack Holidays, more changes in programmes, uniforms, administrative procedures, having three children, etc., were taken in my stride, but I was always looking for a new challenge. So I volunteered to try running a training session at County Day. Encouraged and aided by Elizabeths Weir and Smith, I eventually gained my Training Licence in 1982. Over the next twenty-five years this took me to all parts of Devon and the other counties of South West England, as well as to Foxlease. As a Brownie specialist it also opened the route to becoming an adviser for Devon and South West England; it took me to New Zealand as the UK representative at a Brownie conference, and gave me an insight into the world of CHQ when chosen to be part of a small panel rewriting the Brownie handbook. Chris Tozer must have thought these experiences useful when appointing me

County Programme and Training Adviser and an assistant to her as County Commissioner.

My family have always been extremely supportive, through all the camps, training weekends, evening meetings, etc. And trips abroad sometimes meant weeks away. Most notable of these was three weeks in Kenya helping the Guide Association there on projects for underprivileged girls in Nairobi, Mombasa and a UNHCO refugee camp on the Sudanese border. What an eye-opener that was! There were some wonderful fun trips too, with fellow Devon Guiders – to Our Cabana and Sangam. What a lovely combination, exploring interesting foreign places with good friends from Devon, all in the wonderful spirit of Guiding. So, while I have given large chunks of my life to Guiding, it has given me lots in return.

Being a unit Guider is, I have always felt, the most important job in Guiding. If there were no active units there would be no need for Commissioners or advisers. It is so rewarding to meet women years later who can still recall and enthuse about their time in Brownies or at Guide camp. At a recent reunion of the Guide unit I worked with for many years, women who were the first members in 1953 recounted their exploits, as did those from intervening years and then the Guides of today listed all the things they enjoy doing now. We were all linked by commitment to Guiding and loyalty to our unit.

For over forty years I was part of the leadership team of both a Brownie and Guide unit which met on the same night in the Methodist church hall. I say team, because it takes more than one to do the job properly and developing bonds with fellow leaders is vital; thus I am fortunate to have made such long-lasting and loyal friends. I also held a Rainbow warrant for a time, and also encouraged teenagers to become Young Leaders and complete their warrant by the time they were eighteen, so they could be leaders wherever their lives took them. One year we raised lots of money to take them on a trip to stay with Guides in Vancouver, which for many was a first flight and a never-to-be-forgotten experience.

Goodness knows how many first-aid courses, district meetings,

Brownie Revels, parades, trainings, Thinking Days, parties, service projects, etc., I must have attended over the years. Guide camps, Brownie holidays, day trips, church parades, charity events . . . the list goes on. Then there is the planning, paperwork, form filling, accounts – all the background work that helps to give the girls the best possible Guiding experience, keeping them safe and making it worthwhile and enjoyable for them as well as the Leaders. For a Guider, knowing you have done the best for your girls is rich reward, and, while gaining awards in recognition of services to Guiding is of course satisfying, it is knowing that thousands of girls have been able to enjoy the experiences and activities I have helped provide for them that I feel is my greatest achievement.

Then I was asked to be County Commissioner. What an honour, and a responsibility! Always prepared to take on a challenge, and confident of having family backing, time and plenty of Guiding experience, there seemed no reason to refuse.

My main concerns when taking on the job were firstly the age-old problem of finding people to do all the various jobs involved in running a county, and secondly dealing with any major problems that might arise. There is always backing from Region and CHQ experts, but these issues remained a concern over the whole five-year term. I had to learn to delegate jobs I would have enjoyed doing myself, to be more tactful than ever and to always be aware of useful PR opportunities. A County Commissioner needs to be seen to offer encouragement, praise and recognition whenever and wherever appropriate.

The time commitments of the job were no problem. Just as well, because every meeting also involved thinking time, paperwork, preparation, travelling time (the road to Exeter and on to Salisbury was by then a well-worn path) and follow-up notes, telephone calls, etc. I enjoyed being County Commissioner and willingly took on all it entailed, but writing copy for *Devon Star* did stretch me sometimes – "Surely another month hasn't gone by already! What can I say this time?" Also, I strongly believed that writing thank-you letters when people have given their time to help you or invited you to their special events is one of the major parts of dealing with volunteers and showing that you care.

During my term, the Region decided to hold its Advisers Conference in Tiverton and then another year its AGM in Plymouth, which, while an honour, also involved much work by many Devon personnel. The most distressing part of my time as County Commissioner was the sad loss of our County President, Mavis Budden, following a road accident. She was such a wise mentor and much loved member of Girlguiding in Devon; we organised a special memorial service for her in St Andrew's Church in Plymouth. I certainly missed her quiet, conscientious counsel.

Meeting so many different people, exploring distant and unknown corners of the county, presenting well-deserved awards to dedicated leaders – these were some of the pluses. Events such as the Big County Sleepover, DELTA Camp, BP weekends and Guider residential trainings were a joy to be part of and made me so proud to belong to such a large and vibrant county. I am richer for the experience, for I have many fond memories and have made long-standing friendships throughout both Devon and the Region. I sincerely hope other women will be enthusiastic and continue to promote Guiding in Devon well into the future.

MARY JONES

Devon Guiding began for me when I joined the 38th Exeter St Mark's company in the late 1940s. Meetings started with marching into a horseshoe and colours being paraded. Subscriptions of 1d. were collected by our Patrol Leaders, then badge work and games followed with prayers and taps to close the evening. On the first Sunday of each month we marched to church carrying our world and company flags come rain or shine, our wide-brimmed hats firmly anchored! In the following year our hats and uniforms changed, but we still camped in bell tents, cooked on open fires and hay boxes, and slept on straw palliasses.

Helping with a Guide unit that met each week for patients in the Exeter Orthopaedic Hospital taught me a great deal and formed the service part of my Queen's Guide Award, which I gained in 1951. Miss Dyson began the first cadet unit in Exeter, which I then joined. Four of us went to the International Camp held at Hall Barn in Buckinghamshire as Service Crew (one of the others was Beryl Hitchcock!).

Returning after some years away from Devon in 1966 was a great joy, and with a growing family – like many mums – I soon got involved with Guiding again, at home and in the county. To be Assistant County Commissioner to Beryl Hitchcock was a privilege and, with Elizabeth Smith her other assistant, we had many happy Guiding times visiting units, camps, special occasions and events.

As years go by the Trefoil Guild has always been a wonderful way of keeping in touch with friends in Guiding, and much of what Guiding has to offer. Being asked to serve as County President for some years was both a surprise and a delight for me. Thank you. Guiding in Devon has enabled me to be part of this county's wide range of interest and variety, and to keep in touch with the very special people who make it what it is.

ELIZABETH SMITH

I moved from Hampshire into Devon in August 1982 to take up the headship of St Joseph's Primary School in Newton Abbot. Guiding has been a good part of my life from Brownie days, so I arrived in Devon with Guiding friends already – through my work as a trainer, around the UK and overseas, and was able to become a member of the county team. I enjoyed working with the Junior Council and encouraging the older girls to begin to participate in County decisions and planning. Many of the ideas we formulated in Devon became a prototype for other counties.

Involvement with the Mount Edgcumbe Scout and Guide Jamboree 1986 was another highlight, especially the moment when the clouds dispersed in time for the display of the Red

Arrows team to fly right over the jamboree site!

Another interesting project was the 'Into Europe Challenge' planned with Sheila Wooldridge, who was the County International Adviser at the time. Together we planned a challenge to encourage each unit to find out more about the European countries we were about to join in the Common Market. The winners of each section certainly enjoyed their prizes! Again, other counties were able to make good use of our idea, especially the excellent posters for each country that Sheila was able to organise.

I was particularly fortunate during my time in Devon to be Assistant County Commissioner both to Mavis Budden and to Beryl Hitchcock – jointly with Mary Jones. I enjoyed both these appointments, and the variety of opportunities they provided. I was able to experience the roles of both District and Division Commissioner for myself. I really appreciated the welcome I found around the county.

But the best part of Devon Guiding for me was the time I had as unit Guider for the Kingskerswell Guide Unit, and later as Assistant Leader with the Ogwell Brownie Unit. There are so many clear and happy memories of both these units – from the village butcher spending an evening with the Guides, teaching all of us how to fillet a fish correctly, to the twenty-four Brownies ALL making bread animals, at the same time, for the harvest display in the church! Good times, indeed.

I moved to live in Somerset in August 1999. I enjoyed living and working in Devon, and will always feel that the nineteen years I was a part of Devon Guiding was a highlight of a lifetime in Guiding.

I wish Devon Guiding continuing success, and include my thanks to all who gave me the welcome, and the fun, while I too was a 'Devon Guider'.

RACHEL CORNELIUS

Rachel Cornelius was a stalwart in Devon Guiding with an interesting family history. She lived in Dawlish most of her life and ran Guides there for many years. She was District Commissioner for Dawlish and Starcross from 1961 to 1966, and then County Secretary from 1967 to 1970. She was Angela Graham's Assistant County Commissioner from 1973 to 1975, and Angela wrote in the annual report: 'I have already written in the News Sheet how much her help and support has meant to us all and she will be greatly missed.'

Rachel's nephew Maurice Cornelius was only a few years younger than his 'dear Aunt Rachel', who had helped to bring him up. He was very involved in Scouting, and as Field Commissioner for Scouting in South West England he was invited to become a vice-president of Girlguiding South West England. As such he was involved in the training programme and chaired a committee to raise funds for the purchase of St Ann's Manor in 1996.

Maurice's wife, Maureen, who was a good friend of Rachel's, had an unusual childhood. The family lived in Windsor Great Park and Maureen went to the local school, from where she and several other girls were invited to join the Brownies, who included Princess Margaret, at Windsor Castle. When she moved up to the Guides she was in the Swallow Patrol with Princess Elizabeth as her Patrol Leader. They followed the normal Guide programme, but Maureen remembered there was a lot of emphasis on singing and acting and they all took part in concerts and pantomimes at the castle.

Maureen talked of her frequent association with Princess Elizabeth, especially when they were camping together, which were happy and memorable times, and she succeeded the Princess as Patrol Leader of the Swallows.

For the three or four miles that Maureen had to travel to meetings at the castle, she was collected by soldiers from Windsor barracks and driven in a horse-drawn carriage. The soldiers also helped the Guides with, for instance, pitching tents and digging latrines. The outdoor meetings and camping took place in the grounds of Frogmore.

Maureen was a member of the choir of the Chapel Royal from her schooldays until her wedding in 1955, which took place in the chapel.

Sadly, Maureen died in 2015, having celebrated their sixtieth wedding anniversary, at which she received a special card from her former Patrol Leader.

Maurice kindly gave permission for the above to be taken from a tribute given at the service of thanksgiving for Maureen's life.

BETTY BINDLOSS

Betty Bindloss was involved in Guiding for most of her long life. Growing up in Newton Abbot, she was a Brownie, Guide, Brown Owl, lieutenant, captain, Camp Adviser, trainer, District and Division Commissioner, and at one time ran a cadet company. She said she always wanted to be a Guider because she had such happy memories of Guide activities and the fun of camping.

During the war, as well as doing a lot of nursing, she joined the Home Guard, and when Plymouth was bombed she and other Guiders manned emergency food vans at Home Park and for five days supplied thousands of people with soup and baked beans, etc., cooked on soya boilers.

In 1945 she went with the Guide International Service team to Holland, where they ran a mobile hospital for six months, going to Arnhem five days after the last battle. The team spent three months at Gorinchem, where they fought a typhoid epidemic caused by the bombing of the town sewers. They then ran a hospital for displaced persons in Germany. (Betty's personal diaries are quoted in the little book *A Hospital on Wheels*, by Marjorie Brindley, which tells the story of the Guide International Service).

Betty was given the Beaver Award in 1960. She was County Commissioner for Devon from 1962 to 1970 and then was appointed the first Chief Commissioner for South West England until her retirement in 1975. She remained involved in Devon Guiding through the Trefoil Guild and as warden of Bowerman's, the cottage on Dartmoor that she and her sister had given to Devon Guides.

Outside Guiding she worked for Moral Welfare (the precursor of social work) and from 1952 to 1962 ran the newly formed Diocesan Adoption Society. She was a magistrate for fifty years, chairing the juvenile court, and did much church work.

After a happy retirement on Dartmoor, birdwatching and walking her dogs, she died in 1999 aged eighty-nine.

An obituary writer said of her:

> Betty had a great many friends, who found her friendship bracing and forthright. Never relinquishing her own high standards, derived from her strong Christian faith, she always tried to understand the younger generation, to whom through her Guiding she gave so much.

PATRICIA COWARD

Patricia was a long-serving Guider in Devon who excelled in several different roles and was an inspiration to many, adults and girls alike.

She was a Guide and then a lieutenant in Bathampton before going to live in Rhodesia with her husband, Brian. When Rhodesia became Zimbabwe and life became very difficult for white people under the new regime, Patricia and Brian returned to England with their three young daughters, but they were forbidden to bring anything, including money, with them. Undaunted, they settled in Lapford, and in no time Muriel Foden, the Crediton District Commissioner, was knocking on their door.

Patricia was a draftswoman (among a lot of men) at Exeter University, and managed to fit in a lot of Guiding – including camping, at which she excelled. As County Camp Adviser for North and East Devon, she became a close friend of Laurie Pearson, the County Camp Adviser for South and West Devon, the two having great fun together at Outdoor Team meetings and camp trainings. Laurie remembers the Outdoor Team's first visit to Taw Bottom:

> We hacked our way through undergrowth, both of us muttering that the site was most unsuitable. How wrong we were proved

and over the years we spent so many hours helping to run the Camp Training weekends; both of us would always go home with our cars laden with equipment and the rubbish and Patricia asked, 'why is it always us?' Good training for the County Camp Badger 85 as Patricia was the waste disposal officer!

Patricia and I decided we should get the Licence for running lightweight camps as we would be doing the testing for it, so we took ourselves off to Foxlease for a training weekend and this was followed by an Overnight Expedition into Cornwall. Patricia persuaded her daughter Rachel to be one of the Rangers we took with us. We had found a site on a farm where after a long hike we pitched our tents. We had a good night but woke up very cold (it was the last week in April) and having decided a hot drink was needed I opened up the tent to find the field white with frost. It was then that we learned a hard lesson: do not leave your meths outside at night – it would not light! So being good Guides we gathered up the dry wood we could find and lit a fire. Rachel's reaction was predictable when we took them a cup of tea: who did not know that meths had to be kept in your boots overnight? They certainly did not tell us this at Foxlease.

Patricia was very involved in the running of the County Camp Badger 84 and was Sub-Camp Leader at the Mount Edgcumbe Jamboree in 1986. She was County Outdoor Activities Adviser for a short while before she and Brian moved to Cudham in Kent in 1987 to run the London and South-East England Region campsite, which consisted of ninety-five acres with four camp fields and five Brownie houses, a shop and other amenities. Here she ran a joint unit of Rangers and Venture Scouts.

Back in Exeter a few years later, and having been to Sangam, Patricia helped Sheila Wooldridge with International Guiding. As a member of the Trefoil Guild she was the County Adviser for 'Dark Horse' Challenges, gaining five Dark Horse Venture Awards herself. In 2009 she completed sixty years of Guiding.

Patricia was very proud of the fact that her three daughters and all their families were all involved in Guiding or Scouting. Her husband, Brian, in helping and supporting her in all her Guiding activities, has himself given a huge amount of service to Guiding in Devon. Sadly Patricia died in March 2018 after a courageous battle with cancer. At her thanksgiving service, Laurie in her tribute spoke for all who had known her: "Thank you for your friendship, the fun and of course the memories."

MAVIS BUDDEN

This was a tribute to Mavis Budden following her death in a car accident in 2007. It appeared in *Devon Star*, May 2007:

A Very Special Lady

Mavis attended Bishop Blackall School in Exeter, then read history at London University. She moved wherever her husband Edward's banking career took him, which by the mid sixties was Torquay. They attended Belgrave Church & Mavis taught at the Girl's Grammar School. She reopened the church Brownie Pack & the Guide Unit and was such an enthusiastic leader, both Units were soon on a roller-coaster of learning, enjoyment of the outdoors and especially camping. She was also a District Commissioner whilst in Torquay.

After a spell in Weymouth the family moved back to Devon, Mavis teaching at Plymouth High and later at the hospital school. The strong influence of her Christian faith helped her to inspire & encourage others. Each person was special to her. From 1982 to 1992 Mavis was Brownie Guider of the 12th Plymouth Pack; she also acted as a DC & a Division Commissioner before being appointed County Commissioner in 1987.

During her term as County Commissioner, Mavis crisscrossed Devon, accepting as many invitations as possible, meeting, talking and listening to members in every corner of the country. She really became involved in all that was happening; she knew us and was interested in us. Members of her Executive have memories of well-chaired meetings; everyone recognised Mavis' commitment to her role. She was proud to be the Commissioner for Devon and gave the county her full attention.

She was a people-person. It didn't matter if you were the smallest Rainbow or the oldest Trefoil Guild member, she always made you feel at ease. She encouraged young adults to get involved, revamping the Junior Council. Her great sense of humour will long be remembered, as reflected in DJC's "Mave the Rave" song, written & performed for her CC retirement party.

When Mavis was CC, members of the Region Executive soon realised they had a gem in their midst. She contributed to all discussions & had such superb ideas. If there were contentious issues Mavis always made considered & sensible comments.

She was reasonable and equable; when she felt strongly she never raised her voice – she was always fair, kind and wise. No-one will forget the quiet smile that went with her gentle sense of humour.

On retiring from uniformed Guiding, Mavis became a very active member of the Trefoil Guild, where she was dearly loved. She always seemed to have time – however busy – to listen and wisely advise. Nothing was too much trouble. She served as Chairman for Devon, Treasurer for SW England, as a council member in London and at her death was still National Treasurer. Her humorous tales enlivened many a financial report.

For the last five years Mavis, until her untimely death, was President of Girlguiding Devon – a role she took very seriously. She attended Executive meetings, called in on many county events, served on the Awards Panel and took a leading part in organising AGMs, receptions and liaising with Vice Presidents & Honorary Life Members. Everyone will remember her keen intellect, careful attention to protocol, wealth of experience freely shared and of course that sense of humour – she always had an amusing anecdote to make us chuckle. As a President she was an amazing support and a most reliable sounding-board. She never imposed but was there if needed. Mavis was someone everyone admired; she was much loved and an inspiration to us all.

Baden-Powell said "Your duty in life is to be happy and to make others happy". As well as spreading happiness, Mavis shared the fun & friendship of Guiding among all with whom she came into contact. Four years ago she & Edward moved to Sidmouth, where she continued her service to others by playing a full part in the local church & supporting a nearby home for the elderly, as well as being a loving wife, mother & grandmother. She still found time to be a brilliant ambassador for Guiding throughout Devon, SW Region and the UK.

Chapter 19: MISCELLANEOUS

DEVON STAR

The forerunner of *Devon Star*, known as the county (or Devon) news-sheet, existed since at least 1948. In 1966 Miss K. J. Harper of Torquay took over as editor. Guiders paid for it and complimentary copies were sent to new Guiders. After a year of 'trial and error', which she said had been very enjoyable, Miss Harper wrote this ditty:

> Four hundred envelopes – no addressograph,
> Worn out fifty Biros. . . . Does it make you laugh?
> One side only PLEASE. (What a waste of paper!)
> 'A block of ice, Miss, for your head? Goodness what a caper!'
>
> If I could wave a fairy wand I know what I would do
> I'd wish for all the subs to come the moment they are due,
> Then I'd have time to go and play with Yogi at the Zoo . . .
>
> You wouldn't think I love this task, but honestly it's great!
> To start on next month's News Sheet, I can hardly bear to wait.
> I'm fond of all my readers, too, and now for final yelps . . .
> You needn't be mad to do this job . . .
> BUT GOLLY HOW IT HELPS!!

Miss Harper edited it for ten years. Angela Graham, in the annual report for 1975, wrote:

It was with much sadness that the Newssheet parted from its ten year association with Miss Harper. . . . Happily she is still one of the team as she has succeeded Miss Williams as Queen's Guide Recorder.

She welcomed Mrs Peggy Sawicka in her place, and Miss Gabb, who had taken over from Mrs Whidborne as editor of the annual report. These jobs, she said, like several others such as Badge Secretary and Duke of Edinburgh Award Recorder, receive little publicity, but they are indispensable people 'and they deserve the thanks of all our members'.

In 1977 at Angela Graham's suggestion the news-sheet was renamed *Devon Star*, after the Guide county badge, which was taken from the badge of the Devonshire Regiment.

THE HURDLESTONE CHALLENGE

The Hurdlestone Challenge was started in 1991 by a small group of Scout and Guide Leaders in South Devon, who were inspired by a similar, but much larger, event called the Malvern Challenge. The original organisers were David Wright, Bill Wright and Jeanne Langridge, all of whom had been involved in Scouting and Guiding in South Devon. As Hurdlestone has grown in popularity, so has the number of people organising the event. In 2012 there were over 750 participants enjoying the weekend from all four corners of the county.

The event is held over a weekend, starting on Friday late afternoon with registration, then studying the route and checking kit. Saturday is the Challenge Day itself when members of the Scout and Guide Associations (aged ten and up to fourteen and a half) work in teams of four to six members. They set off for the day and move around the eight-to-ten mile course, stopping at activity bases on the way to gain points towards the Hurdlestone Challenge Trophy. These may include obstacle course, archery, first aid, map and compass work, tug of war, rifle shooting, puzzle corner and water challenge. Over the years, the activity bases have changed and increased in number. In 2012, participants even milked a (model) cow! The 'Sunday FunDay' involves sports and crafts.

Apart from the Scouts and Guides taking part, there is a 100-strong Service Crew of Explorer Scouts, Rangers, Young Leaders and young adults. Mostly these Service Crew members have attended the event in previous years and have chosen to return to ensure the younger members can try some of the things they did themselves as Scouts and Guides.

Units and troops set up their tents on arrival and that's all they have to do. Meals are cooked and supplied centrally to enable leaders to enjoy the event without having to do too much work. Also provided are marquees, water, toilets, gift shop, tuck shop, first-aid cover, safety vehicle, radio control – and lots of fun! It is a great event with teams returning year after year to better their scores.

The vote of thanks to all those who have helped run the event and the presentation of medals and certificates to those teams winning activity bases and being awarded the Hurdlestone Challenge Trophy closes the event at about 4 p.m.

CAMP AT WISCOMBE BAY, near Bigbury-on-Sea
From the Camp Log of Janet (O'Neill) Kirwan, Summer 1951

We went by bus and started walking from Sevenstones to Wiscombe. Miss Lillicrap picked us up near Kingston and took us as far as the farm in her car, and from here we walked down a sloping valley, past some cows and on down to the beach, and here we climbed up some steps and into a small house perched right on top of the cliffs. . . .

Mercy and I had a tent between us and she showed me how to make a bed. Then it was time for tea, and after tea we had a smashing campfire. We washed in the cottage and got ready for bed. . . .

It was a beautiful night and we both lay awake for a long time and then about half past eleven I suggested we go for a walk. So we got up and went to the cottage and sat down. We watched the Eddystone Lighthouse blinking in and out and then we strolled along the beach and back to our tent.

After breakfast on Saturday we went to brail the tents and air the bedding. Ann and Pamela helped me with the tent, and banging in a tent peg I missed the peg and with a mighty wham struck my ankle instead! Oh clever me! I had a lot of trouble with it afterwards.

(*On Sunday morning they went to different local churches.*)

That afternoon we went swimming . . . and had tea on the beach. I had attached myself to Ann and Pamela's Patrol; we walked along the beach and explored some caves, and then decided to explore the cave that night with a torch.

After tea we had a campfire in the woods and I learnt more new songs. By now my ankle was hurting, so I joined the casualty list and had it bandaged. When we went to bed we told Mercy of my idea and she agreed, so about midnight we got up, called for Ann and Pamela and strolled along the beach. Unfortunately the tide was up, and as we could not explore the caves we strolled the other way, munching chocolate and biscuits. It was a bright moonlit night and we sat down on some rocks and watched the lighthouse. About one thirty we all went back to bed. It was sultry.

On Monday we got up early. Had prayers and colours, which we didn't attend. We were all becoming fast friends, so Mercy agreed to shift into the little hike tent with Wendy so that Ann and Pamela could come in with me. . . . Afterwards we went swimming.

After dinner we went up into the woods to cook our tea. We had sausages, bacon and toast. It was lovely. Afterwards, with Anita we got heaps of apples, unorthodoxly. . . . Still, they were very nice, and we had to get more wood for the woodpile. . . . That night, although lights out was at ten thirty, Ann, Pam and I talked for ages afterwards. It was so hot and sultry that we all arranged our beds so that we were half out of the tent, looking up at the clear, starry sky above.

On Tuesday I woke up with a start and lay awake wondering what had woken me up. Casually I glanced above me – on the tent pole and just above my head were a cluster of daddy longlegs; there were twenty altogether because we counted them! Then one moved so with a yell I backed hurriedly out of the tent. Immediately Ann and Pam sleepily enquired what was up. Ann sat up and saw what I saw and also retreated. We dressed gingerly, careful not to disturb them and after breakfast we managed to entice them away from the tent pole!

After dinner we went along to the Bristol Guides further up the River Erme. Our Guides had got friendly with them on Sunday and we had been invited to their camp for the afternoon and 'high-tea-come-supper', finishing up with a campfire. We had a wonderful time and played rounders in the afternoon. After we had a super tea and a super campfire at which I learnt some more new songs. . . . We invited them to come over the next day. They agreed and so we walked back happily to a lovely supper.

On Wednesday we went swimming in the morning and collected more wood and, of course, more apples! Soon after dinner the Bristol Guides came over. We challenged them to the game of rounders. . . . It was very hot playing but the stream cooled us somewhat! Afterwards we had a good tea and then went up into the woods for a super campfire, collecting more apples, and climbing trees to get some wood for the campfire. It was a wonderful day altogether and after the Bristol Guides had left us we had a stew supper and went to bed.

On Thursday after breakfast we got ready a packed dinner and tea to go to Bigbury and Challaborough. . . . We walked over the cliffs to Challaborough. Here we sat down and had our dinner. We tried to open a tin of meat, didn't quite manage it so I tried . . . the tin opener slipped and I cut my finger on the tin!

We looked around Challaborough, then we walked around to Bigbury. We had the germ of an idea – to have a midnight feast Friday night, the night before we go. For this we had to get food. . . . We tried to get some cake and sweets. . . . At last we found a shop and went to buy some cake. As we were purchasing our goods, Miss Lillicrap, Mercy and the cadets came back from their stroll and as we were caught on the hop we looked frightfully guilty, though Mercy said no, when I asked her afterwards.

We had heaps of stuff and carted it back with us in our haversacks. We walked back over the cliffs, having eaten our tea, and got to Wiscombe about seven. Then we had supper. I had over a tin of sardines and we thought of having these the next night, with some bread. But how to get hold of some bread? We managed it! . . .

Friday dawned rather cloudy but still fine though slightly colder. We invited Mercy to our 'Midnight Feast' but she wouldn't come. So in the end we invited several of the others. Everyone was looking forward to it. After breakfast we went swimming and after this Miss Lillicrap nearly gave us a heart attack. You see to have this 'Midnight Feast' we had to sleep in the tent that night, and Miss Lillicrap decided to take in all the tents except three – the little hike tent, the oilskin and the green one. We hoped and hoped ours wouldn't go in, but it did!

Then Miss Lillicrap had the awkward problem of allotting the tents. We awaited the answer anxiously, for if we were in the stable we were sunk. Then she said that as we had helped the most, Ann could have the green tent with two others. Of course Ann asked to have Pamela and me. Were we relieved! Mercy and Wendy had the hike tent, and Janet and Anita and the rest had the other tent.

We had our last big campfire up in the woods – it was wonderful. Then we had our last supper, which was soup, and as there was some bread left over we pinched it, and then someone wanted some, so Miss Peters turned round to get the bread and it was gone. Ann and I grinned at each other and Miss Peters looked rather suspicious!

That night we went to bed for the last time under canvas. Feverish with excitement we talked till about midnight, then we got everything out and ready and the others came over. We had a lovely time and told ghost stories afterwards. They all agreed it was the best midnight feast they'd ever enjoyed. About one thirty we all went to sleep.

About two I was woken by the sound of torrential rain and then I heard the others in the oilskin tent go into the stable – the rain had come pouring through the tent roof! The drumming of the rain slowly became rhythmic and I went to sleep again. Then about two thirty I woke feeling cold and wet, and realised I was lying in a deep pool of water! I yelled and Ann and Pamela woke up and Pamela discovered that she also was in a puddle. It was impossible to remain in the tent as everything was soaking, so wearily we collected everything that was wearable and trudged back and forth in the rain from the tent to the stable. There were no beds left for us, so we laid our beds out on the floor and tried to get some sleep for the rest of the night. The floor was jolly hard and I was wet, but still I did get back to sleep. Mercy and Wendy remained out in the hike tent and were soaked by morning.

After breakfast on Saturday we packed our things away and packed up three tents. The day was quite bright and cool after the storm of the night before. Then we had dinner for the last time, then played rounders on the beach and dammed the stream for the last time. It was wonderful. Sadly we left Wiscombe and followed the track up to Scobbiscombe Farm for the last time. We sang songs all the way home in the lorry, and we waved merrily to two groups of senior Scouts, who waved back. Plymouth came all too soon and I went with Guides to Woodside to help put back the tents, etc. Then I thanked Miss Lillicrap, and went home with Mercy, very happily.

Wiscombe is a wonderful place and I am determined to go there again soon.

Barbara Lillicrap, always a keen and inspirational camper, was a Guider of the Mutley (Plymouth) Methodist Church Guides, and Mercy (Sword) Matthews was a cadet with this company. Mercy and Janet were friends and Guides at Notre Dame School in Plymouth, and this company did not camp, so Mercy invited Janet to join Miss Lillicrap's camp. At this camp, the Roman Catholics did not join in the company prayers and colours; perhaps this was usual at the time. Mercy later became a Guider, District Commissioner and Trefoil Guild member in Ivybridge.

(For more about Wiscombe see pages 255–6)

Patrons

The Countess of Morley	1984–97
Lady Clinton, DL.	1998–

Presidents

The Duchess of Bedford	*
Lady Clinton	1943–53
The Honourable Mrs John White, JP.	1954–66
Lady Amory	1967–78
Mrs Angela Graham	1978–94
Mrs Rosemary Howell, DL	1994–2001
Mrs Mavis Budden	2001–7
Mrs Mary Jones	2007–14
Miss Chris Tozer	2014–

* Dates not known, but included 1928–9.

County Commissioners and Assistants

Lady Clinton	1914–43	
Mrs Dorothy Ledger	1943–6	
Miss E. K. Parker	1946–56	Miss K. Williams (North Devon)
		Mrs Murray, JP (East Devon)
Mrs Shelagh Eastley, MBE, JP	1956–62	Miss M. Wheen
		Miss M. E. Bindloss, JP
Miss M. E. Bindloss, JP	1962–70	Miss M. Wheen
		Mrs Angela Graham (1964–70)
Mrs Angela Graham	1970–78	Miss N. R. Cornelius (1973–4)
		Mrs Vivien Chanter (1975–8)
		Mrs Rosemary Howell (1975–8)
Mrs Rosemary Howell, DL	1978–87	Mrs Vivien Chanter (1978–9)
		Mrs Loveday Fergusson (1979–87)
		Miss Valerie Dampney, JP (1984–7)
Mrs Mavis Budden	1987–92	Miss Valerie Dampney, JP (1987–8)
		Miss Elizabeth Smith (1988–92)
Mrs Beryl Hitchcock	1992–7	Miss Elizabeth Smith (1992–7)
		Mrs Mary Jones (1992–7)
Miss Chris Tozer	1997–2003	Mrs Kate Harding (1997–2003)
		Mrs Sue Brown (1997–2003)
		Mrs Elaine Stevens (1997–2003)
		Mrs Tina Caunter (1999–2000)
Mrs Kate Harding	2003–8	Mrs Tina Caunter (2004–8)
		Mrs Tessa Ricketts (2003–8)
Mrs Sue Bullock	2008–13	Mrs Tina Caunter
		Mrs Tessa Ricketts
		Miss Sue Pinn
		Mrs Deborah Holton

'People often ask "what are Guides doing now?" We don't boast, but we go steadily on and forward, keeping in touch, and often initiating new ideas which appeal to the Youth of to-day. Best of all, we keep our high ideals of love and duty to God and Country, which are the mainspring of all we do.

'With so much quarrelling in the World it is essential that the Young should start life with these great principles which make for Christian Love and Peace.'

*J. G. CLINTON, County President
(From the County Report, 1947–8)*

INDEX

Beevers, Pat 229

Bembridge, Marie 120

Bennett, Helen 144

Bentley, Janet 235

Betts, Sister 38, 252

Biden, Angela 351

Bindloss, Betty 25, 36, 41, 46, 47, 48, 50, 54, 60, 61, 110, 121, 136,
 137, 202, 203, 204, 205, 278, 305, 343, 344, 359, 377, 378, 389

Bindloss, Dorothy 50, 202, 208, 343, 344

Bird, James 297

Blackwell, Angela 96

Blackwell, Joyce 169, 170, 229, 230

Blathwayt, Barbara 60

Blathwayt, Jean 60

Blewitt, Kerry 185

Blower, Sue 134, 135

Boatright, Muriel 28, 29, 127, 160

Bond, Miss 235

Boniface, St 78

Bootherstone, Wendy 69, 244

Bowden, Elizabeth 59, 102, 110, 111, 216

Bowie, David 141

Bowles, Ann Parker 200

Bowles, Diane 223

Boyes, Mr 72

Bradford, Miss 25

Bradshaw, Foky 81, 89, 96, 108, 110, 112, 113, 212, 213, 337, 354

Branch, Margaret 62, 63, 84, 87, 91, 106, 110, 118, 123, 213, 250,
 279

Brice, Molly 359

Brindley, Margaret 377

Bromidge, Sheila 90, 163, 336

Brotheridge, Margaret 53, 56, 60, 63, 64, 68, 76, 83

Brown, Gill 168

Brown, Sue 122, 125, 152, 153, 216, 349, 350, 351, 389

Budden, Edward 109, 143, 380

Budden, Keren 136

Faulkner, Valerie 23, 168
Fear, Sally 333
Fender, Dr Guy 144
Fergusson, Loveday 76, 91, 102, 212, 251, 252, 389
Fitzroy, Ann 216
Fletcher, Jo-Ann 133
Foden, Muriel 56, 173, 378
Folland, Moreen 28
Foot, Sarah 81
Ford, Tina 99
Fortescue, Countess 18, 37
Foster, Chris 155, 157, 238
Foster, Daphne 201, 252
Foster, J.H. 15
Fowler, Claire 215
Fowler, Phyl 69, 76, 121, 278
Franklin, Frances 123, 161, 162, 170, 203
Franks, Captain 71
Franks, Mrs 71
Freeman, Katie 154
Fryer, Lady 34, 233
Furse, Dame Katherine 187
Fyfe, Beryl 51, 71

G
Gabb, Kathleen 123, 382
Gallup, Mary 253
Gardiner, Dorothy 254
Gardiner, Felicity 73
Garside, Jane 150
George V 22, 253
George VI 37, 338
Gilbert, Kathryn 155
Gilbert, P. 51
Gilbert, Sir Humphrey 192, 195
Gill, Margaret 243, 247
Gladstone, Sir William 79

Harper, K. J. 381
Harriet, Ainslie 315
Harrison, Sally 154
Harry, Prince 132
Hartley, Elizabeth 33, 45, 51, 53, 57, 58
Hartley, Ishbel 89
Hartley, Ruth 153
Harvey, Lorna 60, 74
Haskin, Kathy 244
Haskin, Sara 69, 244
Hatherley, Hilary 87, 143
Hayden, Jane 103
Heard, PC 215
Hemp, Ruth 64, 65,
Hermann, Sophie 185
Hewson, Anne 91, 104, 106
Hinchliff, Betty 107, 133, 173, 216
Hinchliff, Brian 133, 216
Hitchcock, Beryl 84, 102, 117, 118, 122, 127, 128, 131, 132, 153,
    163, 173, 305, 343, 367, 368, 374, 375, 389
Hodge, Deborah 222
Hodges, Alice 299
Hodson, Eunice 115
Hogg, Emma 185
Holden, Ian 289
Holton, Deborah 389
Hone, Mr 48
Hood, David 85, 108, 166, 212
Hopkins, Anne 193, 197
Hore, Flik 173
Hore, Rita 24
Hornby, Miss 234
Howard, Hilary 169, 204
Howell, Rosemary 5, 6, 7, 28, 74, 75, 76, 91, 104, 127, 133, 138,
    152, 156, 163, 201, 209, 216, 305, 342, 343, 388, 389
Howell, Ruth 235, 360, 361
Howes, M. D. 60

Morley, Lord 122, 251
Morris, Jennifer 106, 141
Murdoch, Miss 36
Murray, Mrs 389
Myers, Rachel 185

N
Neale, A. 255
Needham, Miss 361
Newell, Corrie 119, 245
Newman, Sally 100
Nicholls, Charlie 39,
Nicholls, Dorothy, 23, 24
Norkett, Sarah 184
Norman, Diana 168
Norris, Lindsey 148

O
Oliver, Jamie 167
Oliver, Miss 31
Ough, Sylvia 131

P
Page, D. 35
Parker, E. K. 31, 34, 220, 233, 234, 255, 343, 389
Parker, Major 250
Parsons, Colonel 48
Parsons, Janet 157, 165, 170
Paterson-Brown, Dr June 138, 143
Paul, Beryl 45, 108, 109, 235, 245, 359, 360, 361
Payner, Pat 64
Pearson, Clive 218, 369
Pearson, Laurie 56, 91, 112, 116, 121, 124, 126, 128, 131, 132, 133,
    143, 146, 214, 216, 218, 315, 368, 369, 378
Pearson, Muriel 194
Pedlar, Karen 147
Peile, Vice Admiral 191

Taylor, Heather 74, 236, 279

Tettersall, Rachel 230

Thomas, Kathleen 55, 56, 69, 76, 82, 104, 222, 223, 224, 225, 244, 281, 336, 356

Thomas, Miss 234

Thompson, Mrs 15

Thorpe, Janet 235, 236, 239, 240, 241

Thorpe, Kay 69

Thorpe, Mr 209

Timmis, Mary 246

Toogood, Miss 279

Towle, Bridget 132, 250

Townsend, Miss 14

Townson, Eve 170, 171

Tozer, Chris 61, 66, 82, 89, 93, 110, 114, 132, 135, 152, 154, 156, 158, 160, 161, 162, 164, 169, 177, 183, 204, 205, 211, 224, 305, 336, 342, 343, 354, 356, 357, 358, 359, 370, 371, 388, 389

Trahair, John 248

Trahair, Pat 248

Travell, Grace 108

Trefusis, Lady Mary 13

Tuckett, Mary 105

Turner, Judith 276

Twelvetrees, Doris 204

Twigg, Susan 95

Tyler, Captain 17, 30

Tyler, Mrs 17, 30

U

Usherwood, June 120, 121, 153, 156, 163

V

Vaughan-Cox, Vivienne 365, 366

Veale, Ann 104, 110, 133, 216

Vickery, Caroline 238, 239, 354

Vickery, Helen 138

Victoria, Princess 20